Also by Archibald D. Hart:

Feeling Free
Unlocking the Mystery of Your Emotions
Depression: Coping and Caring
Children and Divorce: What to Expect, How to Help
Coping with Depression in the Ministry and Other Helping Professions
The Success Factor
The Hidden Link between Adrenaline and Stress
Counseling the Depressed
Fifteen Principles for Achieving Happiness
Overcoming Anxiety
Healing Life's Hidden Addictions
Healing Adult Children of Divorce

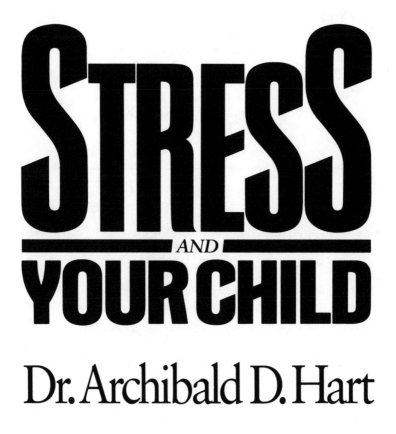

STRESS
AND
YOUR CHILD

Dr. Archibald D. Hart

WORD PUBLISHING
Dallas · London · Vancouver · Melbourne

To my grandchildren

Vincent, Alan, Nicole, and Ashley

and those yet to come

My prayer is that you will all be protected from the
stresses of life and find the same peace and fulfillment
in all your accomplishments as I have.
I also pray that you always keep Isaiah 26:3 close at hand:

"Thou wilt keep him in perfect peace,
whose mind is stayed on thee:
because he trusteth in thee."

STRESS AND YOUR CHILD: KNOW THE SIGNS AND PREVENT THE HARM

Unless otherwise indicated, Scripture quotations in this book are from the King
James Version of the Bible. Other quotations are from the following versions:

The Living Bible (TLB), copyright 1971 by Tyndale House Publishers, Wheaton,
Ill. Used by permission.

The Holy Bible, New International Version (NIV). Copyright © 1973, 1978,
1984 International Bible Society. Used by permission of Zondervan Bible
Publishers.

The Revised English Bible (REB). Copyright © the Delegates of the Oxford
University Press and the Syndics of the Cambridge University Press, 1989.
Reprinted by permission.

Library of Congress Cataloging-in-Publication Data:

Hart, Archibald D.
    Stress and your child : know the signs and prevent the harm / Archibald D.
Hart.
        p. cm.
    Includes bibliographical references.
    ISBN 0–8499–0926–0
    1. Stress in children.   2. Stress in children—Prevention.   3. Child-
rearing.   I. Title.
BF723.S75H37   1992
649'.1—dc20   91–36777
                                                                    CIP

Printed in the United States of America

2349   AGF   987654321

Contents

Acknowledgments

While I am grateful to a number of persons whose support and influence have contributed to this book, including my wife, Kathleen, I am particularly indebted to Ernie and Pauline Owen for their love and encouragement over many years.

It was Ernie Owen who first invited me to write a book, and it is Ernie who has consistently supported my efforts and trusted my hunches about what I could contribute to the healing of persons. Kathleen and I will always be thankful to God for having sent Ernie and Pauline into our lives.

I am also grateful for the labor of love by my secretary, Nova Hutchins, who typed the manuscript for this book while carrying on her many other duties, and for the careful, sensitive, and thorough editing performed by Anne Christian Buchanan.

Introduction

"Would you like to be a child in today's world?" I've asked this question of many adults over this past year. The emphatic response is nearly always no way! When I press for an explanation, the response is, "The world has gotten too stressful for children."

Who can argue? If you are reading this book, you are probably well aware that the days of carefree childhood are history.

Some might think of childhood only as a time for growing up, for learning and fun, for "just being a kid" before the responsibilities and stresses of adulthood set in. And that may have been true seventy or eighty years ago—for some kids.

But times have changed.

The world has changed.

Childhood has changed.

And for most children today, stress is a fact of life.

Expectations are greater. The pressure to grow up is more intense. The competition for success and even for necessities is fierce, and kids are constantly having to prepare for new roles. More and more children live in single-parent or conflict-ridden homes, attend overcrowded, often dangerous schools, and grow up in a paradoxical society where kids seem to make their own rules and yet are not valued.

The effect of this incredibly complex and ever-changing world on our children can be devastating—often beyond the coping capacity of little minds and bodies. The stress in a child's life can create or exacerbate a host of illnesses and disorders—headaches, tics, nervousness, allergies, bedwetting, temper tantrums, stuttering, to name just a few. Just as important, childhood stress can pave the way for future heart attacks, ulcers, and other serious syndromes.

It's a little-known but crucial fact: *Adult stress disease has its roots in childhood.*

But that sobering reality leads to a more hopeful one: *Healthy stress management can begin in childhood as well.* Children who learn to identify and control their stress at a young age will not only be better equipped to grow up happy and healthy; they will also be less likely to experience the debilitating results of stress disease as adults. They will be empowered to turn the unavoidable stresses of life to positive advantage.

And that is the purpose of this book: *to show parents, teachers, and other concerned adults how to "stressproof" their children in an increasingly stressful world.*

My emphasis will be threefold.

Part One focuses on *understanding* stress and how it affects children. This section examines some of the reasons today's children are more at risk than ever before. Drawing on recent studies and my own clinical experience, it will show how the "positive" stress that comes from busy lives, challenging activities, and high achievement can be as dangerous—or more dangerous—over the long term than traumatic stress. It clarifies the intimate connection between childhood stress and the development of stress disease. More practically, it will help you sort out the stress factors in your own child's life and to understand the extent to which stress is a problem in your family.

Part Two is the heart of this book—a practical strategy for helping children manage stress. This section starts out with such basic factors as adequate sleep, physical fitness, and sound nutrition and then continues with specific relaxation techniques you can teach your child and a system of "stress inoculation" to help your child handle future challenges. It tackles the tricky subject of discipline and suggests a (relatively) stress-free approach to correcting and teaching children. Finally, it emphasizes the importance of the home environment and shows how any parent can offer children a home base that is a refuge rather than its own source of stress.

Finally, Part Three of this book examines some of the special stress problems emerging in our society. First, it encourages parents to look at themselves, to consider some ways they may be contributing to their child's stress problems and to discover ways to be part of the solution instead. It looks at the problems of the "hurried child" and offers some suggestions for slowing down a hurried household. It suggests specific strategies for helping angry children handle their stress more positively. It guides parents in walking the delicate balance between giving to their children and spoiling them. Finally, it shows how to help worried children cope with their anxiety and to teach their children safety in a dangerous world without scaring them to death in the process.

Throughout this book, in fact, I will be focusing on *parents* as well as *children*. This is because parents (or other caregivers) play a vital role in the way stress affects children.

First, parents can actually *cause* excess stress in their children—through abuse and neglect and ignorance, but also through wanting the best for their children and pushing them too hard. In this book I will try to approach this problem honestly. My goal is not to add to your stress as a parent or to make you feel guilty, but to help you understand that you, too, can be part of the problem and to show you ways that you can be part of the solution instead.

Second, stressed-out parents almost inevitably *pass it along* to their children. You probably know from experience that when you are under stress you are more likely to lash out at your kids or simply not "be there" for them.

You have probably also noticed that an atmosphere of tension in the home can make it a source of stress rather than the refuge it was intended to be.

Finally—and most importantly—parents who understand stress and learn to manage it effectively will *model* good stress management for their children. When you handle your own stress in a healthy way, you will not only be better able to protect your children from too much stress; you will also be teaching them the skills they need to meet their own challenges. Parents who learn to handle their own stress are the key to stressproofing their children.

Whether you are a parent, grandparent, teacher, pastor, relative, or perhaps even a child yourself, I trust that this book will give you a broader perspective on the nature of childhood stress and provide you with some practical help in building positive coping habits for both yourself and your children. (Since this book could serve as a resource for parent training or adult study groups, I have included a few discussion questions at the end of each chapter.)

A very wise man once wrote, "Train up a child in the way he should go: and when he is old, he will not depart from it."[1] I can think of no more appropriate application of this injunction than in teaching our children how to be less stressed and more at peace with themselves and their world.

Part 1

Understanding Childhood Stress

We hear a lot these days about stress. Unfortunately, *stress* is not a very precise word, nor do most people clearly understand what stress is all about. In this first section, therefore, I will focus on clarifying the true nature of stress, especially as it applies to children, and identifying the major causes of stress in children. In particular, I will identify the arousal of the adrenal system, with its production of the stress hormones adrenaline and cortisol, as the major mechanism of stress disease. In addition, I will guide you in developing a "stress profile" for your child—identifying those elements of your child's world (both innate and environmental) that may make him or her vulnerable to stress damage. Once you understand where the stress in your home is coming from and how it affects your child, you will be well along the road to preventing stress damage in your child.

1

It's Just Too Much!

Four-year-old Lafayette lies on the floor, screaming and kicking his red tennis shoes against the floor. Lafayette's mother sighs; she's going to be late for work again. Both parents and teachers have had trouble coping with Lafayette's frequent tantrums. And it seems clear that his family's recent move must be involved; the "acting out" started shortly after they arrived in their new city. So Mom and Dad are trying hard to give him extra attention, but both are trying to adjust to new jobs and a new home. Too often, they find themselves snapping at him, which only makes them feel guilty and makes Lafayette's behavioral problems worse.

Ten-year-old Sharon sits up in bed—surely she heard a noise. Her heart pounds as she sits there in the dark, straining her ears in the silence. It's been two years since Sharon's parents divorced, and she was doing pretty well until the burglary. But ever since she and her mother returned from an outing to find their apartment "cleaned out," Sharon has been nervous and anxious. Every night she checks all the locks several times before going to bed. Most nights she tosses and turns, "hearing" noises and imagining there is someone downstairs. Even during the day, she is jumpy and easily startled. Sharon's mother would like to get her counseling, but she's afraid she can't afford it.

Fifteen-year-old Gabriella frowns as she rubs her forehead. It's midnight, and her three sisters have drifted off to sleep long ago, but Gabriella still has homework to finish. Her immigrant parents have always encouraged Gabriella to do her best, and Gabriella has never let them down, but it's been harder since she joined the pep squad. The practices are long and tiring, the noise in her crowded house is distracting during the evening, so Gabriella rarely gets started on her homework until after eleven o'clock at night. Still, she is working hard to keep her straight-A average, even if it means cutting back on her sleep. She knows her parents cannot afford college, but she is determined to earn a scholarship and be the first person in her family to go to the university. She refuses to let her frequent headaches pull her down.

Lafayette, Sharon, and Gabriella differ in age, sex, and socioeconomic status, but they have one thing in common: they show signs of being under *too much stress*. And they have millions of brothers and sisters across the nation.

Day by day the world of our children has become more threatening, more conflicted. The stress produced by this rapidly changing social and cultural environment is not friendly to children. It makes growing up more complex. It also produces an accelerated wear and tear on the body that will only show itself in later life—in the form of high blood pressure, heart disease, ulcers, diabetes, colitis, headaches, backaches, skin disorders, depression, anxiety disorders, and susceptibility to disease. Any of these problems can *begin* in childhood and be conditioned by childhood stress. And today's children are perhaps more susceptible to present and future stress damage than any previous generation.

Consider some statistics that hint at the stress levels children are experiencing today. Every twenty-four hours, almost 3,000 children see their parents get divorced; 1,629 children are put in adult jails; 3,288 children run away from home; 1,512 drop out of school; and 7,742 teenagers become sexually active.[1]

Did you get the time frame? It is *every twenty-four hours*.

And those numbers tell only the outside story; they measure only external indications of stress. We have no way of measuring how many children are depressed, anxious, worried, or overstimulated. And we have no way of measuring how many children will develop symptoms of stress as they grow older.

I'm not just talking about the kids of the ghetto, where gang warfare and drive-by shootings are the norm—although the stress levels in poverty areas can be enormous. I'm talking about city kids, rural kids, rich kids, poor kids, kids of every race and neighborhood. From my research and my clinical practice, I am convinced that real, fundamental change is stressing out our kids as never before.

In the pages to come I want to examine some of the factors that make stress such a problem for today's kids. In many ways it's a sobering picture.

But before we proceed, let me remind you: *Your child is not at the mercy of a stressful world.*

High-stress levels are a given in today's society, but the damage it does to children *can* be prevented or minimized. By adhering to a few simple principles, you can completely eliminate the destructive effects of stress on your child. Even more importantly, you can do a lot toward protecting your child from stress disease in his or her adult years. If I didn't believe this I wouldn't bother to write this book. So take heart and read on.

Too Much Too Soon

One of the most extraordinary aspects of childhood stress that I have observed as a clinical therapist is how much *earlier* in life children are being subjected to stressful pressures, and how much earlier they are showing the signs of stress disease.

Depression seems to be occurring earlier in children than ever before. Younger and younger children are attempting suicide. And cardiovascular degeneration is being seen in younger and younger children. What is causing this "regression" of stress disease to earlier stages of life? I can't completely explain this phenomenon except to point to the fact that children are being exposed to major life pressures at earlier and earlier ages.

For instance, kids encounter drugs at much younger ages than before. High school used to be the place where most children were exposed to the availability of drugs. But teachers have informed me that most kids now encounter drugs in junior high and even earlier. Not only is this riskier for children in terms of addictions and physical harm, but the stress that follows this exposure is enormous, even for those kids who "just say no!"

Sexual experimentation also begins earlier these days. Forty or fifty years ago, the average age for first sexual contact was seventeen or eighteen. Now the average is fourteen or fifteen, and it is dropping. So, predictably, is the median age for teenage pregnancy, venereal disease, and AIDS.

Children are also being exposed to violent crime and death at earlier ages. Many adults I have spoken to can barely remember a schoolmate's death while growing up. I can recall one childhood friend who died in a car accident, but not a single suicide and certainly no shootings. Now every child seems to know of a peer who has been killed in some way. Many fourteen- or fifteen-year-olds who live in a major city can recite lists of friends or schoolmates who have been killed in accidents or in gang warfare—or who have killed themselves.

When I was young, we had the occasional bloodied nose when two would-be studs with inflated egos tried to impress a girl in class, but the most dangerous weapons we ever used were our fists. Today children have access to a large arsenal of weapons to settle disputes. I'm talking about *young* children, not just teenagers. And I'm also talking about average neighborhoods, not just inner-city ghettos.

Of course, even those children who don't witness violence firsthand are constantly reminded of it—not only through bloody "action" shows on TV and the movies, but also on the news. And they are warned repeatedly of possible trouble from concerned parents who simply want to keep them safe. From a very early age, today's children are well aware of the reality that abuse, kidnapping, and murder happen every day and that the victims are often young.

Such an environment of violence breeds deep-seated fear and creates extraordinary levels of stress. Most children are being required to cope with such environmental threats before their minds and bodies are sufficiently developed to handle this fear. The result? Stress disease is appearing earlier and earlier.

Too Much of a Good Thing

But it's not only these negative and painful forms of stress that are stressing out today's kids at earlier and earlier ages. Children also feel the increasing pressure of too much stimulation, too much challenge, too much choice, too much opportunity.

The entertainment media offer a smorgasbord of exciting and stimulating entertainment—some "healthy" and child-oriented, some disturbing and inappropriate for children—twenty-four hours a day. Music blares from every street corner. Video games boing and ping in every convenience store. Malls, restaurants, and even grocery stores market a vast array of consumer goods to children, who then feel pressured by their peers to keep up with the latest offerings. Newspapers, books, magazines, and computers present children as well as adults with more details to sort through, more news to digest, more possibilities to consider, more paper to pigeonhole.

The pressure to do well in school is stronger than ever before. College has been touted again and again as the only route to the good life—especially as well-paying, unskilled jobs dry up. At the same time, the cost of education soars, and loans and grants are harder to find. Many young students are acutely aware that their present grades may determine their future.

Even the well-meaning parental desire for their children to be well-rounded and lead an enriched life creates a stressful environment for many children today. Today's children today are busier than ever before. Between after-school activities, sports, church activities, dance and music lessons, their days tend to be full and their nights late. Lazy, unstructured time is a rarity for today's hurried kids. And they are paying the price in terms of stress.

Signs of Too Much Stress

How does all this stress show itself in children? Teachers tell me—and I've noticed it also in the families I have counseled—that illness increases. Some children develop psychosomatic problems—stomachaches, sweaty hands, nervousness, tics, and headaches. Others become more susceptible to colds, influenza, and other infections because their immune systems become weakened. And children who struggle with chronic allergies or asthma find that stress makes their problems worse.

Behavioral problems, too, can be signs of stress. Stressed-out children may be hyperactive or have difficulty controlling their anger. They may have trouble sleeping or concentrating, and they may have nightmares or wet the bed.

Sometimes the situation becomes even more serious. Consider some more figures that hint at what these increased stress levels are doing to children:

- The suicide rate for adolescents has tripled since 1958—and younger children are killing themselves.

- Children as young as five years old are developing ulcers.

- Researchers have noted an alarming increase in depression in children all across the nation.

- Increasing numbers of younger adolescents and children are turning to alcohol, drugs, sex, and violence—either as an escape from stress or a way of "letting off steam."

- Cholesterol levels in children are now skyrocketing, preparing the way for early heart disease.

- Autopsies of children killed in accidents have revealed fatty, fibrous plaque clogging the arteries of fifteen year-olds and beginning to form in children as young as two or three years of age. (We will see in a later chapter that this is not just a problem of diet, but is linked to high stress.)

- Accidents are the number-one killer of adolescents—and stressed adolescents are two-and-a-half times more likely to have an accident.

This does not mean, of course, that every child who experiences stress will get sick, become severely depressed, or commit suicide. But it does point to the fact that stress has consequences—and our kids are experiencing them more and more in our stressed-out society.

Double Jeopardy:
Too Much Stress—Not Enough Family

It is really difficult to comprehend fully the problem of childhood stress without reflecting on the changing nature of family life in our society.

Ron Harris, a staff writer for the *Los Angeles Times,* recently interviewed more than one hundred psychiatrists, psychologists, teachers, social workers, and historians across the United States in order to write a series of stories about growing up today. His sources agreed that childhood today has been transformed primarily because *the family has changed.*[2] With the change to the family have come corresponding changes in other institutions—communities, schools, and societal standards—that nurture our children.

On the whole, home used to be a secure place. Children could rely on it to provide encouragement, to shield them from the threats of society, and to give them a safe and stable place in which to build coping skills. Today that kind of refuge is rapidly becoming scarce. Here are some sobering statistics:

- Out of all first marriages, 60 percent will end in separation or divorce.
- Nearly 25 percent of all children now live in single-parent families (as compared to only 9 percent in 1960).
- Half of these single-parent children will eventually be forced to adjust to a stepparent and a "blended" family.
- Even in two-parent families, 56 percent of all children under six years of age will have both parents working (as compared to 19 percent in 1960).
- 42 percent of children from kindergarten through third grade are regularly left alone to care for themselves.[3]

On top of these statistics is the simple fact that stress in the general population is increasing as well. Many of the factors mentioned above—rising violence, economic pressures, cultural instability—affect adults as well as children. Depression and anxiety are on the rise. And that means there is an increased chance that the parents to whom children look for support and relief from stress will be stressed out themselves.

So children are faced with "double jeopardy." They face a world that is more stressful than ever. In addition, they are forced to depend less and less on their traditional source of support—their families.

Am I making too much of these family factors? Here are some figures that suggest I am not. I include them *not* to make overworked and guilt-ridden parents feel worse, but to help all parents face the issue honestly.

- Children who are regularly left alone are twice as likely to smoke, drink alcohol, or use marijuana.

- Children who are left alone have more problems coping with schoolwork.

- Parents who aren't around much tend to be more indulgent, less likely to set limits, less likely to be consistent in discipline, and more likely to look the other way than have a confrontation.

- Absent parents often fail to establish routine in the household, and lack of routine is stressful for children.

- When parents aren't around, children have to make up their own rules. These rules tend to be shaped more by community standards (or the lack thereof) than by traditional or parental standards.[4]

There is much, of course, that single parents and working parents can do to alleviate their children's stress. Nevertheless, both common sense and clinical experience point to the basic fact that *two parents are better than one* and that, during the very early stages of childhood, *children need a parent close at hand*. Facing this reality honestly is the first step toward overcoming the added stress created by today's changing family situations.

The Stress No One Talks About

In my years as a clinical psychologist, I have worked with many highly stressed families. I have consulted with parents, pastors, teachers, and other professionals and have thoroughly reviewed the available research literature. In the process, I have come to believe that the most dangerous stress in a child's life may be the stress no one recognizes.

A lot of research has probed into the causes and effects of childhood stress. Researchers have spent a lot of time examining the many ways stress can change a child's life. But most research on childhood stress tends to focus on the traumatic or unpleasant areas of life as the source of stress. Very little is directed toward helping parents and children cope with *everyday* stress, *ongoing* stress, and *enjoyable* stress.

A lot has been written, for instance, about how physical and sexual abuse can cause stress problems in later life, but not much about how the pressure of school or problems with peers can lead to heart attacks in early middle age. We know how earthquakes, tornadoes, illness, bereavement, chronic pain, divorce, or chronic illness can cause stress in children, but little about how good parents produce stress through pressuring them to perform.

In plain words, most people clearly understand how unpleasant or traumatic life experiences can stress out a child. But we either ignore or fail to

Theresa's Story: A Case History

Theresa was almost eighteen years of age when she told me her story. At the time, she had just moved into her own apartment and was trying to make it on her own in the world. But something was clearly wrong. Theresa fidgeted constantly, moved around restlessly in her chair, bit her nails, and jumped at the slightest unusual sound. Whenever anyone touched her, she literally leaped to her feet.

"I knew Mom and Dad fought a lot," she told me. "Ever since I can remember they shouted at each other, banged doors, and threw things. In fact, it happened so much that it really didn't bother me that much. I thought all families were like this!

"That's why I was so shocked when my parents announced that they were separating. I was only seven years old at the time, but I felt as if my life had suddenly come to an end. I just stood at the door sobbing as my dad packed his things, hugged us, and drove away. He didn't even say he was going away, much less tell us when he was coming back again.

"About a week later Mom sat us down and explained that she and Dad were going to divorce. She also told us we had to move to be nearer Grandma and Granddaddy, who lived about a thousand miles away. This was even more devastating. My sister became hysterical because she loved her school, her friends, and our house. She was so angry she went into the kitchen and started throwing plates on the floor. I just stood there dumbfounded. I could feel my stomach knot up and my arms begin to shake. I kept asking myself, Why did they have to ruin *our* lives just because *they* couldn't get along with each other?

"The day we moved I don't remember very well. But I do remember sitting in the back of the car as we drove across the country and feeling like I had the shakes. It was at that time that I started biting my nails and haven't been able to stop since.

"When we finally settled near our grandparents, we were so much poorer. Mom kept telling us that Dad wasn't sending us the money that he promised. And then the news came that he had remarried. From that time on, he never ever sent us money again, and I hardly ever heard from him.

"My sister's schoolwork suffered severely. I was able to do fairly well in school, but I hardly ever made any friends; I just kept to myself. Because my mom was also very unhappy, she didn't pay much attention to what we were feeling.

"Now I'm eighteen years old, and I still can't seem to put this behind me. At nights I just lay awake worrying about things. I don't really trust anybody—especially men—and I don't know if I will ever be able to go with a boy and get married. It seems life has lost its pleasure, and there is little left to enjoy. But now and again I get a little glimmer of hope, and my therapy certainly is helping me get over some of the painful things from my past. One of these days I'm going to get up the courage to visit my dad. At least if I understand where he was coming from and why he left us, I might be able to get rid of some of the stress I still feel about my family's breaking up."

understand how the apparently exciting, challenging, and positively demanding experiences of childhood can produce stress.

I am convinced we have focused too much on the catastrophic and not enough on the mundane sources of stress in a child's life. The exciting aspects of a child's life seem so enriching, so good—yet they can easily become the primary source of the kind of stress that later causes early heart and other damage. We fail to understand the devastation that can be caused in the long term by such childhood experiences as overstimulation, thrill seeking, living up to the media's projected images of perfection, fear of peer rejection, or even of neurotic guilt.

I am convinced that these "everyday" forms of stress can be just as significant—and perhaps even more damaging—than the catastrophes. First, they are simply more common and therefore affect more people. Second, these sources are more difficult to identify. They elude recognition and, in some cases, are encouraged by our culture. As a result, they are more likely to continue until significant damage is done. Throughout this book, therefore, I will continually pinpoint these more "normal" sources of stress.

Beyond "Fight or Flight"

The stress response has often been described as the "fight or flight" response. However, I believe there is more to stress than the "fight or flight" picture.

The "fight or flight" reaction occurs only under *certain* conditions of stress. It is the *alarm reaction* of the body that usually occurs in reaction to a threatening or negative type of stress. It usually occurs when a child is threatened in some way—for example, when he or she is frightened by having to walk home in the dark through a bad neighborhood.

I can vividly recall many childhood experiences of this alarm reaction. My heart would pound. My mind would become very alert. I would hear and see things I wouldn't normally notice. This physical response to perceived danger is designed to protect us and to make us capable of either fighting for survival or running for our lives—hence the term "fight or flight" response.

The *fight* portion of the "fight or flight" response is often reflected in anger, and this is one reason children respond with so much anger to anything that threatens them. The *flight* portion is usually reflected in fear, the impulse to get away from danger. Unfortunately, many of the circumstances that provoke these responses in today's children are not helped by physical anger or physical flight. A child is better off learning to understand and control these natural urges than to follow them.

Another way of understanding this is to see the "fight or flight" reaction as a "primitive response" designed for physical threats. It is more appropriate for a primitive and physically threatening world than for modern city life where threats are symbolized in teachers who can fail you, friends who can reject you, or parents who can deprive you of privileges.

As I have said, the "fight or flight" response occurs only under certain conditions—times when something threatening or negative is going on. But this isn't all there is to stress. Stress can also arise out of *positive* and *challenging* conditions—conditions that are neither frightening nor threatening, yet equally destructive. In fact, I believe this stress is *more* dangerous because it is often overlooked.

Allow me to illustrate the difference. A child (let's call her Sue) is afraid of her teacher, who is easily angered and expresses his feelings loudly. This is very threatening to Sue, who has difficulty tolerating any conflict and feels afraid whenever anyone raises his voice. Sue, then, experiences quite a bit of stress when she does her homework because she fears that her work will not please the teacher. As she sits there trying to work her math problem, she grows more and more tense and anxious. The threat causes an alarm reaction, and this arousal makes it more difficult for her to concentrate. Consequently, her work suffers, the teacher responds angrily, and Sue's distress increases. Soon Sue develops a headache every time she tries to do her homework.

Sue's problem is clearly a response of the "fight or flight" kind. Threat and fear cause her body to become overaroused—as if it were facing a life-threatening emergency. Her heart races, her blood pressure soars, her muscles tense. And because Sue has no physical outlet for this reaction—hitting her teacher or running away are not appropriate responses—her body responds to the distress with physical symptoms. Her head hurts.

Now let's look at Janet. She's in the same class as Sue and has the same teacher and homework assignments. Janet, however, likes the teacher, and she does not feel threatened by his volatile personality. She's confident in her ability to work hard and achieve, and she takes her teacher's rare criticisms as challenges to do better. So Janet gives her assignments all she's got. She puts in long hours, writing and rewriting her essays and checking her math. She is a little anxious about doing well and even a little competitive, hoping she'll do better than anyone else.

Now here is the crucial point. When Janet sits down to work on an assignment, *her stress level also rises*—not out of fear or anxiety, but out of sheer challenge. Her heartbeat and blood pressure also go up, and her muscles tense. She feels "racy," even a bit dizzy, every time she sits down to do her homework. And she, too, begins to be bothered with headaches that sap her concentration and worry her parents.

Sue's and Janet's final symptom is the same—headache, but it arises from different reasons. Sue's stress is of the "fight or flight" kind, while in

Janet's case it is the "overstimulation" kind. While both kinds can be damaging, I believe the second is the more common cause of long-term stress disease in our day and age. It is also the most neglected and misunderstood of all the causes of stress. Parents need to know about and be able to recognize both kinds of stress.

Is Stress Always Bad?

Many people are unclear about how they should view stress. Some see it as something to be avoided at all costs. Others see it as not only inevitable, but sometimes positive—a source of strength and character.

Is stress always bad? If not, how much stress is good for a child—and how can a parent know how much stress is too much?

Our confusion is partly due to the many meanings we give the term *stress*. Sometimes it means *simple arousal*—being physical and mentally "stirred up" enough to focus on some activity and carry it out. (I will be explaining the biochemical basis for this arousal in the next chapter.) In this sense, carrying on a conversation or walking to the store is stressful. So is playing baseball or watching a movie. In fact, the only time we are completely free of this kind of stress is when we are dead.

Every child must, therefore, embrace a certain degree of stress. But the stress problem begins when ordinary stress turns into extraordinary—and negative—tension or pressure. We often call this "stress" as well. An example might be a child who sees another child hit by a car. The child who observes the accident might have nightmares for many weeks afterward and may even be afraid to cross a street. Clearly, this type of stress is far more damaging than the stress of simple arousal.

A child's stress, then, can range from listening to music to playing a game to competing in a music festival to observing a catastrophic trauma to experiencing a major earthquake. Quite a range of responses, and they all go by the name *stress*.

In one sense, moreover, these experiences *are all the same*; they differ only in the intensity of the physical and emotional reaction. Listening to music will create some degree of stress, but experiencing an earthquake will trigger massive stress. Of course, other variables will be involved, such as the degree to which a child feels in control or whether there is fear. But I believe these additional factors only serve to reduce or intensify the stress. The basic response is the same.

Stress and Distress

So how, then, do we explain these different stresses and distinguish between the amount of damage they cause? One way to solve this labeling problem is to refer to all stimulation that is healthy and normal as "simple arousal." Stimulation that is above normal but not necessarily harmful we can call "stress" or "overarousal." And stimulation that is both excessive and damaging we can call "distress" or "excessive arousal."

I believe these distinctions can help us be clearer about what we are discussing. We must still decide where the boundaries are, but at least making these distinctions will get us beyond the debate of what is or is not stress.

The simple arousals of life are *good and necessary*—or at least neutral. A child who becomes excited at a game, thrilled at building a soapbox car, challenged to master a difficult piano piece, or energized by cutting out a dress or baking a cake for the first time, is responding appropriately to his or her environment. If you were to eliminate these activities, you would retard your child's development. A world devoid of any challenge or excitement would not only be dull; it would make growth and progress impossible.

The next level of stimulation, stress, involves excitement or pressure that has escalated above the normal level. We use the term *stress* to connote some degree of negativity. But even here, an occasional experience of stress must be considered normal—and is not necessarily unhealthy.

An example of this type of stress would be an examination at school. It's not your everyday fun experience. You would even avoid it if you could. But it can serve a positive purpose—that of motivating study. If limited in its time frame, this kind of arousal will not be damaging.

The final level in the stress response, that of "distress" or excessive arousal, is clearly "bad" stress. This is the *extreme emergency mode*. Our heartbeat and breathing are in high speed, muscles are tense, gastric juices are flowing strongly, hands are cold and moist, and the stomach is in a knot. We are close to panic, and fainting may be the only useful thing we can do. (Fortunately, fainting here is designed as our escape. It helps to restore the body and mind to normal functioning again.)

The third level, that of distress, is nearly always damaging, even when it serves its primitive purpose of stimulating a flight from danger. The surge of terror that causes a ghetto child to run away from the scene of a gunfight can be positive in terms of saving that child's life, but the distress the child feels will almost certainly put excessive and negative pressure on the child's physical systems.

But there's another factor that spells the difference between stress that is normal, healthy, and positive, and stress that is damaging. That factor is *duration*. The longer the body remains in a state of excitement—no matter what the *level*—the greater the potential for stress damage.

As I have indicated, certain experiences in our lives bring us high levels of tension, but that stress is quickly over. Examinations soon pass; there is a time limit to the stress they cause. The same is true of going to the dentist, having surgery, starting school, changing schools, and so forth. These are *short-lived* experiences. Even though they may register in the "stress" range, the shorter duration of these experiences reduces the probability of damage or long-term consequences.

But some life events are different. A child who lives in a neighborhood where there is frequent gang activity or one who suffers a lengthy illness will experience prolonged stress and be at greater risk for stress disease. So will a child who becomes the pawn in lengthy divorce proceedings. And so—importantly—will a child who competes regularly in high-tension swim meets or who is allowed a steady diet of high-stimulation TV.

The longer any kind of stimulation stays around—whether it is simple arousal, stress, or distress—the greater is the potential for damage.

I can summarize what I am saying here quite simply: *The only good stress is stress that is short-lived.* Even simple arousal, if prolonged, will cause stress problems. And extreme states of distress, if prolonged, nearly always produce serious stress damage, especially to the cardiovascular system.

How Much Stress Is Too Much?

Some stress is inevitable—even necessary—in everyday life. In order to function in the world, your child must stay alert, pay attention, and respond appropriately. He or she must go to school and learn. Certain tasks must be mastered and assignments must be completed. Play, too, involves certain challenges—learning to get along with other children, taking on new physical challenges, stretching mind and body. Every child must, therefore, embrace a certain degree of stress. But the stress problem begins when ordinary stress becomes *too much stress*.

Think of the human body as a machine. Of course, a human being is more than this, but the analogy is fitting in that the human body, like a machine, was designed to carry out certain tasks in certain ways. And the human body, like every machine, has its certain built-in limitations.

Take an electric motor, for example. If you examine the label on the motor of your washing machine or refrigerator you will notice that the phrase "duty cycle" is stamped on it, followed by a figure that is usually expressed as a percentage. The percentage refers to the amount of time the motor is designed to run. For example, a motor that is rated as "Duty Cycle 20 percent" is supposed to run only 20 percent of the time. If forced to run more than this, it is likely to overheat and suffer increased wear and tear. If used continuously, the motor could burn out.

The human body and mind also have a "duty cycle." Our "motors" are designed for a certain amount of usage—stress, if you will. When the demand placed on the human machine exceeds this usage, the capacity for normal functioning will be exceeded; the result is "overheating" and increased wear and tear. And this overusage is what we commonly call stress. And this damage comes either from severely overloading the machine or from running a moderate overload for an extended period of time.

When bodies and minds become overloaded, warning signs appear. These include some of the physical and emotional symptoms described earlier. If the distress continues over a period of time, more severe damage occurs. Mild stomach discomfort gives way to ulcers. Vascular headaches give way to hardening of the arteries. High blood pressure becomes heart disease, which in turn may lead to a heart attack. We refer to this damage stage as *stress disease*.

So the sequence is this: *Stress* leads to *distress*, and distress leads to *stress disease*.

The big question, of course, is: How can I tell if the stress boundary is being exceeded? Unfortunately there is no absolute measure for this. Stress tolerance differs from person to person and child to child. Nevertheless, there are some signs that often point to overstress. Stress Test 1, "Is My Child Overstressed?" can give you a general idea of your child's overall stress levels. In coming chapters, I will try to provide some guidance for determining your child's unique tolerance for stress more exactly as well as for helping him or her avoid the damage that comes from ongoing distress.

Meanwhile, I want to reemphasize the "overload" factor. Regardless of what form the stress takes—"fight or flight" or simple overstimulation, one-of-a-kind catastrophe, or the everyday grind—your child's stress becomes distress whenever his or her mind and body reach the overload level. Any stress, if continued too long without relief, will be damaging. And the whole point of stressproofing your child is preventing that damage.

Summary

Stress disease begins in childhood, though it may not show itself until later life. Modern children are under extraordinary pressure—pressure to succeed, pressure to say no to drugs and sexual experimentation, pressure to cope with an increasingly violent world. The family is also changing, so that children no longer have the same protection from premature stress that they once had.

All this means that children are being subjected to more stress at an earlier age. As a result, children are manifesting signs of stress disease at an earlier age or are at increased risk for developing stress disease later in life.

Perhaps the most serious of all the causes of stress is not the "fight or flight" response, which is triggered by perceived threat or emergency, but the more normal—and more pleasant—stress that comes from over-stimulation, overactivity, or constant challenge. This book will focus especially on this form of stress because it is fully as dangerous but tends to be overlooked.

Because there is much confusion about the use of the term *stress*, I have distinguished three separate levels of arousal: simple arousal (playing baseball or participating in a music competition), stress (above-normal stimulation, such as taking an examination or going to the dentist), and distress (excessive stimulation, like being in an earthquake or having surgery). All three levels of arousal can be damaging if prolonged.

Discussion Questions

1. All around us we see evidence that stress is having an impact on children. As you think about your own children, what sources of stress can you identify for them that were *not* a problem for you as a child?

2. Discuss the "fight or flight" response as you see it manifesting itself in your children. Give some examples of what they do when they are in the "fight" mode and when they are in the "flight" mode. Do you see any evidence of stress that doesn't fall in either of these categories?

3. Many pressures, such as sex and violence, are now being felt by children earlier in life than before. In what ways do you think your children encounter these pressures? What can you do to help your children cope more effectively with these pressures?

Stress Test 1: Is My Child Overstressed?

Child's name _____

Carefully review your child's behavior and complaints for the past two or three weeks and rate the following questions using this scale:

0 = My child infrequently feels or experiences this.
1 = My child sometimes (perhaps once a month) experiences this.
2 = My child experiences this often (between once a month and once a week).
3 = My child experiences this frequently (more than once a week).

Rating

1. My child complains of headaches, backaches, or general muscle pains or stiffness.   _____

2. My child reports stomach pains, digestive problems, cramps, or diarrhea.   _____

3. My child has cold hands or feet, sweaty palms, or increased perspiration.   _____

4. My child has a shaky voice, trembles and shakes, displays nervous tics, or grinds and clenches his or her teeth.   _____

5. My child gets sores in the mouth, skin rashes, or low-grade infections like the flu.   _____

6. My child reports irregular heartbeats, skipped beats, thumping in the chest, or a racing heart.   _____

7. My child is restless, unstable, and feels "blue" or low.   _____

8. My child is angry and defiant and wants to break things.   _____

9. My child has crying spells, and I have difficulty stopping them.   _____

10. My child overeats, especially sweet things.   _____

11. My child seems to have difficulty in concentrating on homework assignments.   _____

12. My child reacts very intensely (with angry shouting) whenever he or she is frustrated.   _____

13. My child complains of a lot of pain in many places of the body.

14. My child seems anxious, fidgety, and restless, and he or she tends to worry a lot.   _____

15. My child has little energy and has difficulty getting started on a project.   _____

Total Score _____

Test Interpretation

0–5   Your child is remarkably low in stress or handles stressful situations extremely well.

6–12   Your child is showing minor signs of stress. While it is nothing to be concerned about some attention to stress control may be warranted.

13–20   Your child is beginning to show signs of moderate stress. Some attention should be given to how your child copes with stress.

21–30   Your child is showing significant signs of stress. You should give urgent attention to helping him or her reduce stress levels.

Over 30   Your child appears to be experiencing very high stress levels. You should do everything possible to eliminate stressful situations until your child can learn to cope. You may want to consider getting professional help.

Note: You may want to go over the test items that have been answered with a rating of 2 or above to better understand the signs of stress in your child's life. See where you can provide relief and help your child build more resistance to stress. If you feel that your child's problems, no matter what his or her score on this test, are beyond your ability to handle, then seek immediate professional help.

2

The Adrenaline Connection

Beth and Michael Riggs awoke to hear mysterious pings and whistles coming from their living room. Groggy with sleep, they glanced at the clock on the bedside table; the glowing green digits spelled out 3:00 A.M. Then they realized what was going on. Six-year-old Kenny had snuck downstairs again to play his video game.

What had come over Kenny, they wondered. He had always been a bright, lovable, easy-to manage boy. But ever since they had bought that game, Kenny's personality had changed.

They had laid down rules from the beginning. Kenny was to share the game with his sister, and he could not play for longer than forty minutes a day. But despite those limitations, Kenny had become irritable and bossy. When he couldn't get to the next level in the game, he cried and stomped his feet. He balked at having to go to school, fought with his friends, and sassed his teachers. And recently—like tonight—he had begun to sneak in extra time.

"First thing tomorrow, I'm getting that game out of the house," Beth told Michael as they stumbled toward the den. "I don't like what it's doing to Kenny; it's almost like he's addicted to it."

Beth Riggs was partially right. In a sense, Kenny *was* becoming addicted, but not to the video game.

Kenny had come to depend on the pleasurable surge of adrenaline the exciting video game triggered in his small body—and he was willing to go to great lengths to experience it.

Kenny is not that unusual. Kids—and adults—all over the country have come to depend on the "rush" of adrenaline-arousing activities, and in the process, are setting themselves up for childhood and adult stress damage.

After extensive thought and research, in fact, I have concluded that *overarousal of the adrenal system* is the essence of the stress problem. That physical system that releases stress hormones, including adrenaline, into the bloodstream to create a state of alertness and to prepare us for an emergency also is the mechanism underlying most of our stress and leading to most stress disease.

Recent research clearly points to this overarousal of adrenaline as the essential causative factor in such stress diseases as heart attacks and coronary artery disease. Too-high adrenaline also influences many other physical and emotional disturbances, including headaches, ulcers, gastric distress, panic anxiety, chronic fatigue, and depression.

In this chapter, therefore, I want to explore this vital connection between adrenaline and stress.

Adrenaline: The Stress Hormones

Adrenaline is the term we commonly apply to any of an important group of hormones produced by the adrenal glands, the tiny glands above each kidney. These organs produce a whole array of hormones that help us cope with stress by mobilizing our systems into an "emergency" mode. The leader among these hormones is the hormone called adrenaline.

Adrenaline is well known by every layperson as the "fight or flight" hormone. It is the substance that gives us that extra energy to make that special effort. Dangerous or threatening situations, especially, make our adrenaline levels soar. In times of threat or, say during an accident, we pump extraordinary amounts of adrenaline. In response to that surge of adrenaline, our heart pumps harder. Blood rushes to our brain and other vital organs. Muscles tense and prepare for action.

During times of adrenaline arousal, our senses are heightened, our energy levels are up, our strength is at its greatest. We hear stories about tiny mothers who lift automobiles off their injured children, or bystanders who expend superhuman effort to rescue a drowning person. Adrenaline is what makes such extra effort possible; it is the hormone of survival and action.

But adrenaline is also known as the "spicy" hormone that gives zest to life. The rush of adrenaline is what fuels the surge of excitement we experience as we zip down a ski slope or step onto a stage. It's the hormone of excitement, and it can make us feel more competent and alive. It's the physical source of that feeling of being "psyched up" and ready to function. High adrenaline provides a heightened sense of well-being, increases energy levels, reduces the need for sleep, and provides an added sense of security— *but at a price*.

Human beings were not designed to live in a constant state of arousal. Instead, we need a *balance* between low and high arousal. We need "mountaintops" of stimulation and arousal not only to handle emergencies, but also to grow and to find meaning. But we also need "valleys" of rest and low arousal—so that we can *recover* from those periods of high stimulation. We need the valley times in order to understand our mountaintops and to keep them in perspective.

What happens if we don't maintain this balance between high and low arousal? For one thing, we become accustomed to abnormally high levels of adrenaline. If we are constantly stimulated, that level of stimulation begins to lose its pleasure value and our need for stimulation gradually increases; it is like building a mountain on top of a mountain.

More importantly, the long-term overarousal of adrenaline is what causes stress disease. Recent research clearly points to this overarousal of adrenaline as the essential causative factor in such stress diseases as heart attacks and coronary artery disease. Too-high adrenaline also influences other hormonal changes that can produce physical and emotional disturbances, including headaches, ulcers, gastric distress, panic anxiety, chronic fatigue, and depression. It also weakens the immune system, increasing the risk of infection.

Briefly, then, let me review some of the long-term damaging effects of high adrenaline:

- It increases the production of blood cholesterol by triggering its release in abundance from the liver.
- It decreases the body's ability to remove cholesterol from the bloodstream.
- It increases the blood's tendency to clot. (This is part of the "fight or flight" reaction and is designed to prevent us from bleeding to death.)
- It increases the release of fatty plaques that deposit themselves on the walls of our arteries.
- It keeps the blood pressure elevated, thus putting a strain on the arteries.

The clear link between high adrenaline arousal (with the accompanying stress hormones) and heart disease is now well documented. Allow me to make one quotation to support this link. Meyer Friedman and Ray Rosenman, the cardiologists who identified the personality type most prone to heart disease, clearly found in their research a connection between prolonged adrenaline arousal and heart disease. They state:

> The chronic excess discharge and circulation of the catecholamines [the hormones adrenaline and noradrenaline] . . . may be the chief factor in the total process of arterial decay and thrombosis. We have seen coronary heart disease erupt in many subjects whose blood insulin levels and metabolism of cholesterol, fat, and sugar were quite normal. But rarely have we ever witnessed the onset of this disease in a person whose rate of manufacture and secretion of catecholamines [adrenaline and noradrenaline] we did not know or suspect to have been increased.[1]

This connection between high levels of circulating adrenaline and the development of cardiovascular disease is not only the most serious of all stress diseases. I believe it is also *the most neglected connection in medicine and stress psychology*. The prevention of heart disease continues to focus on the treating of symptoms (lowering cholesterol and blood pressure with drugs, thinning the blood with aspirin, and so forth). I would like to switch the emphasis to treating the underlying problem—the stress and excitement that cause the overproduction of stress hormones such as adrenaline.

And because childhood is the time that most people begin overproducing adrenaline in response to stress, I am convinced that childhood is the place to start in reducing and preventing stress damage.

The Causes of High Adrenaline in Children

What are some of the factors that stimulate a high level of circulating adrenaline in children? They are no different from the causes in adulthood. As I describe these causes, you may not at first think of them as arousing or stressful. Bear in mind, however, that many of these apparently innocent adrenaline stimulators compound and build on each other. Any one of them, by itself, may not be a problem, but when one follows another they can build the adrenaline to a high pitch. Here are some of the primary culprits:

Noise

Noise, especially aggravating or loud noise, is received by the body as a threat and therefore stimulates the release of adrenaline. No doubt you have observed how irritable you feel when you are exposed to high levels of noise while you are trying to concentrate on something or when you are tired.

The body simply cannot cope with too many simultaneous demands, and noise makes demands on us *even when we are not aware of it.*

The body tries to ignore noise when it persists. The brain tries to adapt to the noisy environment and cancels out our awareness. But the body is still responding by feeling threatened. Prolonged exposure to noise—even the noise we no longer "hear"—causes significant and prolonged arousal of the adrenal system.

Many kinds of noise raise the stress level of today's children—city noises such as that caused by traffic and construction; the "white noise" made by appliances and computers; high volume on televisions and radios; and, of course, loud music.

Most children don't appear to be bothered by loud music, but it stimulates adrenaline nevertheless. In addition, children—teenagers in particular—*use* loud music as a form of stimulation. The arousing effects of loud music will eventually produce stress disease through adrenaline overstimulation (not to mention hearing problems).

Television, Video Games, and Such

Following close on the heels of loud music as causes of arousal in children are visual media such as television, movies, and video games. And of all these, television is the most common culprit, simply because it is more widely available and because most children spend many more hours of the day in front of the TV. (The advent of videocassette recorders, for the most part, has simply broadened the range of choice and increased the amount of time when television stimulation is available to children.)

Some programs, particularly violent ones, are directly stimulating. There is hardly a child these days who escapes seeing violence portrayed on television (and in the movies). Not only does this encourage violent behavior by teaching that violence is an acceptable way of resolving conflict and resolving stress, but it causes high arousal as well.

But violent programs are not the only ones that cause overarousal of adrenaline. Some experts believe that contemporary TV programming encourages hyperactivity. The frequent changing of scenes (often every few seconds in a typical movie) prevents children from learning to concentrate. They try to duplicate the rapidly changing sensation of the TV screen with their own hyperactivity, and this also causes adrenaline arousal.

Even if today's quickly moving visuals don't make children hyper, they are clearly designed to be stimulating. Music videos—the constant diet of many teenagers—are in the forefront of this trend, but even some of the best children's programs, including "Sesame Street", have been criticized for moving too fast and overstimulating children. Commercials, especially, aim at catching consumers' attention by fast moving, high-stimulation visuals. And television is, of course, a primary source of noise in almost any household.

Less directly, television promotes stress damage by reducing children's ability to cope with stress and to enjoy low-arousal alternative activities. When glued to the set, children usually do little else—except to change the channel or fight over what to watch. Their verbal ability, social skills, and motor development may be stunted. Because typical children's programming does not encourage precise or interactive listening, children who watch a lot of TV often fail to develop good listening skills. And because TV watching is mostly a passive activity, children easily lose the ability to structure their own play activity. All of these losses can rob children of the resources they need to fight stress disease: physical health, proper perspective, and a balance of activities.

Although television is by far the most common source of audiovisual stimulation among children, video games have become increasingly popular among older children and teenagers. Those children who don't own home video-game systems can frequent the arcades that have sprung up in shopping malls or can locate games in convenience stores or fast-food restaurants. Clearly the appeal of most games—with their flashing lights, noisy sound effects, and often violent themes—is excitement and stimulation. They are major sources of adrenaline arousal for many children.

Overcrowding

One of the unfortunate consequences of our migration to the cities is overcrowding. Wherever I go, in our big cities particularly, I tend to feel "crushed." Freeways are crowded. Shopping malls are crowded. In Los Angeles, where I live, even the parks are crowded. Some children feel the effects of overcrowding primarily at school and public places, but they may also experience it at home. Inner-city children, particularly, feel the effects of overcrowding and pay for it with increased stress.

What happens when children are crowded together even for short periods of time? One fascinating study, conducted at Rutgers University, examined the effects of overcrowding on school children and adolescents. After putting children together in high-density situations, they monitored their arousal levels and demonstrated that crowding caused negative physiological, behavioral, and social consequences for these children.[2] Their blood pressure and pulse rates went up (indicating higher adrenaline arousal). They became more competitive, even though they had more to gain by being cooperative. They reported feeling tense, annoyed, and uncomfortable. And interestingly, males were more affected than females, showing the highest levels of stress in response to crowding.

Clearly, then, crowding increases a child's stress levels. When over-crowded, children's bodies react as if they were being attacked; their adrena-line surges. The result is more conflicts, higher competitiveness, increased irritability, and a higher incidence of physical distress. This reality has sig-nificant implications for inner-city or even urban school settings, where crowding is becoming the norm. It contributes significantly to the early for-mation of stress disease in children.

Pressures, Threats, and Dangers

There are several sources of pressure for children: the pressure to per-form, the pressure of living in an unstable world, and the pressure of threats, both natural and social.

Many of today's children feel tremendous pressure to perform, to com-pete, to succeed, to be the best. Take Cathy for example. The youngest of three children, she has been competing with her older brother and sister all her life. Her parents are both professionals and superachievers. And while they have never overtly said to her, "We will only love you if you live up to our standards," she has internalized that message nevertheless.

Cathy's older brother is a star. Not only is he a brilliant student, but he is good at sports, has excellent social skills, is well liked. He is "going places," as his father says. Cathy's older sister excels at math and music. (She plays several musical instruments.) While not very studious, she nev-ertheless manages to bring in straight A's.

Over the years, poor Cathy has come to feel very inferior. Even though she is well above average in intelligence, she just can't shine in her family. She is a little comet trying to compete with superstars—the competition is just too good. And the pressure is getting to Cathy. She feels she has to work harder and longer just to survive. As a result, she undertakes every task with great seriousness and intensity. Nothing she does gives her any pleasure; everything feels like hard work.

Competition is not just a problem within high-achieving families like Cathy's, of course. Kids are pitted against one another in school and in sports. As they grow older, they are warned about the competition they will face to get in college and then to find a job. It's a competitive world out there, and for many kids it feels like a pressure cooker. No wonder their adrenaline levels are up.

And not only is it a competitive world; it's a dangerous one as well. Local and world events can be very frightening to children and can keep their adrenaline levels high. Crime, disasters, wars—all vividly portrayed in the media or enacted on their doorsteps—can be terrifying to children. Many children tend to internalize the almost nonstop, subconscious sense of threat and danger in the world, and they pay the price in terms of elevated stress levels.

In Los Angeles, we live in the context of regular earthquake preparation drills. Our children feel the presence of this threat, even when they are not consciously aware of it. For others the threat involves living on the coast—in the path of hurricanes—or in "tornado alley." It can mean living too close to a nuclear power plant or a toxic-waste dump. Or it could mean living in a neighborhood overrun with gangs and drugs. For many children, life easily comes to feel like one constant threat.

And children don't get much help from overstressed adults, who are trying to cope with the same threats themselves. And when these adults turn to alcohol, drugs, sex, violence or other forms of escape, they are not only inadequate models of stress management for their children, but can also become sources of intimidation themselves.

Emotions

Certain emotions are notoriously bad for creating high levels of adrenaline arousal. They include:

- frustration,
- irritation,
- resentment,
- hurt,
- fear,
- anxiety,
- threat.

But all these emotions are variations on two themes: *anger* or *fear*.

Whenever these emotions are triggered, large amounts of adrenaline are released because the body believes it is being attacked and must protect itself or get away. This triggers the "fight or flight" reaction—with emphasis on the "fight" in the cases of anger or hurt and on "flight" in cases of fear and anxiety.

The purpose of adrenaline, remember, is to mobilize our actions. It energizes our muscles and makes us stronger and more able to flee or to defend ourselves. Unfortunately, the physical retreat or defense is seldom necessary in our world, which is less physical and more social. A high-adrenaline response usually only gets us into more trouble!

Children naturally tend to be quick to anger, quick to fear. One reason for this is that they have not yet learned to control their emotions. Another reason is that children usually feel so helpless. A major reason, I believe, is that they have an *instinctive protective mechanism* built into them.

Whatever the reason, when a child becomes fearful or angry, adrenaline floods his or her system. And there are times, of course, when this adrenaline serves a purpose; it motivates the child to protect himself or herself. In our culture, however, the surge of adrenaline often serves no purpose; it only creates a heightened state of stress.

Adrenaline-producing emotions, furthermore, can become habits and may even become addicting—and this is especially true of anger. Because the state of adrenaline arousal can be enjoyable, a child easily makes it a permanent part of his or her psyche. We call this the "angry child syndrome." The child reacts to even the mildest of frustrations with anger because "letting off steam" feels good. The anger gives the child a sense of power and of being in control. But it can easily become a bad habit that not only destroys relationships but also, eventually, damages health. The angry child easily develops into an adult with the so-called Type A personality—the hurried, hard-driving, easily frustrated type that is especially prone to heart disease.

Don't misunderstand me. The emotion of anger serves a very important function in protecting us. It is a "signal" alerting us to a violation of our rights or to a threat. It mobilizes our energy to "fight or flee" when appropriate. But anger is a dangerous emotion. It can kill us if it is left unattended.

The signal of anger, then, must be heeded at the earliest possible moment, and steps must be taken to deal with the threat or violation and disperse the anger. It is not without significance that the apostle Paul wrote, "If you are angry, don't sin by nursing your grudge. Don't let the sun go down with you still angry—get over it quickly"[3] Unresolved anger is like a kettle left boiling. Sooner of later it runs dry and burns you up.

In a later chapter I will provide more specific help in teaching children how to deal with anger. Suffice it for me to say at this point, that anger *as a behavior* is seldom healthy in our culture, although anger *as a feeling* is an important signal that must be heeded, understood, and talked about. If children can be helped to *talk* about their anger, rather than being left to just act it out, they not only will be less stressed, but will also be healthier and happier in other areas of their lives as well.

The Dangers of Adrenaline Addiction

I have alluded several times to the fact that adrenaline arousal is highly pleasurable. It provides a sense of well-being that energizes us. But there is more to the adrenaline story. As the opening story of this chapter indicates, I am also convinced that this marvelous hormone is highly addicting—as addictive as some of the most powerful drugs available today. In this age where we are extremely concerned about addictions and see scores and scores of people in every neighborhood abusing alcohol, nicotine, and even "hard drugs" such as cocaine, I believe we must pay more attention to the dangers of adrenaline addiction.

Research into the so-called "hidden addictions" in recent years has highlighted the fact that many *addictive behaviors* such as workaholism, gambling, thrill seeking, compulsive shopping, sex, and certain sporting activities may actually have an underlying biochemical basis in the body.[4] Two important groups of hormones are currently implicated in these hidden addictions. One is the set of substances known as endorphins, those tranquilizing substances released in the brain in response to physical exercise. And the other is the group of related hormones known under the collective name of adrenaline.

Adrenaline provides pleasure and energy—a "rush" that makes people feel competent, energetic, challenged. It is, quite literally, a chemically induced "high," and many people find it highly pleasurable.

A drop in the level of circulating adrenaline, however, produces a "letdown" or a unique form of depression. When adrenaline has been flowing strongly for a while, this letdown can cause a fairly classic set of withdrawal symptoms:

- irritability,
- restlessness,
- strong compulsion to "do something,"
- poor concentration,
- feelings of depression.

Most of us have experienced this feeling of letdown at one time or another, after we've been caught up in a period of high excitement or challenge. Given time and rest, they will subside on their own. Some people, however, try to escape these unpleasant withdrawal symptoms by returning to the behavior that originally triggered the adrenal system. So the workaholic sneaks back to work, the gambler to the card table, the thrill seeker to the Bungee cord, or the shopper to the sale. They continue to indulge in adrenaline-recruiting behavior because they need their "fix."

For many people, adrenaline addiction begins in childhood. At a very early age, they come to enjoy the surge of adrenaline and to seek out the behaviors that produce it.

An Adrenaline-Addicted Culture?

Thrill-seeking behavior is particularly dependent on adrenaline, and we are coming to understand more and more just how addicted to thrills and excitement our entire culture is. Sports, especially dangerous sports, are worshiped by many, both as participants and spectators, precisely because these activities help get their adrenaline juices going.

A particular type of personality has been identified as being prone to thrill seeking.[5] Known as the Type T personality, it identifies people who are driven by temperament (with a lot of help from their biological makeup) to a life of constant stimulation through risk taking. These people seem to "need" arousal like other people need air—the more, the better. Ordinary life seems too dull to them, so they are constantly on the lookout for new hobbies, new activities, new "toys." They have a penchant for daredevil activities. And they pursue pleasure not for pleasure's sake, but because the pleasurable activities stimulate the production of adrenaline. This drive for stimulation easily leads them to experiment with drugs. And some Type T's are also known to become delinquents as teenagers and later to seek a criminal life—just for the kicks.

What's the problem with all this? In addition to the fact that much thrill-seeking activity is inherently dangerous, Type T's are basically adrenaline addicts. As with all hard-driven people the major source of their stimulation comes from their own adrenaline. Later in life, therefore, this prolonged surging of adrenaline can cause early heart disease and a tendency toward heart attacks.

But a person doesn't have to be a Bungee-cord diver or skydiver to have a problem with adrenaline. I am alarmed, in fact, that our entire *culture* seems to display Type T characteristics. Many of us ordinary folks are, to some degree, susceptible to stimulation and addiction to our adrenaline. We need excitement. We love a challenge. We avoid boredom at all costs, and we pay a price for this overstimulation in stress disease.

Many activities can provoke high stress through the superabundance of adrenaline they can produce. Could this possibly be the foundation on which teenagers will later turn to stimulant drugs for their kicks? I think so. Addiction experts are coming to believe that there is a "crossover" effect between stimulating behaviors and stimulating drugs. Excessive engagement in stimulating behaviors could very well prepare the way for addiction to stimulating substances.

Learning to Live on Less Adrenaline

What does all this mean? Simply that many events in a child's life can stimulate high levels of adrenaline arousal and even lead to adrenaline addiction. When children are stimulated for long periods of time, the body adapts to this higher level and *high adrenaline becomes the norm*. However, the wear and tear on the mind and body increases dramatically under higher levels of general arousal. Headaches increase. The stomach begins to act up.

Most seriously, cardiovascular disease has its beginning. The high level of circulating adrenaline will work its damage insidiously but permanently.

To help our children protect themselves from stress disease and to prevent the establishment of the habits that will lead to stress-related illness, we must teach our children how to control their level of arousal and literally "switch off" their adrenaline when it is no longer needed. They must learn how to moderate and control their use of adrenaline and become less dependent on being "psyched up."

Children who naturally love excitement and enjoy the thrill of challenge may have to work especially hard at controlling their adrenaline. But because overstimulation is such a given in our culture, all children—even the most easygoing ones—can benefit from learning to enjoy life at lower levels of arousal. All children—and adults!—need to learn to come down frequently from the "mountaintop" and enjoy the peace of the valley, where recuperation and healing can take place. The accelerated pace of modern living tends to rob us of natural recovery time, so that it must be planned into our lives by deliberate design.

Even Jesus was aware of this need for recovery. After a particularly busy time, when "there were many coming and going, and they had no leisure so much as to eat," he told his disciples, "Come ye yourselves apart into a desert place, and rest a while."[6] And that is good advice for our adrenaline-addicted society as well. We will certainly be giving our children a great life-gift if we can teach them how to "come apart and rest."

Summary

The essence of the stress problem is overarousal of the adrenal system. This is the system that releases a group of hormones, including adrenaline, to mobilize us for an emergency. This reaction is commonly known as the "fight or flight" response. The excessive circulation of adrenaline is the primary cause of stress disease.

Among the causes of high adrenaline arousal in children are noise, television, overcrowding, pressures, and certain emotions. The potential for adrenaline addiction is a hazard for children and adults who constantly seek stimulation.

An important goal in reducing stress disease, therefore, is teaching children to balance high arousal with low arousal.

Discussion Questions

1. What is the essence of the stress response? Discuss how this evidences itself in your family's life.

2. Of all the causes of high adrenaline arousal in your children, which one or two can you identify as being a major problem? What changes can you make to reduce this problem?

3. What are some of the socially acceptable things children do to give themselves an adrenaline "fix"? Where should parents draw the line?

3

Is Your Child Overstressed?

Sandra's mother closed the door gently on her daughter's sobs. With a worried expression, she pulled her robe around her and padded to the bedroom, where her husband was beginning to dress for church.

"She says she's not going."

"Again?"

"Yes. She just can't stop crying. And she says she's just too depressed to be with people."

"Well, I think this is just a ploy to keep from going to Sunday school. There was nothing wrong with her on Friday; she aced her algebra test."

"That's true. Come to think of it, she gets this way on the weekends. Do you think she's under too much pressure at school?"

"Sandra loves school; you know that. And besides, kids are *supposed* to be under pressure at school; that's the way they learn to compete in the world.

"Well, maybe you're right, but I'm worried. I think I'll call Dr. Watson in the morning. I'm sure that this isn't normal."

———

Sandra's mother was right to be concerned. Sandra's weekend depressions were clear symptoms of overstress in her life—in her case, a stress that was largely self-imposed.

But how can you tell if a child is overstressed? Or, more to the point, how can you tell when a child's stress is just "normal" pressure and when is it excessive or damaging?

These are important questions. In this chapter, therefore, I want to look at some of the physical and emotional (psychological) manifestations of overstress—the physical and emotional symptoms a child may display when the stress becomes too much.

It's important to recognize, however, that some overstressed children show no overt symptoms. Children are remarkably resilient, and some can endure a lot of stress without showing it on the outside. However, stress damage may still be taking place, as we will see in chapter 6 when I discuss the threat of high cholesterol in children.

For this reason, it is important to evaluate not only a child's stress symptoms, but also his or her stressors—the pressures or challenges that stimulate the stress response in his or her life. In this chapter, therefore, we will be looking at both the *symptoms* and the *sources* of overstress in a child's life.

Physical Symptoms of Distress

The human body is an awesome creation. And nowhere is its complexity and intricate functioning more evident than in the way it protects itself from self-destruction. The body has an intricate warning system to alert us to danger and protect us from damage—and the stress response is part of that system.

How the Body Protects Itself

The symptoms of overstress are intended to *warn us of overuse and danger*. But as we grow up, unfortunately, we begin to see our stress symptoms more as obstacles trying to thwart our progress, so we try to blot them out with painkillers or sedatives. But our symptoms are not enemies; they are our allies. They are intelligently designed for our benefit and protection. We need to heed them and to teach our children how to heed them. Be thankful, therefore, every time you get a headache. You are receiving an intelligent warning that something needs to change.

There are three components to the body's *protective system:*

(1) An activating system. This system, which includes the adrenal system, is designed to prepare us for action when confronted with an event or circumstances that threaten or challenge us. As I explained in chapter 2, one of the things that happens when we are stressed is that adrenaline starts to flow quite strongly. This increases our pulse rate and raises our blood pressure; the heart pumps harder to send blood to our brain and large muscle groups. The heightened flow of adrenaline also stimulates our muscles to tense up in readiness to "fight or flee."

The activating system, remember, is the body's emergency apparatus. Our bodies are not designed to operate in a state of emergency for long.

Overstress happens when the activating system remains "on" for too long a time—when adrenaline continues to flow at a high level.

(2) An alarm system. This system is designed to alert us to imminent danger to our bodily safety or well-being. It sounds the warning whenever we are beyond the safety zone and entering dangerous territory. Destruction and damage is about to take place.

Pain is the primary signal in this part of the system. It tells us that tissue damage is occurring—usually because the tissue is overextended. Many parts of the body are designed to rebel and send out warning signals—in the form of pain—whenever stress has gone too far.

The alarm system operates closely in conjunction with the activating system and eventually lets us know when the activating system has been engaged for too long and our "motors" are "overheating." For instance, if high levels of adrenaline continue to course through the body and the muscles remain taut, the fibers in our muscles will begin to rebel by sending out pain signals. Many aches and pains, and especially tension headaches, are the alarm system's way of saying, "You've gone too far this time."

(3) A recovery system. The final system in the sequence is designed to provide healing. When the stress demand or the emergency is over—or when we heed the message of the alarm system—the brain turns off the activating system and allows the organs, muscles, and glands to rest, rejuvenate, and repair themselves.

Sadly, many people—children included—seldom or never get back to this stage. For them, life is one long emergency, and their activation system remains "on" at all times. Without adequate recovery times, their stress becomes distress and then stress disease. Damage eventually becomes pervasive and even permanent. The most common and serious final consequence of this lack of adequate rejuvenation may be the classic heart attack.

We neglect this system, therefore, to our peril. Learning to use it is one of the most dependable ways of preventing stress damage.

Physical Manifestations of Stress

The *physical* signs of stress, arising from either the activating system or the alarm system, are targeted to certain parts of the body. Some children will show their stress signs in one part, while others will show it elsewhere. Whatever physical manifestations it takes, parents must learn to "tune into" and recognize it as soon as it occurs. The organs of the body most commonly affected are as follows:

(1) Brain. The brain is implicated in *all* stress because it is the "executive director" of the whole stress-response system. However, the brain can also be the site of certain specific stress reactions.

A child who is about to take an examination, for instance, needs her brain not only to work for her in recalling facts and figures, but also in directing the rest of her mind and body. As her body responds to the stress she is under, blood rushes to the brain to make it more efficient. But this heightened flow of blood can easily start a migraine headache process.

When under stress, the brain may also lose its innate capacity to calm us down. When the chemicals in the brain that provide us with a sense of tranquility become depleted under prolonged stress, anxiety and even panic may result. A highly stressed child, may not only have an intense headache while trying to take the examination, but may also feel extremely anxious and even get panicky, forgetting all the facts she has memorized. In an extreme instance, she may collapse with fear.

Not only have I observed such a reaction in the examination room as a student, but through the years I have counseled with many children and college-aged students who have experienced a panic reaction during an examination. There is nothing mysterious about it. It is the normal consequence of pushing the brain too far and too fast.

(2) Heart. The heart with its many pipelines (known as the cardiovascular system) is the next most essential organ that helps us respond to stress. Stimulated by the flow of adrenaline, the heart pumps harder, pushing blood to the brain and other vital organs of our body. In moderation this system works fine. Human beings have never engineered a pump that is as gentle, yet efficient as the heart. But when we become overstressed, several things happen to our heart:

- Our heart thumps, and we might even feel pain in the center of the chest.

- Our heart skips a beat or may beat very rapidly for a brief period.

- Our blood pressure goes up, and we might feel light-headed or dizzy.

These symptoms, in and of themselves, are not dangerous. They are warning signs. But, as we will see later, more insidious destruction could also be going on—hardening of the arteries and the depositing of fatty plaques in the blood vessels. This is what finally leads to heart attacks.

(3) Stomach and Intestines. These digestive organs, known together as the "gastrointestinal system," also play a major role in stress. Under "normal" stress this system is activated to speed up digestion and provide us with the energy we need to cope with the emergency situation. But in many highly stressed children this system also goes haywire because it gets "arousal" messages from high adrenaline. Heartburn (stomach acid being forced up the esophagus), general stomach discomfort ("My tummy hurts!"), nausea,

acute and chronic diarrhea, indigestion, constipation, and churning sensations ("I've got butterflies in my stomach!") are very common symptoms of overstress. Over longer periods of time, when too much stomach acid is released for too long, the lining of the stomach can be eaten away and ulcers can form.

(4) *Muscles*. The muscular system is extremely important in the "fight or flight" response. We need muscles for both fighting and fleeing, so every muscle tightens and tension rises throughout the body when we are under stress. After a while, however, these muscles rebel and send out pain signals. How else can they tell us that they are tired and need a rest?

Prolonged muscle tension brought on by stress can result in all sorts of pain complaints. Lower-back pain and stiffness of the joints are common. Tension headaches result when the muscles of the neck and forehead remain too tense for too long. Teeth grinding and general pain in the jaw can also be related to muscular tension.

(5) *General*. A number of other physical systems can arise from overstress. For instance, the hands get cold because blood has been diverted to more vital organs. (This phenomenon is an important one; in chapter 7, I will show how it can be used as a diagnostic and a stress-reducing device.) The child may break out in a cold sweat or experience skin eruptions. Some children suffer respiratory problems, including aggravation of asthma.

Overstress, in fact, will *aggravate almost any existing physical problem* because it unbalances the body's natural disease-fighting capability. The body cannot fight battles on two fronts. Usually the body shifts its focus to the stress threat and temporarily gives up the battle against the disease. Reducing stress, therefore, will help the body to refocus on fighting real disease.

Physical Effects of Chronic Stress

The body responds to *acute* stress differently than to *chronic* stress.

In *acute stress* the onset is sudden and the stress doesn't last very long. An accident, taking an examination, or going to the dentist would be examples of acute stress for a child.

Chronic stress is different. The arousal is ongoing and unrelenting; it doesn't go away. When a child's parents separate and divorce, for example, that child will suffer from chronic stress. The pressure doesn't go away easily or quickly, but may last for years. Long-term illness, ongoing conflicts with peers or teachers, or abusive home situations would all be examples of chronic stress.

Because it is short-lived, acute stress tends to be less damaging than chronic stress, so I will focus on the latter here.

How does chronic stress affect a child's body?

(1) Chronic stress weakens the body's natural immune system. Important cells that fight disease are depleted. The result? The child gets sick a lot. Colds, influenza, stomach viruses—almost any of the infectious diseases—can take hold. The microbes that cause these infections are around all the time, but our natural immune systems keep them under control. When we are under too much stress for too long, the body focuses on fighting the stress, and we suffer from having no "immune army" available to protect us. There is even evidence that tumors grow faster when the number of our natural "killer cells," part of the immune system, is down.

What does this mean in terms of identifying overstress in your child? Simply that it pays to be alert. Every child gets sick from time to time, but frequent illnesses may be a symptom of too much stress.

(2) The brain's natural painkillers are depleted. The brain produces a wonderful group of hormones called "endorphins" (short for "endogenous morphine") that block pain and make us feel good. When we are under stress, the brain at first increases its production of endorphins to help fight the pain. But when stress continues without a break, the endorphin level begins to decline and we feel more pain.

I frequently encounter a patient who has been under a lot of stress and who complains of feeling "pain all over my body." Some report pain that shifts from one location to another. When there is no disease to explain this pain we can assume that it is evidence of depleted endorphins.

When the brain's supply of endorphins is diminished, everyday aches and pains become magnified, and more significant pain can be excruciating. Going to the dentist when you have been under a lot of stress can be a harrowing experience. Everything hurts more, no matter how gentle the dentist's hands are. Every part of the body suffers from this depletion of endorphins under prolonged stress.

When your child complains of a lot of pain, therefore, pay attention; his or her body may be showing evidence of overstress. Of course, there is always the possibility that your child is exaggerating some discomfort or converting emotional pain into a physical complaint—but doing this can be a sign of stress as well. So before you reach for the medicine bottle, consider that your child may be overstressed. Simply relieving the pain without correcting the underlying stress will not be helpful to the child in the long run.

(3) The brain's natural tranquilizers are depleted. This is perhaps the least understood symptom of stress. Our brains have "receptors" for natural tranquilizers that are produced within the brain. When we feel calm, stress-free and happy, it is because we have an abundant supply of natural tranquilizers. They keep us peaceful, calm, and unruffled, and they also provide us

with a feeling of well-being. When we are under chronic stress, however, these natural tranquilizers are diminished. We become restless, fidgety, and anxious.[1]

The reason artificial tranquilizers are in such high demand today is that people are too stressed. We have to replace our natural tranquilizers with bottled calmness because our brains cannot keep up with the demand. Unfortunately, introducing these artificial tranquilizers may cause the brain to stop producing its own. That is why it is so easy to become "hooked" on artificial tranquilizers.[2]

Parents should pay very careful attention, therefore, to fluctuations in a child's anxiety levels. They can be important clues to the presence of high stress. (I will cover the problem of anxiety more fully in chapter 14.)

Emotional Symptoms of Stress

Children who are under too much stress may display emotional symptoms as well as physical ones. Emotional symptoms can exist by themselves or they can coexist with physical symptoms. In fact, because our bodies and our minds work closely together, many emotional effects have physical causes and results. The more important emotional symptoms are depression, self-esteem problems, anger, and anxiety.

(1) Depression. Depression is a common symptom of too much stress. Periodic bouts of sadness and diminished energy are quite common among teenagers and are often accentuated by lack of sleep. However, children as young as five or six can also suffer from depression.

Sandra's depression, which I mentioned at the beginning of this chapter, was a clear response to overstress. Sandra was about fourteen when she came to me for help with her depressions. Sandra liked people, but her shyness and self-consciousness prevented her from making many friends. To compensate, Sandra relied on academics as her primary source of satisfaction and self-esteem. She worked long hours, always completed her homework to perfection, and often sought out extra-credit projects—just to be sure.

Sandra's depressions first began to hit her after periods of intense academic activity. The day after an exam, for example, Sandra would be tearful and would not want to go anywhere or do anything. Then Sandra's depressions started to strike her almost weekly—beginning on Saturdays. Sandra dreaded weekends. She would wake up with a mild headache and eventually the tears would come. All Saturday and most of Sunday would be spent in morbid self-reflection. She avoided her friends, and finally she refused even to go to Sunday school. By Sunday afternoon, however, Sandra would begin to feel better.

Keeping a Stress-Watch on Your Child

What are the common symptoms of too much stress? Be alert for the following symptoms:

- headaches

- anxiety and panic reactions

- irregular or accelerated heartbeat

- dizziness or lightheadedness

- heartburn

- stomachaches or a "churning" sensation

- intestinal upset

- generalized body pain

- teeth grinding or jaw pain

- cold hands

- skin eruptions

- frequent infections or minor illnesses

- flareups of chronic disorders such as asthma or allergies

- depression

- general lethargy

- outbursts of anger

- loss of appetite

- irritability

- restlessness

- sleeplessness

Sandra's particular kind of depression is a very common one in people who are under a lot of stress, even when this stress is self-imposed. They become intensely involved in some activity, and their activating system springs into action. Adrenaline courses through their bodies, and they feel strong, excited, intensely alive. Then, when the challenge is over, these people experience a massive shutdown. Their adrenaline level drops, and a feeling of anticlimax or even sadness follows. This emotional "letdown" is known as "postadrenaline depression."

I know the experience well. You probably do, too. A person suffering from postadrenaline depression feels "down in the dumps"—sad and generally "blue." Irritability, restlessness, loss of interest in normal activities, loss of appetite, sleeplessness, feelings of worthlessness, and withdrawal from social contacts are the common symptoms of this kind of depression. In Sandra's case, the period after a test and later on the weekends was a time of adrenaline shutdown. Because her response to the challenge of her schoolwork was so intense, her depression was especially deep.

Not every depression is caused by a drop in adrenaline following a period of high challenge, but other kinds of depression can be stress-related as well. Sometimes prolonged stress can disturb thyroid or other glandular functions, causing depression. Sometimes sleeplessness and fatigue, also brought on by stress, can cause depression. A wise parent, therefore, will consider *any* type of depression in a child a sign of stress.

And don't be surprised by an occasional outburst of "I wish I were dead." Such an outcry isn'tnecessarily a warning of dire consequences, but it probably is a cry for help from a child who is overstressed. It is an attempt to be taken seriously and to say, I can't cope anymore. Will someone please pay attention?

(2) Self-esteem problems. Closely associated with depression are problems involving self-esteem. Not only is lowered self-esteem a side effect of depression, but too much stress, especially when associated with failure or disappointment, can erode self-esteem and create in a child a profound sense of unworthiness, which in turn causes more stress.

Lowered self-esteem can actually change a child's personality if allowed to continue. When children are bombarded with thoughts about how stupid they are or how everyone else seems to have it together but they don't, they begin to write a "life script" for themselves. This script tells them how to behave and feel and can make low self-esteem a self-fulfilling prophecy. It can begin to shape their personality into being withdrawn, negative, and prone to failure. For some children the script moves them toward wearing outrageous clothes, experimenting with drugs, or joining a gang as a way of building a personal sense of value.

Possible signs of stress-induced self-esteem problems include the following:

- The child seems to be unhappy, doesn't smile or laugh much.
- The child is easily upset, pushes others away, and refuses to be comforted.
- The child engages in a lot of comparisons, always seeing other children as superior.
- The child complains a lot and criticizes other family members.
- The child teases or attacks others to boost his or her self-image.
- The child refuses to try new challenges or to learn new skills.

(3) Anger. A major part of the "fight or flight" response in stress is the emotion of anger. And this anger serves several useful functions *if* the stress is caused by actual danger. If it is caused by the normal pressures of life, however, the anger not only is of little value; it may even become a further cause for stress. People are less likely to be helpful or friendly toward a child who attacks them every time he or she is stressed.

In really dangerous situations, the anger we feel helps us to get up the courage to fight; it mobilizes our energy to do what is necessary to protect ourselves. If I am suddenly confronted by a mugger, for instance, my anger will help me deal with the threat. But when my stress is caused by overwork or by a teacher who may be too demanding, my anger may not be helpful. It needs to be channeled to some constructive outlet.

Because anger is a built-in emotional adjunct of the activating system, children who are highly stressed will probably also be expressing a lot of anger. It may manifest itself in any of the following ways:

- hostility at any attempt to be helpful,
- aggression toward friends and family,
- instability at even small frustrations,
- picking fights at inappropriate times (such as in restaurants, where it is embarrassing to others),
- temper tantrums (even by teenagers),
- scapegoating or blaming others,
- always playing the role of the victim ("You made me do it" or "It's all your fault"),
- destructive behaviors such as breaking things or throwing valuables away.

Childhood anger can also show itself in less obvious ways. It can come out as excessive passivity, brooding, and even as self-destructive behavior. Some children pinch themselves, cut or mutilate parts of the body that are normally covered or, in more severe cases, starve themselves. In such cases, the children usually feel that they cannot express anger outwardly and so turn it inward, toward themselves.

(4) Anxiety. Anxiety is an important emotional symptom of overstress for two reasons:

- Prolonged stress can dramatically increase anxiety because the stress depletes the brain's natural tranquilizers.

- Anxiety arises when we have too many fears or when we feel we cannot control our lives.

How does childhood anxiety manifest itself?

- increased tension, restlessness, inability to relax,

- nail biting, facial tics, and jumpiness,

- excessive worrying, even about petty problems,

- increased fear and avoidance of any activity that involves a risk of failure,

- increased nightmares, fear of falling asleep,

- morbid apprehension that something terrible is going to happen to someone close to the child,

- fears of animals, certain toys, or certain places,

- inordinate questioning about situations, seeking constant reassurance,

- complaints of gastrointestinal distress or headaches, when no underlying biological cause is suspected,

- marked feelings of self-consciousness and fears of embarrassment or humiliation.

A high level of anxiety is a very clear signal that stress is out of control in a child's life. To relieve this anxiety, the stressors in the child's life must be identified and the stress level reduced.[3]

Your Child's Stressors

Although physical and emotional symptoms can be helpful signposts in detecting overstress, just looking for the symptoms of distress is not enough. Your child may be made of steel and show no obvious sign of stress disease—yet! A careful review of the stressors in your child's world will help alert you to the presence of potential distress even if no symptoms are yet evident.

Remember, the best time to deal with stress is *before* it becomes distress. Some forms of stress damage are hard to reverse. Once the damage is done, it is a lot more difficult to control.

Generally speaking, stressors fall into two categories: *external* and *internal.* A child can be stressed not only by what is going on in his or her external world, but also by thoughts and expectations that are created internally.

Below are some samples of external and internal stressors. I will touch on many others as we proceed.

External Stressors

As we pointed out in chapter 1, children today live in a stressful world. Here are some of the circumstances in a child's environment that may put a child under too much stress:

(1) Conflict. Conflict may arise in the home, at school, or in social settings. They may be "cold wars," where no one shouts but everyone is hostile or indifferent. Or they may involve open warfare—yelling, pushing, even physical violence. Either kind of conflict can put inordinate stress on a child.

Tommy's situation is a good example. Tommy was the youngest of three brothers in a rather undisciplined home. Neither the mother nor father exercised any control over how the boys treated each other. And the lack of discipline had taught the boisterous older brothers disrespect for each other and a rather cruel way of putting each other down. Their language was quite shameful, but neither parent paid much attention. "Boys will be boys" they would say, to appease their guilt and excuse their poor parenting.

Destructive and unruly, they showed no respect for anyone else's property. Neighbors cringed when they saw the boys emerge from the house. But the greatest victim was Tommy. He could never own anything of his own; one of his older brothers would snatch and keep it. They appropriated birthday gifts, a transistor radio he saved for and bought himself, and even clothing his parents had bought him. Tommy tried to fight for his rights but was always beaten up. He became the butt of his brothers' jokes and the scapegoat for all their problems. By the time he was thirteen, Tommy was an overly anxious, highly stressed, and deeply angry boy.

Conflict, especially where there is a lot of anger and hostility, is extremely stressful for children. Parents should work hard to minimize their own conflicts as well as to exercise appropriate discipline in the home to minimize conflict caused by other members of the family.

(2) Life Change. We have known for decades that life change of any kind increases the possibility of illness.[4] Today we know that stress causes this increased susceptibility by weakening the immune system. Stress, in other words, is a natural by-product of change. And any child, of necessity, will face a number of life changes before reaching adulthood.

Growing up itself is a series of changes—from childhood to adolescence, from hating girls (or boys) to liking them, from carefree living to responsibility, from dependence to independence. These developmental changes, together with illnesses, deaths, moves, changes of schools, new friends, and finally leaving home, are all quite normal in a child's life—and many are quite pleasant—but they are still stressful. They call on a child to adjust, find new ways of behaving and thinking. If a child makes the appropriate adjustments, health ensues. He or she learns skills that help in later life. If the child does not adjust well, however, stress increases dramatically.

Some life changes, by their very nature, produce extraordinary stress in children because they add the element of change to a situation that is difficult in itself. Here are some examples:

- parental separation or divorce,
- death of a parent or sibling,
- severe injury or serious illness,
- developing a disability or a handicap,
- injury, illness, or disability of a sibling,
- one or both parents becoming alcoholic,
- changes in discipline, especially an increase in abuse.

Parents need to be particularly sensitive to how a child adjusts to or copes with any of these highly stressful situations. But parents need also to recognize that *positive* life changes can also be highly stressful to a child. A move to a new and bigger house, being put into a "gifted" class at school, getting a new pet, a week's visit to Walt Disney World—these, too, elevate stress levels.

All this means that change in a child's life—even positive change—should take place *as slowly as possible* and *should be limited*, if at all possible, to one or two changes at a time. Allowing a child time to adjust to change will minimize the stress consequences.

(3) Excessive competition. We live in a highly competitive culture. From our earliest years we have to compete to get what we need and to feel adequate. Too many children are bombarded from babyhood with the popular wisdom that "winning is everything." But the "win at all costs" philosophy

Change Is Stressful!

Any life change—positive or negative—can add to a child's stress. Here are some examples of stress-causing changes in a child's life:

- Death of a family member

- Birthdays or holidays

- Developmental milestones (such as the onset of puberty)

- Marital conflict or separation of the parents

- Injury or illness to the child or someone close

- Remarriage by either parent

- Mother's return to the workplace

- Birth of a baby into the family

- Change of school

- Move to new town or neighborhood

- Family member—such as a sibling—leaving home

- Older relative—such as a grandparent—moving into the home

- Unemployment in family

- Change in family's standard of living

- Change in church activities

- Change in sleep schedule

- Going on a vacation

is not only morally questionable; it carries undeniable stress consequences. If too much competition is injected into a child's life too early, a child may become compulsive and develop a distorted fear of failure. Both can cause intense stress.

Toni had developed an exaggerated fear of failure by the time she was ten years of age. Pushed by an overzealous father to "be the best," Toni had become a compulsive overdoer. She pushed herself very hard, fearing that someone else would do better. And she lived in constant fear of being second; she could not accept any place but first in anything.

As a result of her excessively high standards, Toni was destined to fail, because nobody can be first in everything. More importantly, Toni's competitiveness got in the way of her social development. She was too preoccupied with how others were doing and whether or not they were "right on her tail," as she put it, to develop normal friendships. She became a very lonely person, always fearing that the people around her would somehow outshine her.

It was no surprise, then, to see that Toni was already "burned out" by the time she reached puberty. Her overly competitive life had worn her young body out. She developed chronic headaches and feelings of exhaustion.

Competition can be healthy, but it must be balanced. Children must learn that some failure is inevitable and normal, and that sometimes failure can be more conducive to growth than constant success. Children must also learn to cooperate, to be good team players, and to celebrate the accomplishments of others. These are tough assignments, but they are absolutely necessary for a child's healthy, happy, and stress-free maturity.

Internal Stressors

Not all stressors are external, of course. Many arise from a child's internal beliefs and attitudes. Here are some examples:

(1) *Unrealistic or unreasonable expectations.* Every child needs to understand what is expected of him or her. And every child needs something to strive for, a sense of where he or she is going in life. In the beginning, the expectations and aspirations come from the parents, and they are easily internalized by the children; the parents' expectations often become the children's expectations. Of course, they also add a few of their own, just to make life a little more complicated.

A parent may begin by setting out very reasonable expectations. They communicate certain values: Work hard. Don't steal. Show respect for others. They also communicate their hopes and dreams for their children's future: Get a good job. Marry the right person. Do something valuable with your life.

Many of these expectations are incorporated into the child's value system and are healthy and necessary. But sometimes the expectations that parents communicate and their children internalize are unreasonable.

Parents often try to live out their unfulfilled dreams through their children. I know I have done this. When my three daughters were small, I would often daydream about what I wanted each of them to become. Then one day I woke with a start. I realized that all my dreams for my daughters were really my own dreams that I had never fulfilled—at least at that stage in my life. I changed my expectations. And I do believe that I have given each of my daughters the freedom to be themselves! However, now that they are mothers, I notice that they are repeating the same pattern. So I quietly remind them that they, too, need to let their children "go free."

What happens when a child's internalized expectations don't match his or her abilities, interests, or sense of calling? The inevitable result is stress.

I know one older teenager who is under a lot of stress because he has always been expected to take over his father's business one day. The son is terrified. He doesn't have his father's brains, he tells me; he is much better at outdoor work. Deep down he would rather be a park ranger than a businessman. But he believes that his father's expectations are superior, so he is doing everything he can to meet them. As a result, this young man is experiencing severe internal conflict. And the more he fails at the activities his father values, the more stress he feels.

Now the fascinating point is this. When I talk to the father about the reasons for his son's high stress, the father insists, "I have never once told my son that he has to take over my business." It's true. The father had never ever said this in so many words. But he had taken over the business from his father, so it was quite natural for the son to think the same was expected of him. And this expectation had been reinforced by many subtle cues and innuendos. Finally, through conjoint therapy, we were able to clear up both father's and son's expectations and to relieve the son's high stress.

As this father-and-son story shows, unreasonable expectations do not need to be overt to be stressful. Unstated expectations can control a child just as fully as those that are spelled out. In fact, it's often what we *don't* say that can set up unreasonable expectations in our children's minds.

Sharon, my middle daughter, taught me this lesson. Shortly after starting in college she called late one night. She had been experiencing intense stress symptoms, including headaches and sleeplessness. Her first examinations were approaching, and she felt tremendous pressure to succeed. As we talked, I realized that part of the problem was that she feared disappointing me.

I protested, "But my darling, I have never ever told you that you must pass every examination to please me!!" Her response was most enlightening, and absolutely on target: "Dad, you may not have told me I must succeed, but you have never ever told me it was OK to fail." We cleared the air that night. And she went on to complete her studies—the better because the stress of overly high expectations had been relieved.

(2) Learned helplessness. The concept of helplessness is a very useful one in understanding childhood stress. Children naturally feel powerless. After all, everyone else tells them what to do, and they have very little real say-so in their lives. Many children feel they have to comply with the demands of parents even to get their basic necessities met. This can create an intense feeling of helplessness. And when this sense of helplessness continues too long, it can become a "learned" response. Even as the children grow and reach the point that they should have more control over life, they continue to believe they have no power, that they cannot change anything. Too often, they just give up.

Teenagers, especially, easily develop this sense of helplessness when they are subjected to a lot of stress, but the process of "learning" can begin at a much earlier age. Whenever stress undermines a child's ability to develop confidence and responsibility at his appropriate age level, he is likely to feel powerless and, over a period of time, to learn helplessness. Unfortunately, because the learned helplessness reduces a child's ability to take control of life, it also becomes a cause of further stress. A vicious cycle is easily established—with stress leading to helplessness, helplessness causing stress, and stress further reinforcing the feeling of helplessness.

Parents who understand the nature of helplessness can deliberately take steps to empower a child and help him or her feel more in control. Whenever possible, for instance, parents can allow children to make their own decisions. Even a preschooler can choose between several outfits to wear for the day or choose whether to go to the park or take a walk in the neighborhood. Teaching children from an early age how to manage money, be more assertive, or take more responsibility for important family functions can all help counteract the development of learned helplessness.

(3) Sexual identity issues. As children approach puberty, and for several years afterwards, they become preoccupied with sexual issues. Quite a few become confused about what their perceived roles must be.

Our culture, which bombards children constantly with contradictory messages about sex, compounds the confusion. Different sources in the family, at school, and in the media, send loud but very different messages: "Just say no!" "Do it now!" "Wait until you're married." "Wait till you're ready." "Sex is dirty." "Sex is cool." "Sex is dangerous." "Sex is everything."

The combination of natural inquisitiveness and provocative and contradictory messages from society can cause a preteen or an early teen to become quite stressed over sexual matters. The stress comes from not know-ing what to do with the stimulation one begins to feels at this age.

Clear guidance and the laying down of sexual boundaries and values is extremely important in minimizing sex-related stress. But it is also impor-tant to strike a balance between clear guidelines and overly rigid restrictions. An overly strict attitude in this area can create as many problems for a child as a very lax one. For many children, especially girls, the topic of sex can easily be colored with fear and disgust. Other children, especially boys, can develop an unhealthy preoccupation with sex and exaggerated sense of guilt.

Many boys, for example, are treated with disgust when they want to talk about masturbation. Parents avoid the topic like the plague. This can create a lot of stress and confusion in children who come to believe that there is something very shameful or evil about sex. Rather than helping boys to control their sexual urges, these feelings of guilt act to heighten the ten-sion and may even create an obsession with masturbation. The disapproval children feel creates anxiety which, when paired with sexual arousal, makes the relief of masturbation even more exciting. Taboos around sexuality al-ways do this; they turn a normal and healthy part of life, created for appro-priate expression in marriage, into an obsessive and compulsive drive.

The general subject of sex, of course, is much too large for me to ad-dress adequately here. Suffice it to say at this point that parents must do everything in their power to communicate a healthy sexuality to their chil-dren. Children need open, balanced communication about sex. I urge par-ents to talk about sex as naturally and frankly as they can. Remember: If you don't talk to your children about sex, they will find out about it from some-one else.

Summary

I have discussed the more common symptoms of stress and the variety of external and internal sources of stress that a child can experience.

The human body is equipped with a wonderful and efficient self-pro-tective mechanism that consists of (1) an activating system, (2) an alarm system, and (3) a recovery system. Most physical symptoms of overstress oc-cur when the activating system, meant for emergency use, is engaged for a prolonged period, triggering the alarm system. These symptoms may take the form of pain or other forms of discomfort and may involve the brain, the heart, the gastrointestinal tract, or other areas of the body.

Emotional symptoms of overstress may also have physical under-pinnings. They include depression, self-esteem problems, anger, and anxiety.

Since not all children show overt symptoms of overstress, it is important to evaluate the stressors in a child's life as well as the symptoms. External stressors include conflict, life change, and excessive competition. Internal stressors include unrealistic expectations, learned helplessness, and sexual identity issues.

Discussion Questions

1. Review the physical and emotional symptoms of distress. How many can you recognize in your child, and how many in yourself?

2. Of the many external sources of stress that a child can experience, which can be controlled? How could you help your child cope with external sources of stress that cannot be controlled?

3. Because helplessness is a major cause for stress in a child, children should be given a feeling of control over some aspects of their lives. Suggest some actions or decisions you can let your child take that can reduce these feelings of helplessness.

4

Your Child's Stress Profile

Rose and Peter stood at their front door, dressed and ready to leave—ready, that is, except that eighteen-month-old Peter, Jr., was throwing another fit. Desperation was written all over his little face as he sat crying in his grandmother's arms, reaching out piteously for his mother and father. Feeling a familiar mixture of concern and irritation, Rose kissed him once more, turned a resolute back to her screaming son, then followed her husband out the door.

"I just can't understand it," she told her husband as they walked toward their parked car. "We've done everything right according to the experts. We only leave him with my mom or your mother. We tell him we're going and when we'll be back. We don't leave too abruptly. But he *still* acts like this every time we go anywhere—even for a little while. Barbara and Jeff's little boy isn't like that at all, and neither is Sandra's little girl. What's wrong with Peter?"

My first task, when Peter and Rose consulted me, was to help them accept that their child was different from others—not inferior, just different—and to learn to understand him. Like every child, young Peter is a particular human being in a particular set of circumstances. In order to help little Peter handle his stress, this couple needed to understand his unique "stress profile"—the way the "stress ingredients" in his life fit together.

There are basically two ingredients to childhood stress:

- the child—especially his or her particular sensitivity to stress, and

- the child's world—the particular stressors in his life that trigger the stress response.

Understanding how these ingredients interact can take you a long way toward preventing stress damage in your child.

The Key to Understanding

Human behavior, after all, is not really that mysterious. In fact, nearly all behavior has an explanation. Even those children who seem to react unpredictably in certain situations are probably reacting in a way that is consistent with their unique personality and physiology, their distinctive history, and the particular stresses in their life. Understanding the reasons for your child's behavior, therefore, is an important step in helping him or her handle stress more positively.

Remember that as a parent you have at least two qualifications that make you supremely capable of understanding your child. First, you probably know your child better than anyone else, including a professional counselor. Don't minimize this knowledge. You live (or have lived) with your child; you observe his or her reactions on a regular basis. You probably know well the people who contributed both to his or her genetic makeup and his or her environment. With a few additional tools, you should be uniquely qualified to assess your child's distinct stress-proneness.

Second, you were once a child yourself. While the outside world has changed, the inner workings of a child remain the same. With a little effort you can recall your own childhood experiences and responses.

I can vividly recall what it was like to have my parents separate and divorce when I was twelve. I can easily relive my feelings following the divorce and my mother's remarriage and what it felt like to be "adopted" by a stepfather.

You have similar "feeling memories." Draw on them as you try to understand your child's stress. Recollect your own experiences and recall your own thoughts and how you reacted. Then try to slip into your child's way of thinking and feeling. This will help you to be empathetic and understanding. Your child will feel understood and accepted at a very deep level.

It can be useful to actually ask yourself, "How did I feel when I faced this challenge as a child?" Ask your child how he or she feels also. Trust your common sense, and don't overlook the obvious. A little patience and a lot of listening will make you the expert in understanding your child's unique stress response. And with understanding, solutions will quickly become more obvious to you.

Understanding Your Child's Unique Stress Response

Your child is unique. No two children share exactly the same genetic makeup. No two children have gone through the exact same set of life experiences. And no two children will respond the same way to a given stressful life situation. This basic fact is key to understanding the role stress will play in any child's life.

Many parents make the mistake of wanting their child to be just like—or better than—all other children. They have difficulty accepting that their child's response to stress may be very different from that of other children. And they especially have trouble accepting that some children are simply more prone to stress than others.

But susceptibility to stress does vary substantially, even between children in the same family. These variations are caused by differences in (1) personality, (2) physiology, and (3) life experience.

The Child's Unique Personality

One important factor in a child's unique susceptibility is his or her personality or temperament. This is so important that I will devote an entire chapter to helping you understand the role personality can play in a child's ability to tolerate stress.

The Child's Unique Physiology

Physiology is as important as personality in determining a child's susceptibility. Different children respond to the same bombardment of stress stimuli with substantially different physiological reactions.

Physical health, for instance, affects how well children tolerate stress. Any parent who has spent the day with a sick child understands this. A six-year-old with an earache or intestinal infection just can't handle frustrations as well as he normally would. His little body is struggling to cope with the invasion of some microbe. His temperature is up, and all his immune resources are mobilized to fight the illness. His body can ill afford to mobilize the physical resources for coping with additional stress—say, a bout of teasing from his big sister. When stress is superimposed on physical illness, the child will be much more likely either to "lose it" emotionally or to become physically sicker.

This helps explain why children can appear to take on different personalities when they are sick. A child who is usually quite calm and able to cope with stress may suddenly become extremely out-of-sorts, irritable, and unmanageable—or much quieter and more withdrawn.

Understanding parents will make plenty of allowance for such variability in stress tolerance due to physical factors. During those times, they will also make special efforts both to reduce the stress the child is exposed to and to bolster his resources for coping. Children who are under the weather or physically weakened have a particular need for plenty of rest, nutritious food, and moderate but not overstimulating exercise. They should steer clear of excess sugar and caffeine and avoid activities that recruit excess adrenaline. Protecting a child from excess stress when he or she is physically ill or run-down is both a kindness and an important stressproofing tool.

But health is not the only physiological factor that affects children's responsiveness to stress. Even healthy children will vary in their physical reaction to stress. Some children are physically "programmed" to react more dramatically than others; they respond to a challenge or threat with high excitement and energy. We call these children "hot reactors."

Charlie is a hot reactor. He is a bright boy, just turned twelve years of age. Quick both in body and mind, Charlie can almost always anticipate what you are going to do and gets there before you do. He moves quickly, eats fast, and seems always to be in a hurry. He never sits still for very long and easily becomes bored. His whole family sees him as a "chip off the old block" because his father is exactly the same. ("Hot reactors" tend to run in families.)

Hot reactors tend to be "hot headed," "hot blooded," and "hot tempered." They are quick to respond to changes around them, and they easily become irritable, frustrated, or threatened in response to stress. Hot reactors also experience significant physiological changes in response to challenge. Their adrenaline surges, and their blood pressure rises dramatically. Pulse rates speed up, stomachs churn, muscles tense, and even hands grow colder or sweatier. And as we have seen—all these changes can be bad for the body if allowed to continue.

Clearly, hot reactors enjoy certain advantages in the world; they frequently beat others "to the draw." But these "high octane" people also pay a penalty in terms of greater stress. Hot reactors tend to recruit more stress hormones and suffer more from stress disease. They are more prone to panic attacks in later life and run a greater risk for early heart disease. Because the long-term consequences for being a hot reactor are quite serious, this type of reactivity needs to be understood and brought under control.

And control *is* possible. Hot reactors may be genetically predisposed to overrespond, but they *can* learn to regulate their physical and emotional responses. I know. I have been a hot reactor all my life—but I have learned what it takes to cool down this basic physiological response. If your child is a hot reactor, you can help him or her learn do the same.

Tim's Story: Case History

Tim is fifteen years old, small for his age, and very timid and unassuming. He always stands in the back of the crowd. He seldom asserts himself, and as a result gets pushed around a lot by his friends.

Tim is quite adamant that he is the way he is because of the tremendous stress he has lived with most of his life. His stress has a single root: alcohol. Ever since he can remember, his parents drank. They describe themselves as "social drinkers," but from Tim's description they passed that point long ago.

Tim has come to dread weekends, which is when the trouble usually starts. All week long, Tim worries about what will happen come Friday. And it usually does. It starts on Friday afternoons, when Tim's father goes out drinking with his friends. His mother, left alone at home, starts drinking by herself. Then, around midnight, Tim's father comes home, and the bickering begins. Tim can't sleep, and he is frequently drawn into the arguments by one or the other parent, who is trying to gain Tim's support for their respective sides of the altercation.

The drinking and fighting goes on for hours—well into Saturday morning—until finally, to Tim's relief, his parents fall asleep. As soon as he wakes up, Tim takes off for somewhere—anywhere—just to get out of the house. He walks down to the neighborhood sports ground to watch whatever activities are going on, or if in summer, he grabs his swimming trunks and heads for the local pool.

What causes Tim the most stress is the stark contrast between his parents' sober behavior and the way they act when they are drunk. When sober both parents are loving, kind, considerate, and attentive to him. When they drink, however, their personalities change dramatically; they become hateful and abusive. When they are sober he is drawn to them. When they are drunk he is repelled by them. The constant alternation between his parents sober and drunk behavior creates an ongoing inner tension for Tim—a constant state of anger and fear. While he loves and wants to respect his parents because they are basically good when they are sober, he has slowly come to hate them, especially his father, when they are intoxicated. And then he feels extremely guilty.

"I wanted to run away from this horrible and painful side of my life," Tim once told me, "but another part of me wanted to stay and be happy and secure in my home. I felt so helpless at times. I am sure that if I were bigger than my father, I would have beaten him up many times because of what he was doing. I know my parents are not aware of the deep stress they cause me, and I also know that they basically love me. But it is very strange how parents seem to think that children just forget it all when it's over. They treat me as if I must accept what is going on and fit into it. I try to do so but it sure takes a toll on me."

The Child's Unique Stress History

Every child brings to a particular stress event in his or her life a history of past experiences with stress. This history influences how he or she copes with stress in the present.

Billy is a good illustration. He is now eight years of age and has been forced to adjust to his parents' lengthy and painful separation and their impending divorce. Over the past few years, he has faced intense family conflict almost daily and has received very little support from either parent. Not surprisingly, Billy is having trouble in school. He finds the struggle to cope with his schoolwork much more stressful than does his best buddy, Paul, whose family life and history have been much more stable.

The contrast is quite noticeable. Because Billy has been exposed to a stressful home situation so long, he quickly gives up, has few coping skills, and seems depressed much of the time. Paul, who has fewer battles to face at home, is far more confident, brave, and outgoing. The difference in the two boys' stress histories dramatically affects the way they respond to new stresses.

In considering a child's stress history, we must remember that adults and children don't always see things the same way. An event that an adult considers low-stress may seem very stressful to a child. A quiet visit by grandparents who live far away may be a just a pleasant interlude for a parent, but a major event for the child.

Even more important to remember is the fact that a life event does *not have to be unpleasant* in order to be stressful. Many highly pleasurable experiences may produce more stress problems than unpleasant ones. A death in the family, a marital separation, or an intense conflict can certainly cause huge amounts of stress. But so *also* can a wedding, the purchase of a car or a home, starting school, or coming home for the holidays.

Any activity or experience that triggers adrenaline arousal—pleasant or unpleasant—increases stress. That stress then becomes part of the child's history and helps determine how successfully or how unsuccessfully the child copes with future stressors.

Understanding Your Child's Stressful World

Just as every child is unique in his or her personality, physiology, and stress history, every child faces a unique combination of "stressors"— the pressures or challenges that stimulate the stress response in his or her life.

Any stimulus that is personally threatening or highly arousing to a child becomes a stressor. Stressors can be:

Stress Test 2: My Child's Stressors

Child's name _____

Some stressors are internal, that is, they come from who the child is, while some are external or environmental. This test will help you consider both types of stressors in your child's life. Carefully review the circumstances in your child's life for the past three or four weeks and rate the following questions using this scale:

0 = My child infrequently feels or experiences this.
1 = My child sometimes (perhaps once a month) experiences this.
2 = My child experiences this often (between once a month and once a week).
3 = My child experiences this frequently (more than once a week).

Rating

1. My child feels pressured by too many demands and feels that there isn't enough time for relaxing or playing. _____

2. My child quarrels a lot with peers or siblings. _____

3. My child has difficulty expressing how she or he feels about people or situations. _____

4. My child has disturbing dreams or nightmares. _____

5. My child is exposed to family quarrels and arguments. _____

6. I or my spouse tend to use strict punishment on our child. _____

7. My child feels that other children have things he or she does not have. _____

8. I or my spouse shout at my child whenever he or she is disobedient. _____

9. My child is under a lot of pressure to do well in school. _____

10. My child tends to be tardy and is often late for school for no legitimate reason. _____

11. My child has difficulty keeping up with schoolwork. _____

12. My child worries about what his or her teacher thinks of him or her. _____

13. My child feels rejected or excluded by other children. _____

14. My child does not handle delays or being told to wait for something very well. _____

15. My child is sensitive to noise, cold or heat, tight or itchy clothes, dirt, or dampness. _____

Total Score _____

Test Interpretation

0–5 Your child is remarkably free of any significant stressors in his/her life. Continue to monitor these stressors from time to time in case they change.

6–10 There are some minor sources of stress in your child's life, but he/she may be coping with these quite effectively. Review these again to see if you can make any improvements for your child.

11–20 Your child's stressors are moderate and may be producing unpleasant or unmanageable stress. Some attention should be given to relieving some of these stressors.

21–30 Your child is being subjected to a significant number of stressors. If your child is vulnerable, he or she may respond with a high level of stress. You should give urgent attention to relieving your child of many of these stressors.

Over 31 Your child is being subjected to a high level of stress. He or she requires urgent relief because of the overload. You should do everything possible to reduce the number and intensity of stressors your child is experiencing. Seek professional help, if necessary, but your child's situation needs prompt attention.

Note: Review again the test items that have a rating of 2 or more to better understand the stressful world of your child. See if there are any "themes" or features of your child's world that you can change and thus reduce the likelihood of overstress.

- physical (cold, heat, noise, bacteria, viruses, or chemicals),
- psychological (conflict, tension, pressure, rejection, failure, or excitement), or
- spiritual (a sense of sinfulness, meaninglessness, or failure).

The range of possible stressors in any child's life is enormous. Unfortunately, many are often overlooked even by caring parents. Many children suffer in silence, unwilling or unable to talk about the problems that bug them and the sources of stress in their lives. They feel ashamed or fear being scoffed at by adults, so they bottle up their fears and internalize their stresses. It may take a little time and some careful observation for parents to "tune into" the unique world of stress in their child's life.

Stress Test 2, "My Child's Stressors," can help you understand your child's world better. You may want to take it before we examine in more detail the stresses of a child's world and the resources that can help him or her cope with stress.

An Increasingly Stressful World

The world of the child has always been stressful—but the stresses are different today, at least in middle-class America. In past times—say, more than one hundred years ago—physical stress was perhaps greater. Children carried out heavy physical labor at an earlier age and were more at risk for malnutrition or from diseases like typhoid, smallpox, and appendicitis. And there were always certain groups of children—say, the urban slum dwellers and child factory workers of the nineteenth century—who lived lives of constant pressure.

Nevertheless, the overall pace of life in earlier centuries was slower—without electricity, automobiles, or telephones, it had to be. There was more drudgery, but also less excess stimulation. People competed against one another at the workplace or the local fair, but not in the world marketplace. For most people, darkness and winter dictated enforced rest periods.

For today's children, *psychological* stressors are perhaps greater than they have ever been. Children of the "information age" must learn more, compete more, cope with more demanding moral temptations, and work harder than at any time in our history to achieve even the bare essentials of life. The media makes them far more alert to the dangers they face in the world. And the stepped-up pace of modern life gives them very little "downtime" for recovering from this stress. Growing up has never been easy, but I am convinced it has never been harder than today.

Just think about it for a moment. Perhaps in your childhood, and certainly in your parents' or grandparents', children could limit their worries to simple concerns like what to wear for "trick or treating" or what bait to use when going fishing with Grandpa. Today's city child must know not to eat the Halloween candy until Mom or Dad has tested it for razor blades and to watch out for hazardous waste down at the pond—not to mention avoiding strangers while walking home from school, and to stay indoors after dark to avoid gang activity. In many ways, our world has become more dangerous, and it has certainly become more stimulating. The result is an overall stress level that can be very hazardous to children.

Stress Factors

Several factors influence what your child's "stress world" is like. Perhaps the most important of these is their *stage of development.* Stress and development interact in several ways.

First, the tasks of growing up—such as potty training for a toddler, learning to read for a six-year-old, or "separating" from the family for an adolescent—are inherently challenging and therefore stressful. A child who has difficulty negotiating any of these tasks will feel the additional stress of disappointing others or not measuring up to his or her standards.

Second, the specific way a child reacts to stress will reflect his or her stage of development. For instance, a preschooler who is first learning to venture out into the world and experience the world outside her family may respond to additional stress by becoming overly shy or anxious about strangers. A preteen who is at an extremely self-conscious stage may respond to stress with excruciating embarrassment, while a teenager who is trying to separate from her family of origin may react with open rebellion. The sidebar on p. 62 outlines some of the specific stress issues children at each stage of development may encounter.

There is also evidence that *birth order* may affect a child's vulnerability to stress. In some ways, first-born children tend to be more vulnerable.[1] They are their parents' first "experiment" in child rearing and therefore bear the brunt of both their parents' mistakes and their high expectations. As a whole, first-born children tend to be more serious and "responsible," and this sense of responsibility can carry a heavy degree of stress.

But each place in a family can carry its own special kind of stress. Middle children may experience psychological stress of feeling "forgotten," and both middle children and the "baby of the family" may feel the pressure of trying to "keep up" with an older, more accomplished sibling.

Each child in a family may experience a family crisis differently. For instance, first-born children typically experience more stress when divorced parents remarry, but last-born children tend to become more vulnerable as a stepfamily becomes established. It is not difficult to see why this happens. First-born and last-born children experience some degree of privilege in the family, and they also tend to be closer to their parents than middle children. When the parent remarries, the oldest child feels the displacement of affection first, but being older learns to adjust to the change sooner. The younger child may at first get extra comfort from the mother, but as the stepfamily develops, begins to feel the loss of the mother's special attention.

When the effect of *gender* is examined, different types of stress seem to affect the sexes differently. Girls, for instance, are more likely to experience abdominal pain and loss of appetite as a reaction to stress, while boys tend to respond with poorer concentration, fighting, and conduct disorders.[2] In other words, girls are more likely to direct their stress inward, while boys direct it outwards.

In addition, a particular stressor may affect one gender more than the other. For instance, the stress of marital separation and divorce seems to affect boys more than girls. This may be due to the fact that the father is more likely to leave the family and that boys feel this loss more acutely—at least at first—than girls.

What this all means is that not only must we understand and allow for differences between children in stress vulnerability, but we must also take into account the age, birth order, and sex in helping a child cope with the stressors in his or her world.

Stress Issues for Different Age Groups

How do children of different age-groups experience stress? This depends partly on the child, of course, but certain stressors are predictable at different stages of development. Let me highlight some of the experiences and developmental issues that may contribute to the stress of each major age-group. Note that these issues may include both *causes* and *manifestations* of stress. Note also that the inclusive ages for each stage overlap, especially in the stages surrounding adolescence. This is because the onset of puberty and exposure to issues such as sex and drugs begin so much earlier for some children than for others.

Stress Issues for Preschoolers (Birth to Age Five)

- Discovery of autonomy and resistance to discipline
- Shyness and stranger anxiety
- Learning to share
- Learning bladder or bowel control
- Fear of the dark
- Separation anxiety
- Day care problems
- Destructive behaviors (hitting or biting)
- Temper tantrums

Stress Issues for Middle Childhood (Ages Five through Seven)

- Transition to school environment
- Heightened expectations for performance
- New competency issues: reading, writing, arithmetic
- Curtailment of physical activity—need to sit still
- Stubbornness and refusal to obey
- Jealousy over parents' love and attention
- Self-criticism
- Increased self-consciousness
- Excessive boasting to boost self-esteem
- Heightened interest in sexual matters
- Difficulty in handling rejection or failure

Stress Issues for Later Childhood (Ages Eight to Ten)

- Moodiness, sulking
- Acute body awareness—demand for privacy, modesty when dressing
- Overt anger
- Increased self-criticism and self-rejection

- Resentment of parental authority
- Growing sense of independence and autonomy
- Beginning of some rebelliousness, lying
- Deepening of school curriculum; higher academic expectations
- Exposure to drug and substance-abuse issues
- Popularity, formation of cliques
- Heightened sense of competition—who can and can't, has and has not
- Concern over athletic success—performance and body image

Stress Issues for Preadolescents (Ages Nine to Thirteen)

- Self-consciousness over physical signs of development
- Increased concern over social pressures and acceptance
- Confusion about sex roles and opposite sex
- Concern about overdevelopment or underdevelopment
- Intense introspection
- Conflict with parents over amount of freedom
- Testing of boundaries by rebelling
- Continuing pressure about drugs and sex

Stress Issues for Early Adolescents (Ages Twelve to Fourteen)

- Intense group pressure—need to belong
- Entry into high-school environment
- Testing of boundaries of control
- Acute self-esteem issues
- Continued concern with physical development
- Dating issues and sexual pressures
- Ongoing drug pressures

Stress Issues for Older Adolescents (Ages Fourteen through Sixteen)

- Conflicts over desire for independence
- Increased financial pressures—clothes, cars, etc.
- Peer pressure
- Disappointments over not achieving ideal self
- Experimentation with drugs and sex
- Continuing belongingness issues
- Growing sense of reality about who she/he really is
- Worry about the future—further education, career, marriage

The Big Stressors

Stress seems to be everywhere in most children's lives, but certain common experiences seem especially fraught with tension for many children. Here is a quick overview of some of the "stress biggies" in a child's life:

(1) Home Stress. As I pointed out in chapter 1, stress at home carries a "double whammy" for children. Tension on the home front not only adds to the stress level; it also robs the child of the secure "home base" that helps them cope with the stress.

Parental strife and divorce, of course, is a number-one ingredient in home stress. But children can also be stressed by other crises at home: unemployment, illness or death in the family, financial difficulties, overcrowding, strife between siblings, and even a cluttered environment can be stressors in the home environment.

(2) School and Day-Care Stress. The school environment can be a major source of stress for children, who must spend years and years in this environment.

Except for the few parents who have the skills (and courage) to undertake home schooling, most must rely on schools to educate their children. Relatively few can afford private schools—not that these are necessarily less stressful. Private schools do at least give parents a measure of freedom to choose where to place their child. With public schools, parents and children must take what they get—and it's not always good!

How do schools stress kids? This varies, of course, from school to school, but here are possible sources of school stress:

- tests (most children hate them!),
- grades and the pressure to perform,
- pressure to conform,
- nonsupportive or abrasive teachers,
- indifferent school systems,
- overdemanding extracurricular activities,
- ridicule of youngsters who are "different,"
- crime at school (theft, weapons, drugs).

For small children whose parents both work—and their numbers are increasing—day care can also be a significant source of stress.

For some children, day care means being cared for by underpaid, undertrained workers, adjusting to frequent changes in caregivers, adjusting to a chaotic or overregulated environment, being exposed to communicable diseases, or even—in a few cases—outright abuse and neglect. But even under the best circumstances—and many day-care facilities and preschools provide superb care—day care means children must cope with the stress of separation from their parents for a significant portion of the day. It must be considered as a significant source of stress.

(3) Peer Pressure. Children learn how to get along with other people primarily through intense peer relationships. With their peers they learn how to give and take, love and hate, and balance their autonomy with communality. These are important lessons, but they are fraught with stress.

The key to keeping peer-related stress at a minimum is to help the child develop *flexibility* and the ability to *adjust.* The child who refuses to adjust or just doesn't know how will usually be the most stressed.

There are times, of course, where adjusting is not healthy—when the child experiences the stress of resisting peer pressure. Drugs, sex, and delinquent behavior can be major pressure points for many children, and "just saying no" is tremendously difficult. Children need strong emotional support from parents and the right sort of peer support to resist these pressures.

Stress As a Stressor

One of the important things to understand about stress is its "circular" effect. Stress tends to build on itself; that is, a little stress produces more stress. Not only is a child subjected to life stressors, but any *experience* of stress will set up consequences that will produce more stress. In a sense, the stress itself becomes a major stressor in a child's life.

Let us suppose, for example, that Mary is under a lot of pressure at school. It is near the end of term, with examinations looming and class projects due. And Mary is also caught up in rehearsing for a play at church.

Feeling the stress of too much to do, Mary burns the midnight oil. For several days in a row, she works well into the early hours of the morning on her projects, overloading on sugar and caffeine to stay awake. Eventually, Mary begins to develop a major headache. At first it is just at the back of her head, but it soon becomes more generalized. As she tries to sleep, Mary's head throbs and keeps her awake. She takes a painkiller, but this causes her to feel woozy the next day. She has trouble concentrating in class and worries that she will get sick and miss the play. So her headache gets worse, her sleeplessness increases, and her stress is even more intense.

Suddenly, sitting at her desk late one night, Mary begins to feel alarmed. Suddenly she is overwhelmed by a sense of impending doom. Her heart is racing. There is an intense pain in her chest. She can't get enough air, so she goes to the window and throws it wide open—even though it is quite chilly outside.

Mary is experiencing a very common stress reaction—a panic attack. In recent years this acute anxiety response has become very common among young girls and women. And the panic attack is so frightening that it becomes a source of stress itself; the symptoms are so scary that the sufferer begins to be afraid that they will recur. This is known as the "fear of fear" response; the anxiety feeds on itself.

If this cycle is left to itself, it self-perpetuates. The only way to slow it down is to break into it somewhere, to reduce the symptoms of stress so they do not become sources of further stress. This can be done through relaxation, sleep, or if necessary, the use of medication. As we continue, much of what I will be presenting will be focused on interrupting the stress cycle and on improving the child's coping skills—teaching him or her how to manage time better, filter out stressors, not take on too much, and heed the early warning signs of increasing stress.

The Child's Resources for Coping

There is a limit to what a parent can do about a child's personality, physiology, stress history, or even life circumstances. In fact, you may feel pretty helpless in these areas. Certainly you can't change your child's genetic makeup or past experiences. And you may not be able to remove current stressors from his or her life.

Nevertheless, there is a lot you can do to help your child build a happier and less stressful life—by providing the child with coping resources. These resources for coping both *support* the child through a stressful period and *teach* coping skills.

What are the resources that can help any child cope with stress? As I list them, take inventory of your own home to get a picture of its strengths and weaknesses in terms of coping resources.

As this book proceeds, I hope to help you take advantage of the strengths and reduce the weaknesses.

Resource #1: Caring, Involved, Supportive Parents

Parents who care deeply about their children, who are "present" for them and support them in their endeavors, will give those children the strong foundation they need for handling the inevitable stresses of life. Conversely, parents who are distracted, selfish, uncaring, or absent will produce highly stressed children.

Most parents, of course, fall between the two extremes. They love their children deeply and want to help them. But because they have trouble coping with their own stress or because they don't know how to help, they either add to their children's stress or rob them of the understanding and skills they need to handle stress well.

Because the quality of parenting is so essential to stressproofing children, I will address it in more detail in Part Two and chapter ten of this book.

Resource #2: A Caring and Loving Extended Family

Grandparents, uncles, aunts, cousins and even siblings (believe it or not) can be resources for teaching a child to cope. Children with healthy extended families and lots of involvement in these extended families have always seemed healthier and happier to me. In fact, I can often detect the presence of such a loving extended family from a child's level of happiness.

Grandparents are a particularly wonderful resource; they can provide support and listening ears when parents are too busy trying to cope with their own stress. Not only are they more experienced than most parents in dealing with stress, but they tend to be more relaxed and tolerant in dealing with their grandchildren.

In the absence of an extended family, some wise parents develop a network of friends or neighbors who fulfill a similar role—providing mutual support and caring. Churches, too, can take on the role of an extended family. And some families even arrange to "adopt" a lonely senior adult as an "honorary grandparent." Any of these "family building" strategies can provide children with important resources for coping.

Resource #3: A Safe and Abuse-Free Environment

Child abuse—whether physical, emotional, or sexual—is inexcusable and devastating to a child. When abuse overlays normal childhood stress the consequences can be disastrous. Our clinical practices are full of adults who have suffered as children at the hands of careless, if not deliberate abuse.

Just to be free of abuse is a wonderful resource for coping. It leaves a child free to concentrate his or her coping efforts on normal life pressures. Every child *deserves* an abuse-free environment.

Resource #4: Supportive and Understanding Schools and Teachers

Although the school or day-care environment can be a major source of stress for children, a good school or day-care situation can provide important coping resources for both parents and children. An educational or care facility which emphasizes creativity cooperation, and healthy life skills instead of intense competition is an invaluable resource for any child.

Teachers are an especially important resource for helping a child cope with stress. Although teachers can be both the *recipients* of stress ("burnout" is very high in this profession) and the *cause* of stress, they can also be instrumental in stressproofing your child.

Parents, therefore, should maintain a close working relationship with their child's school and especially with their child's teachers or caregivers. It is important to listen to what the teacher has to say and to keep the lines of communication open. Don't take everything your child says about his or her teacher too literally. Check it out. Talk to other parents and arrange a conference with the teacher. Then, if you still feel there is a problem, *express your opinion* to the principal if necessary.

Of course, choosing the right school or day care is of paramount importance—if you have a choice. Since the quality of day-care and private-school facilities in a community varies widely, research and planning will pay dividends. Talking to other parents and "dropping in" on likely prospects to observe day-to-day operations can help you determine what facilities will provide a maximum of learning and growth with a minimum of stress for your child.

If your child seems to be under undue stress at school, here are some ways parents can ease the anxiety:

- Don't put undue pressure on your child to make better grades than he or she is capable of making.

- Monitor the number of extracurricular activities with which your child is involved.

- Let your child talk about the anxiety. Sharing one's worries helps to relieve them.

- Watch for signs that a very young child is under stress at day care—unusually "clingy" behavior, regressing to an earlier stage of development, an increase in temper tantrums and other stress-related behavior.

- Arrange for tutoring or counseling if your child seems unduly stressed about grades or other school-related problems.

- Be alert to security problems at your child's school and be prepared to work with the school and other parents to solve these problems.

- Encourage your child to learn and practice a relaxation technique or a hand-warming exercise (described in chapter 7) every time he or she is anxious about a school activity.

Resource #5: Esteem-Building Activities

Every child needs to develop a sense of mastery and competence, and ordinary school or neighborhood activities help every child do this. To maintain and build a sense of self-esteem, parents should expose a child to enough variety in activities that he or she can find something to feel good about.

No child can be expected to be competent in every activity or sphere of life, but exposure to a variety of activities can help a child pinpoint where he or she can shine. A child who does not have strong academic aptitudes, for instance, may thrive at making clay pots, playing the guitar, or even cleaning up polluted ponds. If your son does not have the physique to be a star football player and this is the only sport he knows, his self-esteem is bound to be eroded. But if, in exploring a wide variety of activities, he learns he can be a star table-tennis player, his self-esteem will soar.

Exposure to individual hobbies such as electronics, computers, painting, weaving, sewing, carpentry, gardening, and music can help your child discover his or her talents, build a sense of self-mastery and esteem, and teach low-adrenaline relaxation. Group activities such as Scouts and Campfire groups, choirs, bands, dance troupes, and organized sports provide exercise, relaxation, peer interaction, and social opportunities to round out a child's sense of self.

I would add two caveats at this point, however:

(1) *Keep the competition level down.* Too much emphasis on winning breeds tension, anxiety, and stress and can negate the benefit of a given activity. The wise parent will heed the stress reactions of a child and back off from fostering too much competitiveness.

(2) *Don't overload a child's schedule with activities.* Every child needs some "downtime" in his or her life—time to just "mess around" and do nothing. Even beneficial activities can become stressful when there are just too many of them. Exposure to a wide variety of activities does not have to mean exposure all at once.

Resource #6: Supportive and Caring Church
Activities

For many parents, a supportive, caring and vitally alive church involvement has been the salvation of our children. We can love them, cajole them, preach to them and pray for them. But without the peer support and influence that Sunday school (or Sabbath school) or a youth group can give, we'd be sunk.

Having raised three children (who are now parents themselves), I thank God for this resource. I believe that secular school activities need a counterbalance. Our children need to see and relate to adults and other children who care about the spiritual dimension of life. If your child does not have such a resource, I urge you to find one. It can be an invaluable coping resource for you, too.

Conclusion

In this chapter I have explored the two main ingredients of childhood stress: the child and the child's world. Parents must accept that each child is unique and different. Each child brings a unique personality, physiology, and history to his or her encounter with stress. And each child experiences a unique set of stressors. While specific stressors differ according to age, birth order, and gender, the stress most children experience originates in the home, at school, or with peers. Stress itself can also be a stressor, creating a cyclical effect. The resources a child needs to cope with stress come primarily from the family and supportive groups such as schools and churches.

Discussion Questions

1. In what ways is your child unique and different from other children? Make a list of these differences.

2. Honestly examine each of the differences you listed. Take stock of how you feel about them.

3. Discuss ways in which you might become more accepting of your child's unique personality or physiology.

4. List three stressors in your child's world that you think affect him or her most. Then, beside each stressor, list three ideas for helping your child cope with it.

5. Review the resources you can provide your child for better coping. Are there any resources you are not adequately utilizing?

5

Personality, Character, and Stress

I recently counseled with a client I consider to be extremely intelligent. A successful businessman in his middle thirties, he holds a senior executive position in a large company. He and his wife are parents of three beautiful daughters.

Two of the girls, aged ten and eight, are extremely well-behaved, well-mannered, and easy to get along with. They are cheerful, patient, and slow to anger. Ever since they were small, they have shared toys, clothes, and friends without problems.

But seven-year-old Alison is a different story. She's quick-tempered and impatient, prone to tantrums. As an infant, she cried longer, louder, and more desperately than her sisters, and now she slugs other children as easily as Rocky Balboa slugs his opponents.

My client was worried and confused. He had bought into a common misconception in our society that purports that if parents were raising their child correctly, this wouldn't happen. "What are people thinking of me or my wife when they see Alison behaving so badly? They must think we are abusing her or something."

"If that were true," I asked him, "then why are your other two girls such model children?"

No reply. My client just sat there thinking.

"Besides," I went on, "I know from experience that a child who is difficult to manage early in life will not necessarily be a problem the rest of his or her life. Many 'problem children' turn out to be remarkably effective and successful adults. Their conflicts with the world teach them how to be winners. They learn how to overcome obstacles and build great strength of character."

"Furthermore," I told my patient, "I think you should just relax and accept the fact that much of Alison's disposition was inherited. There's no point in blaming yourself—or her—for it. Instead, I think you need to work at understanding Alison and treating her appropriately. For whatever reason, she came into this world with a more stress-prone (and stress-causing!) personality than her sisters, but you can help her learn to react to stress more positively."

Some Kids Are Just Born Difficult

No matter how patient, consistent, or firm parents are, some children are just more stress-prone and difficult to manage than others. My client learned this through painful experience, and research backs up his personal testimony. Stanley Turecki, in his book, *The Difficult Child*,[1] states that about 15 percent of children under age six are temperamentally difficult and hard to raise. In most cases, this "difficult" personality is evident almost from the cradle. This high percentage and early occurrence indicate that these children's difficult—and therefore stress-prone—personalities are genetically determined to one degree or another.

The old idea that a child is born a *tabula rasa*—a "blank slate" on which his or her environment "writes" a personality—is now out of date. Most researchers agree that each human being comes into this world with a distinct personality and a unique response to his or her environment.

There is little point, therefore, in blaming yourself or feeling guilty if your child is cranky, slow to adapt, negative, or contrary—or, for that matter, congratulating yourself if your child is cheerful, adaptable, and relaxed. To a certain extent, your child's personality is a given. If you are responsible, then it is mainly because of what you give your child through your genes. And the only way to prevent such responsibility is not to have children!

Even without the guilt, however, parenting becomes more of a challenge when you are raising a child who is naturally negative, unpredictable, nervous, or angry. Such children not only experience more stress themselves; they are "carriers" who inflict stress on those around them. Parents of "difficult" children need all the wisdom they can muster and the patience that only God can give.

But this is *not* to say that difficult children are a lost cause. Although personality is innate to a certain extent, it is far from fixed and unteachable. Experts today believe that only 20 percent to 50 percent of a person's personality is inherited.[2] This means that while parenting skills and child-hood experiences do not wholly determine the kind of person a child be-comes, there is still a lot of room for shaping and improvement.

This is good news not only for the parents of difficult children, but for all parents and caregivers. Any child, even the most stress-prone, can be made more stress-resistant. And a basic understanding of your child's unique personality will make stressproofing far easier.

Personality, Temperament, and Character

Up to this point, I have used the terms *temperament* and *personality* somewhat synonymously, and they are indeed used interchangeably in much popular literature. I am not sure that I need to make too much of the dif-ference between the two here, since I doubt if any two psychologists can really agree on the distinction. Here I will try to explain what each one means to me but, more importantly, I will try to show how personality/temperament differs from *character*.

Personality

This term comes from the Greek word *persona*, which means "mask." In ancient Greece, actors wore masks on the stage—a different mask for each role. Each mask assumed a different personality—that is, different ways of talking and behaving. When an actor changed masks, he became, in a sense, a different person.

Your personality, therefore, can be thought of as the *sum total of what you are*—how you tend to think or behave as you adjust to life. It involves and shapes your values, motives, beliefs, intelligence, and emotions.

Temperament

This term comes from a Latin word, *temperare*, which means to "regu-late, soften, or balance." A blacksmith "tempers" his steel—he softens and makes it less brittle. We "temper" an argument by criticizing softly. An art-ist may "temper" her colors or a musician might "temper" his tones. Your temperament, therefore, is your customary frame of mind or natural dispo-sition—the way you *regulate yourself*. It involves how you choose to respond to someone who hurts you—you keep or lose your "temper." If you act re-spectfully toward other people, we say you have a "polite temperament," that is, you regulate or moderate the way you respond to them.

Temperament, then, is clearly and inextricably tied to personality. Some psychologists never refer to temperament, only to personality. I, however, find it helpful to think of personality as the car (Buick, Chevrolet, or BMW), and temperament as the driver. One may have a similar personality (or car) to someone else, but drive it differently (fast, slow, or impatiently), depending on his or her temperament.

For my purpose here, however, let us think of personality and temperament as closely allied and differentiate them from character.

Character

And now, what is "character"? The term comes from the Greek *charassein*, meaning "to scratch or engrave;" it often refers to any writing or printing or symbol. I use the term to refer to the *patterns* of behavior that arise from personality or temperament. *Character* refers to the "marks" an individual makes in his or her own life and the influence he or she has upon others.

We speak then of a "sterling character" or of "weak character." Character goes beyond basic personality and even temperament. If personality is the car and temperament is the driver, character is the "route" you take and the use you make of the "car"—a drive in the country, a race down the freeway, a bank robbery and escape. Character has to do with what you *do* with your personality and your temperament.

As parents, we should be concerned about all three in our children: personality, temperament, and character. And obviously, the three are closely interrelated. A child's personality and temperament will affect the kind of character he or she develops; for instance, a little girl who is inherently bold and inclined to take risks will be more likely to develop a crusading, courageous character. And just as the way a car is driven and the route it takes will eventually affect the way the car looks and drives, an adult's developed character will eventually become incorporated into his personality. For instance, a basically shy teenager who develops the character traits of honesty and assertiveness may eventually become *less* shy.

In the realm of stress, *all three* psychological dimensions will influence the way your child experiences stress. Learning to assess your child's personality, temperament, and character will help you prevent unnecessary stress and teach your child to cope with the inevitable stressors of life.

In terms of our power to influence and change, however, parents have *significantly more* ability to influence character than temperament or personality. (It's easier to decide where to drive the car than to change the way one drives or to rebuild the car.) It makes sense, therefore, that parents should focus more on shaping a child's character than on trying to change his or her basic personality. As character is shaped, however, this shaping can begin to foster changes in personality and temperament.

Your Child's Stress-Prone Personality

To help you understand your child, let's begin with personality.

Stress Test 3, entitled "Assessing Your Child's Personality," will help you to obtain an overview of your child's personality. Please remember there is no "rightness" or "wrongness" about a given personality. The test is not intended to show where your child is deficient but rather to help you understand your child's distinctive approach to life. There is no scoring of this test, therefore. What you will have, if you join all your crosses together, is a "profile" that describes your child's major personality characteristics. If you have more than one child and you complete a profile for each one, you can compare the different profiles to get a picture of the distinctive differences between your children.

The *interpretation* of your child's personality profile is quite straightforward. If you have rated your child honestly, you should not have a line down the center of the profile—such a child would have no "personality" to speak of. Children *should* score to one side or another on a test like this, and it is these distinctive deviations from the middle point that help describe the child's unique personality.

As you examine the deviations to one side or another, you might be able to identify a theme. For instance, a child who scores strongly toward "thinker," "follower," "introvert," and "nervous" may clearly be someone you would not want to push into high-risk situations. Such a child may be highly reliable and do high-quality work, but will probably perform best when left to go at his or her own pace, alone and without pressure. A wise parent, then, would create these optimal conditions to reduce stress and maximize the child's growth and learning.

Another child, however, may have a profile that leans toward "doer," "leader," "high achiever," "daring," and "bold." Such a child probably enjoys pressure, likes to be pushed to perform harder, and may even lose interest in study or a project if not highly challenged. To optimize this child's performance (and minimize stress) a wise parent may set up a study schedule, appropriate reinforcements for achieving goals, and even some consequences for not achieving them.

Another way to interpret the personality profile is to take the *four* strongest deviations to the left or right and use these as a way of describing the child's dominant personality characteristics. Let's say, for instance, that your son scored highest as a "thinker," "moody," "works slow," and "shy." These four characteristics would be a helpful way of summing up William's personality. Your daughter Marianne may score highest on "doer," "never breaks rules," "shy," and "trusting." These characteristics would then be a way of describing her.

Stress Test 3: Assessing Your Child's Personality

Child's name _____

This is not really a test, but an assessment device. There are really no "right" or "wrong" personality styles, although some personalities can be more stressful for parent and child than others. The purpose here is to help you *describe* your child's personality so you can understand it better. Keep in mind, as you fill out the test, that it is hard to draw distinctions between personality traits and temperamental characteristics.

The test contains pairs of personality opposites. Each line is graded with a zero in the middle and two opposite characteristics on each side. Place a small cross somewhere along the continuum at the point where you think your child best fits. (See text for the interpretation of the test.)

If you have more than one child, photocopy the test so that you have a copy for each one.

		3 2 1 0 1 2 3	
1.	Thinker	_____	Doer
2.	Follower	_____	Leader
3.	Introvert	_____	Extrovert
4.	Low Achiever	_____	High Achiever
5.	Shirks Responsibility	_____	Welcomes Responsibility
6.	Moody	_____	Consistent in Mood
7.	Accepts Losing (as in a game)	_____	Resents Losing
8.	Cries Easily	_____	Never Cries
9.	Never Breaks Rules	_____	Always Breaks Rules
10.	Selfish	_____	Unselfish
11.	Timid	_____	Daring
12.	Downbeat	_____	Upbeat
13.	Often Depressed	_____	Never Depressed
14.	Nervous	_____	Relaxed
15.	Self-assured	_____	Unsure of Self
16.	Works Quickly	_____	Works Slowly
17.	Highly Motivated	_____	Low in Motivation
18.	Trusting	_____	Suspicious
19.	Shy	_____	Bold
20.	Self-conscious	_____	Not Self-conscious

Remember, however, that the final point of assessing your child's personality is to help you understand his or her particular mix of characteristics. It is *not* to show where your child does not match up to your personality or where you would like your child to be different. If you try to alter your child's personality by putting pressure on him or her to change, you are bound to create more stress and to set up tension between you and your child.

This is not to say that a child should not try to compensate for some personality extremes. When a child's personality brings him or her into conflict with others and thus brings more stress, a little honest feedback and instruction may help him or her become a little more balanced.

For instance, a child who is introverted and slow to make friends can be taught some social skills. Being friendly and considerate *is* a skill anyone can learn. But to expect this quiet child to become the life of the party or to make "being friendly" a condition for love (which is often how we try to force change) is both cruel and counterproductive. Love, understanding, acceptance, and appreciation for the child's unique gifts are much more likely than criticism and rejection to keep stress levels low and to prepare the way for growth.

As you evaluate your child's personality (and the temperament characteristics described in the next test) you may realize that there is a wide difference between who your child is and the demands of your home or the school environment. This is bound to cause stress.

A child like Elliott, for instance, who tends to be quiet, reserved, shy, and nervous, may not do well in a home full of boisterous, energetic, and disruptive siblings. Or a naturally ebullient child like Suzanne, who tends to speak loudly, move quickly, and act without thinking may be constantly in trouble if the rest of her family is quiet, reserved, and precise.

In such cases, parents should reckon with the mismatch between personality and environment. They can do this by adjusting the environment, and by teaching the child to manage the stress better. Elliott's parents, for example, could make a point of setting up (and enforcing) rules about privacy and personal boundaries so that Elliott has the quiet haven he needs in his noisy home. Suzanne's parents may need to make sure there are "kidproof" areas in the house where she feels free to be her slapdash but charming self.

Children whose personalities clash with teachers or peers may also experience extraordinary stress and need a little special help. A child like Jermaine, who cries easily and is unsure of himself, may make a very poor adjustment to a teacher who is demanding and strict in her methods. Parents should be alert to this kind of conflict and discuss with the teacher any tensions they observe.

Teachers, by and large, are skilled at "reading" a child's personality, but not every teacher makes adequate allowances; therefore, a frank discussion with a demanding teacher may be in order. In a few cases, a change of teachers or even schools may be justifiable, but in most cases this won't be necessary. Keeping the lines of communication open, helping your child modify his or her extreme responses, and teaching the child some stress-management skills will usually reduce stress for everyone involved.

Your Child's Stress-Prone Temperament

Your child's *temperament* may also be the cause of stress. Take Sandy as an example. She has a dominant personality, that of a leader. She likes responsibility and never shirks her chores. Teachers like her because they can depend on her.

But Sandy is easily irritated when others are asked to do things ahead of her. She has become so used to being "teacher's pet" that whenever someone else is asked to take a file to the principal's office, fetch a book, or even clean the chalkboard, Sandy sulks.

Sandy always expects to be number one, and there is no room for being number two. She easily becomes angry, offended, and jealous. And when she gets into her angry mood she hates everyone—not surprisingly, she has few friends.

Quite often, then, Sandy goes home from school feeling rejected and angry, all because someone else got asked to do something. Stress is obviously at work in Sandy's life—and her parents don't help much. Instead of responding with understanding to Sandy's ravings about not being teacher's pet for that day, they try to encourage her to be more assertive. "When your teacher asks Mary to clean the board, just speak up and tell her that's your job."

Of course it never works. The teacher knows better than Mom or Dad what is going on. Gently but deliberately, she has been trying to wean Sandy from the privileged role she has claimed for herself.

It has been a slow process of change for Sandy, but over the past few months the parents have begun to cooperate with the teacher, and Sandy has slowly changed her behavior. She still has a dominant personality, but she is learning to lead instead of forcing herself in front. She has begun to share with others more and even to celebrate the achievements of her friends.

Stress Test 4, entitled "Assessing Your Child's Temperament" will provide you with a temperament profile similar to the personality profile. Marking each continuum with a cross, joining the crosses to form a profile, and studying the deviations to the left or right will help you see the shape of your child's temperament.

Temperament is different from personality in that whereas personality characteristics are neither good nor bad (your child is who he or she is), temperament characteristics have values attached to them in our culture. It's usually considered better to control anger than to lose it, to be persistent than to give up easily, to be adaptable than inflexible. I have arranged the "negative" temperament traits on the left and the "positive" ones on the right.

Interpretation of the profile, therefore, should be quite straightforward. The more the profile "leans" toward the left, the more likely your child's temperament is to be problematic, and—everything else being equal—the greater the child's experience of stress. The further right the child's profile reaches, the more "positive" your child's temperament and the less stress he or she is likely to experience.

At this point, however, let me caution you not to be disappointed with your child—or at least not to show disappointment with your child—if he or she seems more "negative" than "positive." First, try to be accepting of where he or she is. Then, with a lot of love and patience, you might be able to influence your child in a more positive direction if you consider the trait to be undesirable and stress-producing.

Your ultimate goal should be to help your child become a healthy and stress-free person. Praise and acceptance are far more conducive to such an end than criticism or rejection. So affirm the positives and be very gentle in drawing attention to the negatives. If you don't consider a negative to be important, you would do better to ignore it.

The temperament characteristics I have described in the profile are all amenable to some degree of modification—through teaching and through example. In fact, the most powerful way to teach a healthy, balanced temperament is to model it yourself. For instance, you will have a hard time convincing your child to stick to projects or to be loving if you give up easily or model hate.

You can begin to influence your child's temperament, or at least teach him or her how to compensate for a high-stress temperament, by identifying the traits you see as a problem (because they bring on stress) and then focusing on those traits one at a time.

Let's say, for example, that Sara's mom is concerned because Sara tends to give up easily, so she chooses that aspect of Sara's temperament to work on. First, she looks at all of Sara's activities and picks one in particular—for instance, Sara's tendency to leave craft projects unfinished. The next time Sara expresses interest in a project, therefore, Sara's mom determines to work with Sara to be sure she completes it.

First, she helps Sarah *plan ahead* for the project. Often, we just assume that a child knows what is needed to complete a project and we fail to teach good planning. Together, mother and daughter make a list of *all* the materials and tools Sara will need and they gather them together ahead of time.

Stess Test 4: Assessing Your Child's Temperament

Child's name _____

    This is not really a test but an assessment device designed to help you *describe* your child's temperament so you can understand it better and, where appropriate, provide some guidance on how to improve it. It is just a sample of temperament characteristics and is not intended to be exhaustive. Unavoidably, some of these traits also overlap with personality. Once cannot always draw clear boundaries.

    As in the personality test, each line is graded with a zero in the middle and two opposite characteristics on each side. Place a small cross somewhere along the continuum at the point where you think your child best fits. (See text for interpretation.)

    If you have more than one child, then photocopy the test so that you have a copy for each one.

```
                 3   2   1   0   1   2   3
```

1.	Can't Control Anger	_____	Controls Anger Well
2.	High Anxiety	_____	Low Anxiety
3.	Dislikes Challenges	_____	Likes Challenge
4.	Gives Up Easily	_____	Perseveres
5.	Serious Minded	_____	Fun Loving
6.	Very Much a Loner	_____	Enjoys Being with Others
7.	Hateful	_____	Loving
8.	Always Tries to Please Others	_____	Balances Pleasing Others with Pleasing Self
9.	Self-rejecting	_____	Self-accepting
10.	Offended When Teased	_____	Takes Teasing Well
11.	Doesn't Take Embarrassment Well	_____	Takes Embarrassment Well
12.	Not Adaptable	_____	Adaptable
13.	Tries to Change Rules	_____	Cooperates with Rules
14.	Dislikes Change	_____	Accepts Change
15.	Dislikes Meeting People	_____	Enjoys Meeting People
16.	Easily Distracted	_____	Concentrates Well
17.	Sulks Easily	_____	Never Sulks
18.	Hurries Everywhere	_____	Never Hurries
19.	Always Jealous	_____	Never Jealous
20.	Irritable/Touchy	_____	Unflappable/Insensitive

Once the project is started, Sara's mom *removes all distractions*. Painting T-shirts and watching TV, for instance, are not compatible activities. Sara's mom also sets *time limits* for each painting session. She helps Sara *break down the project* into clear steps and stands ready to assist Sara if she needs it. Nothing is more frustrating to a child than outrunning her own skills and not knowing what to do!

Most important, Sara's mom *pays attention* to what Sara is doing. She shows interest, reinforcing each accomplishment with lots of praise. When Sara's attention lags, she encourages her to give it another try. And she is especially lavish in praising the finished project. Gradually she is teaching her child the thrill of seeing a job accomplished.

Adjusting a child's temperament to cut down on stress obviously takes time and attention—I don't know any other way to teach children how to be whole and healthy. But the payoffs in terms of lowered stress and reduced chance of stress disease for both parent and child can be enormous.

Your Child's Stress-Prone Character

What kind of *character* is your child developing as he or she grows? What are your child's values? What sorts of choices does your child make? How will you remember your child when he or she is grown up? As an honest child? A child who keeps promises? Or perhaps a courageous child?

These are all character traits—positive and negative patterns of behavior that characterize a child (and eventually the grownup child). They are qualities that, by and large, transcend personality and temperament, although they may be influenced by personality and temperament. The most significant aspect of character traits, in my opinion, is that they are *almost all learned*—which means that we can model and teach them to our children. What we teach or show helps our children make better choices, and making the right or healthy choices helps shape their character.

Stress Test 5 is designed to help you assess your child's character. It is by no means exhaustive. You can probably add many character traits of your own you would like to see in your child.

The test is also value laden; in other words, it is based on my own set of biases. I see the world through the values of my Christian commitment, and my choice of positive and negative characteristics reflects this value system.

As in the temperament test, the pairs of traits I present in Stress Test 5 are arranged so that the negative traits all appear on the left side and the positive traits (by my value system) appear on the right. If you join your crosses down the page, you will get a profile of your child's character. The more the profile leans toward the left side, the more negative or undesirable

Stess Test 5: Assessing Your Child's Character

Child's name _____

Once again, this is not really a test, but an assessment device. The purpose here is to help you *describe* your child's character so that you can understand it better and begin to shape it in a positive, stress-free direction.

Each line is graded with a zero in the middle and two opposite characteristics on each side. Place a small cross somewhere along the continuum at the point where you think your child best fits. (See text for interpretation.)

If you have more than one child, then photocopy so that you have a copy for each one.

                    3   2   1   0   1   2   3

1.	Unfeeling	Compassionate
2.	Dishonest	Honest
3.	Disregards Obligations	Fulfills Obligations
4.	Never Keeps Promises	Takes Promises Seriously
5.	Avoids the Truth	Values the Truth
6.	Irreverent	God-fearing
7.	Criticizes Others	Praises Others
8.	Ungrateful	Grateful
9.	Mad at the World	At Peace with the World
10.	Does Not Respect Others	Respects Others
11.	Careless	Thoughtful
12.	Unforgiving	Forgiving
13.	Makes Bad Choices	Makes Good Choices
14.	Inconsiderate	Considerate
15.	Vengeful	Never Takes Revenge
16.	Cowardly	Courageous
17.	Hasty/Rash	Thinks Before Acting
18.	Indifferent/Detached	Concerned/Responsive
19.	Overly Compliant	Healthily Assertive
20.	Stifles or Represses Feelings	Expresses Feelings

your child's character traits are. The more it leans toward the right, the more positive the overall character.

It is important to understand that *you can do a lot to shape your child's character*. And as in the case of temperament, the most powerful teacher is your own example. You may want to take the test for yourself just to get a feel for where you stand. If both you and your child evidence the same weaknesses, you may want to devise a joint self-improvement project.

Why should we attend to our children's characters and deliberately try to shape them? Because, to a large extent, their characters will determine what sort of persons they become—whether they will be happy, whether they will fulfill their life's ambitions, whether they live their life with courage and integrity, notwithstanding what happens to them.

In many ways, I fear, we are becoming a "characterless society"—and that trend carries serious stress consequences. How? When a society's values weaken, so does its citizens' overall sense of meaning and purpose. And people without a sense of purpose quickly become angry, frustrated, disillusioned, and bitter. When we build our children's positive characters, therefore, we strengthen their abilities to withstand the stressors of life. When they can see beyond the here and now, they are better equipped to handle the pain, suffering, anger or disappointments of life with dignity.

Helping Your Child Build Character

How can you "grow" more character in your child? Your most important strategy, of course, will be to work on developing your own character. In addition, you might find it helpful to take each of the traits I have listed in Stress Test 5 and write it on a 3 x 5 card. Take one of these cards at a time and, for a period of one week, attend very carefully to your child's (and your own) behavior, attitudes, and manner as they relate to the topic on the card.

Whenever you find your child evidencing the negative side of the trait, *gently* discourage the behavior. Don't criticize; don't punish—just gently and lovingly suggest that your child do the opposite.

And now, the more important task. Whenever your child *does* evidence the positive trait—*reinforce it with praise*. Don't hold back; give it all you've got. Praise is the most powerful shaper of correct behavior. When people praise me for doing something they like—I always want to do it more. Children are exactly the same.

Let me illustrate this. Let us suppose that Mark, who is nine years old, tends to be a little detached and indifferent to others, doesn't value the truth (in other words, he lies a lot), and continually criticizes his little sister. What you would do is to write down each of these on a 3 x 5 card so that you can have them readily available as a reminder.

Take the first card (let's say it is indifferent/detached), and for one week monitor *this behavior only* in Mark's goings and comings. Ignore the others. That afternoon you hear Mark saying good-bye to his friend out on the street as they come home from school. The friend invites Mark to play, and Mark rudely declines. As he comes in the door you might say (being *gentle* in your discouragement of his behavior), "Mark, your friend tried to be nice to you. Think about how you responded." Then leave it at that.

Later, you hear Mark call his friend and invite him over to play. You go to Mark and praise him with, "You know, Mark, that was a very nice thing you just did. You showed your friend that you really cared for him. I am very proud of your behavior." A hug and a kiss will round out the praise. Mark may shrug off the compliment, or even do the typical kid's thing and say, "Aw, don't embarrass me Mom," but deep down he will bask in the praise. Believe me, he will repeat the behavior just for the praise. After a while, he will begin to learn how to behave this way naturally.

After a week, move to the next trait. After you've cycled through all those that concern you, go back to the beginning or add a few more. But remember to keep reinforcing the previous behaviors even while you work on new ones.

It's really not difficult to be intentional about building your child's character. As you do so, you will also discover that you are lowering your child's stress level. This is because, on the whole, positive character traits *minimize* stress. Negative traits, like being dishonest, selfish, never keeping promises, or criticizing others *always create stress*—and the stress they create could one day kill your child.

Type A and Type B Personalities

No discussion of the stress-prone personality would be complete without some reference to what has now become a very popular way of characterizing personalities—Type A and Type B personalities.

I have always seen myself as a classic Type A. I get impatient when I am delayed. I don't handle frustration very well. I am always in a hurry, become angered easily, and have a deep sense of justice. These traits pretty much sum up the Type A personality. In many ways, they are the psychological and emotional characteristics of the "hot reactor" described in the previous chapter.

The Type B personality is exactly the opposite. My wife is a Type B. She is patient, slow to anger, and easygoing—a classic "cool reactor." (Type A people, in fact, always seem to marry Type B's. God must think we need some help in changing!)

These ways of categorizing personality were devised very early in the research into what caused some people to develop premature cardiovascular disease and have heart attacks while they were still young. Personality quite clearly played a role in the development of this, the most serious form of stress disease. People with the Type A personality style were found to have a three to four times greater risk for developing early heart disease than their opposites, Type B people.

Furthermore, the correlation between Type A personalities and heart disease corresponded to the correlation between adrenaline arousal and Type A characteristics. The two go together. In other words, people who are always in a hurry, impatient, and angry also pump a lot more adrenaline than other people. And these "stirred up" personalities are the ones who generally have high cholesterol and the fatty build-up in arteries that lead to heart attacks.

The classic Type A/Type B distinction is obviously too simple, of course. Most people are a *mixture* of the two (sometimes known as Type X). More importantly, one cannot easily distinguish the two types from outward behavior. A person may seem calm, placid, and easygoing, yet be churning with adrenaline on the *inside*. In other words, one can really only tell who is at high risk for stress disease by carefully evaluating their "inner" workings, including their biological reactions to stress. Their level of arousal can only be reliably monitored through measuring adrenaline levels in their blood or urine. I have discussed this matter at length in chapter 3 of my book *The Hidden Link Between Adrenaline and Stress*.[3]

As far as children are concerned, parents ought to pay attention to what is known about the Type A or Type B personality styles. They cut across the personality, temperament, and character types I've already presented and represent combinations of all of these.

Stress Test 6 is a test to help you determine whether your child evidences those Type A personality characteristics that could lead to greater stress and higher levels of adrenaline arousal. You should be able to get enough clues from knowing your child so well to answer the test fairly accurately. Keep in mind, though, that your child may appear to be calm and cool on the outside, yet feel very much like a Type A on the inside.

How does a Type A child come across? Stan is a good example. If you have ever watched a film or video on fast forward, you will know what Stan looks like. He is always doing something. I don't mean he is hyperactive; that disorder is quite different from Type A. I mean Stan is always busy, always on the go. He eats quickly, thinks fast, and acts impulsively. He tends to do more than one thing at a time—like finishing his homework while watching TV and talking on the phone. He loves challenges, hates being delayed or standing in line anywhere, and can never find the time for a haircut or to tidy his room. He is quite competent, bright and energetic. And he never reports feeling tired—until, exhausted, he finally falls asleep. He is an adrenaline junkie par excellence.

Stess Test 6: Is Your Child a Type A Personality?

Child's name _____

Determining whether a child is or is not a Type A personality really requires a more careful evaluation by a professional. But the following questionnaire will assist you in spotting whether or not your child is prone to this personality style. If you have any serious concern here, consult a child specialist for a more thorough evaluation.

Rate each statement as it applies to your child according to the following scale, and enter the rating in the right-hand column.

0 = My child shows no evidence of this behavior.
1 = My child shows only slight evidence of this behavior or only behaves this way some of the time.
2 = My child is like this most of the time.

	Rating
1. My child gets angry very easily.	_____
2. My child eats very quickly.	_____
3. My child cannot tolerate frustration very well.	_____
4. My child cannot sit still or relax.	_____
5. Winning is everything to my child.	_____
6. My child does several things simultaneously (like homework *and* talking on the phone or watching TV).	_____
7. My child detests waiting in line.	
8. My child goes into a rage whenever he or she cannot open a drawer or door.	_____
9. My child seems to be in a hurry.	
10. My child talks rapidly.	_____
11. My child thinks for others and finishes their sentences for them.	
12. My child's mind doesn't seem to stop.	_____
13. Going to bed is a hassle because my child doesn't seems to feel tired or to need sleep.	
14. My child enjoys being the leader or telling others what to do.	_____
15. My child gets mad at others for being slow or being held up.	_____
16. My child refuses to give up on a project even when it seems hopeless.	
17. My child talks and gestures with a lot of emphasis and inflections in speech.	_____
18. My child seems to get injured or to have more accidents than other children.	
19. My child seems hostile a lot of the time.	_____
20. My child seems to get into fights or arguments more often than other children.	_____
Total Score	_____

Test Interpretation

0–10 Clearly your child is a Type B personality (see text for explanation) and not Type A. This may change as he or she gets older, however.

11–20 Your child may have a few Type A characteristics or may function as a Type A in some situations and a Type B in others.

21–30 Your child evidences strong Type A tendencies.

Over 30 Clearly your child is a Type A personality. The higher the score, the stronger the trait and the greater the risk that your child will continue to function this way into adulthood.

Zachary, on the other hand, is Stan's exact opposite. Also quite intelligent, Zachary doesn't let anything bother him. He is late for everything and displays no irritation when someone delays him. He loves doing "quiet" things—reading, listening to soft music, working on crafts. When everyone else is upset, he just sits there calmly, wondering what the big deal is all about. He takes things one at a time, and he often leaves things to the last minute so they don't get done. Flexibility is his thing. "Hang loose, man," is his favorite expression. Zachary is pure Type B—not overly stressed himself, but a source of stress for his Type A friends.

Who is the better off? Clearly, there are drawbacks and benefits to being both, but Zachary clearly has the edge when it comes to stress disease. A person like Stan lives at a pace that is too fast for his or her body. Wear and tear accelerates. The body literally ages faster, since the Type A lifestyle maintains an internal state of "emergency" that not only elevates adrenaline but disturbs the whole balance of the immune system.

"Hurry sickness" is a common way of describing the stress disease that Type A people tend to develop. These days, however, "hurry sickness" is not just confined to those individuals who, by nature, tend to resonate with it. Instead, hurry sickness is a cultural malady. In many ways, we are a Type A society, and time urgency has become a distinguishing characteristic of our age.

Those who study cultural trends and try to anticipate where we are headed as a culture warn us that in the next century, which is not too many years away, time will become our most limited and precious resource. That may be true already. Most of us—even Type B's—find that there simply isn't enough time to get in what we want to do. And all the technology that was supposed to *save* us time has merely created a greater demand on us to do *more* in the time we have. We are pushed to walk, talk, work, and eat faster. The pace of life is accelerating dramatically for all of us, and it is hard to succeed unless you move as fast as everyone else.

The development of our Type A culture will have serious implications for all our children when they grow up. Obviously the time for them to learn how to balance their lives and prevent stress disease is now. (I will look at the particular problems of the hurried child in chapter 11.)

Let me interject a personal note here. I greatly regret that I, as a classic Type A, did not learn as a child how to monitor my arousal level, sleep better, slow down, take time to rest, and control my anger. For the past ten or twelve years, however, I have made dramatic changes in every one of these areas—and I hope that these changes have come in time to prevent permanent damage. In the past decade, my attitude to being delayed has changed. My reaction to frustrating people has mellowed. I am finally able to control my sense of urgency and not let it run my life.As a result, I feel more efficient. My thinking is clearer, and I am extremely happy and content with my life, notwithstanding its unsolved problems.

One major factor in my own stress management is that I have learned to travel through life at God's pace, not my own. God has no affinity with our hurried and hassled modern lifestyle. I have found no better program for managing one's stress than learning how to use the resources God has provided and to try to see life from the perspective of the eternal.

I believe that we all need that long-term perspective to protect us from hurry sickness. A Type A lifestyle inevitably takes its toll in terms of stress disease. If we are going to prepare our children for less stress, therefore, we must begin by teaching them how to find their peace even as the world speeds by in the fast lane.

This does *not* mean our children must disengage from life or live without challenges. I know from experience that one can engage in life fully and fulfill one's ambitions *without* suffering the destructive consequences of stress disease. But it does mean paying attention to the consequences of the hurried lifestyle and learning to ameliorate Type A tendencies. In coming chapters we will look at some practical strategies for "slowing down" your child without holding him or her back.

For now, as you evaluate your child's vulnerability to stress and discover his or her weak points, try to develop a better understanding of your own stress vulnerability. Understanding yourself will help you to understand and guide your child toward more effective stress control. It will also help you not to contribute to your child's stress by working against his or her unique individuality. If you improve your own stress management in the process, you will serve as an effective model that your child can emulate.

Summary

In this chapter I have examined three aspects of your child that can contribute to his or her stress-proneness: personality, temperament, and character. In addition, I outlined the traditional Type A/Type B personalities and their connection with stress disease.

While there is little a parent can, or should, do to change a child's basic personality or even temperament, character is clearly amenable to change. Unlike personality and temperament, character is almost entirely learned.

Type A characteristics are tied to hurriedness and adrenaline arousal—and make one more vulnerable to stress disease, especially cardiovascular disease. But being Type A is not an inevitable fate. By changing one's behavior—by learning to slow down, to be more patient and less hassled—one can learn to be more like a Type B person—and have the best of both worlds.

Discussion Questions

1. Take the tests for personality, temperament, and character yourself. What do you see? Where would you like to change?

2. As you compare the tests results with each of your children, where do you see similarities and where do you see differences? (If you only have one child, compare profiles with other parents.)

3. The damaging characteristics of the Type A person, as described in the items of Test 6, all have to do with *behavior*, even though they have strong personality underpinnings. These behaviors *can* be changed to lower the level of adrenaline arousal. Identify three of these characteristics in your child and discuss ways you can begin to influence change in the behavior underlying these characteristics.

6

Cholesterol and Childhood Stress

Ronnie is the picture of health. To look at him, you would say that he was the all-American boy. Intelligent and diligent, he gets good grades in junior high. He loves playing games and sports, and he is good at almost anything he does. Skateboarding is his favorite pastime, but he also does well in baseball. Ronnie is in good physical and mental shape. He hardly ever gets sick, and he is well liked by peers, neighbors, and teachers.

Ronnie's father is also the all-American type. In his late forties, he holds a good—if stressful—job. For years he has played racquetball three times a week and made a point of eating "healthy" food. He's always been in "great shape"—that is, until his recent heart attack. That's why everyone in the family was so shocked when the doctors told Ronnie's father he needed a triple bypass operation to restore the function of his heart.

Shaken up, Ronnie's mother took the whole family in for physical checkups and asked to have their cholesterol levels checked. The family physician was somewhat skeptical about checking Ronnie's cholesterol level; at that time there were very serious questions about how predictive these tests were on children. But the test was finally done, and you can imagine everyone's surprise when the results showed that Ronnie's "bad" cholesterol (known as low density lipoprotein or LDL cholesterol) was extraordinarily high. His young blood was swimming with destructive fats.

Of course, Ronnie's high cholesterol level is not life threatening at this stage in his life. Left unaltered for many years, however, it will work its damage by helping to carry and deposit the fats on the lining of his arteries, especially those in the heart. His arteries will continue to narrow and harden until one day, probably at quite a young age, he may well have a heart attack like his father.

Ronnie is fortunate. He has discovered very early that he has a problem with cholesterol, and with the help of his parents he has begun to change his eating and his lifestyle. Already, after a short period of time, the "bad" cholesterol has begun to decline and the "good" cholesterol (known as high density lipoprotein or HDL cholesterol) has begun to increase.

And just in case you are thinking, But the poor kid probably had to forfeit everything that helps childhood be a happy time—like hot dogs at the baseball game, pizza on special occasions, or snacks and desserts, let me reassure you.

No such drastic steps have been necessary. Diet is only one of several sources of bad cholesterol. While Ronnie has had to alter his diet somewhat, a lot of his recovery has involved changes in how he handles anger, how long he sleeps, and how he deals with challenge and excitement. In other words, he is lowering his "bad" cholesterol by improving his response to stress. Such strategies are what this chapter—and the rest of this book—is all about.

The Dangers of High Cholesterol

We have known for several years that adults must watch their cholesterol levels to avoid heart disease. Until recently, we have totally neglected to keep an eye on cholesterol levels in children. We now know, however, that although cholesterol buildup is slow, it is certain, usually goes unnoticed—and it starts a lot earlier in life than adulthood. We also know that there is a close connection between high cholesterol levels, heart disease, and stress.

This understanding had its beginning in 1951, when the Pentagon sent a team of pathologists to the combat zone of the Korean War on a grisly mission to learn from the bodies of dead young Americans killed in action. These were not sick young men, but vigorous, well-trained, and physically fit young men. So everyone was surprised when the pathologists began to discover signs of heart disease in an age-group that typically doesn't die of heart disease.

The pathologists found that the network of tiny arteries that nourish the heart muscle were becoming clogged by fibrous fatty deposits. Seventy-seven percent of the Korean War casualties, young and fit, showed gross evidence of coronary heart disease.[1] This news shocked the medical world—and high cholesterol was discovered to be the culprit.

In subsequent years, regrettably, diet became the major focus of subsequent research into cholesterol, with exercise and fitness in close pursuit. But the very discovery that started the research points to the fact that diet and exercise are not the only pieces in the cholesterol/heart-disease puzzle.

These young soldiers, after all, were neither abusing their diets nor sitting around like couch potatoes watching "I Love Lucy". They were many years removed from an age in which normal wear and tear on the body could be considered as a factor.

So what explains the clogged arteries and the high cholesterol levels in these young men? The missing component in the chain of causes was *stress*—the stress of battle, of the long hours of enforced boredom between battles, of being far away from home and being surrounded by death and destruction.

Stress, more than any other factor, predisposed those young soldiers to early heart disease. And that vital fact is important for parents to keep in mind as they seek to stressproof their children.

The Problem with Cholesterol

Cholesterol, like adrenaline, has a positive and indispensable function to perform in our bodies. Cholesterol helps build up cell membranes and serves as the basis for the bile acids in the liver and for certain hormones. Eighty to ninety percent of the body's total cholesterol is manufactured by the liver—and the rest comes straight from the foods we eat. As we saw in chapter 2, stress triggers a surge of adrenaline in our system, which then causes the liver to release an "emergency supply" of cholesterol into the bloodstream to help build up the body's resources.

All this is very important and beneficial in a true emergency. Both the extra adrenaline and cholesterol help the body respond to the threat. But we now know that if high levels of cholesterol remain circulating in the blood for an extended period of time, arteries eventually become clogged and heart disease results.

I doubt if anyone these days questions the connection between high levels of "bad" cholesterol in the blood and the onset of early heart disease. The famous (and ongoing) Framingham Heart Study, which has tracked five thousand residents of a Boston suburb for a number of years, has clearly established this connection.

It is also widely agreed that *reducing* cholesterol levels can help prevent heart disease. In 1984, a panel of experts came to a consensus, stating that "it has been established beyond a reasonable doubt that lowering definitely elevated blood cholesterol levels will reduce the risk of heart attacks caused by coronary heart disease." Furthermore, they recommended that everyone down to age two should be advised to reduce fat intake to reduce cholesterol.[2]

The Problem Begins in Childhood

But can cholesterol really be a problem for children? Evidence to that effect has been around for at least thirty years. In 1961, a pediatrician by the name of Holman first posited that diet was somehow linked to cholesterol levels in children.[3] The habits that could lead to high cholesterol and cardiovascular catastrophe before age sixty were established in childhood, he argued, and children need to be protected from this destructive way of life.

Since Holman's study, evidence has accumulated slowly but indisputably that there is a link between stress, high cholesterol, and early heart disease in children. For example, the Orange County Health Education Department, in conjunction with the University of California at Irvine, recently screened about 450 children ranging in age from nine to eleven. Fourteen percent of these children had cholesterol levels considered to be excessive and alarming.[4]

Evidence of incipient heart disease is showing up in autopsies of children killed in accidents. Fatty fibrous plaques have been found clogging the arteries of fifteen-year-olds, and fatty deposits have been found along the aortic walls of children as young as two or three.[5]

If high cholesterol can begin in childhood, therefore—and the evidence is convincing that it can—then childhood is the logical time to begin fighting high cholesterol. That is the conclusion of a report issued by the National Cholesterol Education Program of the National Heart, Lung and Blood Institute. They state categorically that the best way to avoid heart trouble in later life is to take steps to reduce cholesterol levels *in childhood*.[6]

Diet Isn't the Only Answer

The evidence is convincing that something must be done about cholesterol if we are going to stop the rising tide of stress-related heart problems—and that childhood is the place to start. But what concerns me is the emphasis that has been placed on the role of diet as the sole cause of high cholesterol, to the neglect of understanding how diet interacts with stress to cause the problem. Without neglecting the importance of diet, I want to take this opportunity to show how stress—particularly overarousal of the adrenal system—contributes to the cholesterol picture.

There has long been evidence that diet is not the only cause of high serum cholesterol (cholesterol in the blood). The Korean War studies hinted at that conclusion, of course. So did the findings of early researchers in the diets of different cultures.

These researchers, trying to understand the correlation between cholesterol in the diet and cholesterol in the blood, compared the cholesterol levels in people of different cultures. And some of these studies showed a clear link between dietary cholesterol and blood cholesterol. For example, people in countries that consumed high amounts of animal foods were observed to have high cholesterol levels, while those consuming grains, vegetables, fruits, fish, and poultry had relatively low levels. But paradoxes abounded in these studies. Eskimos, who ate nothing but high-fat animal foods, had low cholesterol and virtually no heart disease. In another culture, young men fed extra eggs in their diets showed no rise in cholesterol.

This last phenomenon was partially explained by the "saturation effect"— the fact that the human body can only take in so much fat and cholesterol before it reaches saturation level. If you never eat eggs and then eat one, your cholesterol goes up. If you eat them all the time, however, your blood is likely to remain at saturation, and one egg will not increase the amount of cholesterol.

But other factors besides the saturation effect play in the diet-cholesterol picture. This was clearly evidenced by studies showing the effect of a reduced-cholesterol diet on the level of cholesterol in the blood. The National Heart, Lung and Blood Institute, for instance, picked out 3,806 middle-aged American men who had high cholesterol levels and followed them for ten years. And while the study showed that for every 1 percent drop in cholesterol level there was a 2 percent drop in the risk of heart attack, *diet control alone* lowered cholesterol by only 4 percent.[7] Other studies put the figure at between 10 and 13 percent.

According to this evidence, diet is responsible for between 4 and 13 percent of our cholesterol. And this is not a lot. It means that if your total cholesterol is 250 milligrams per 100 milliliters of blood serum (250 mg%), you might be able to drop it to 225 or 220 mg% by eating only lettuce. Not much of an improvement when a bout with stress could easily send it soaring again to 300 mg%.

Clearly, then, diet, is only a *part* of the picture. The other part—the missing link in solving the cholesterol problem—is stress control.

Abundant evidence indicates that stress raises cholesterol levels.[8] Accountants have been shown to have their highest cholesterol levels during tax season. Medical students register a 10 percent increase in serum cholesterol at examination time, and employees fired from their jobs show a 10 percent drop when they finally secure work.

Emotional reactions such as fear, anger, and anxiety also cause a rise in cholesterol levels, and certain personality characteristics also cause it to rise. A person who is competitive, aggressive, and impatient, for instance, or who has an exaggerated sense of responsibility, typically runs high levels of cholesterol. These characteristics go along with the Type A personality, who is known to be higher in adrenaline arousal as well.

Clearly, in my opinion, the stress that pushes up adrenaline will also raise cholesterol levels, especially the "bad" cholesterol. They are both part of the emergency response. And here is where a pattern of *continued* life-stress is a problem. If we, or our children, only occasionally triggered this "emergency" response, the consequent rise in cholesterol and adrenaline would not put us in jeopardy. But for most people today, stress is *not intermittent*. It is this continued stimulation of the adrenaline and cholesterol, through our hurried and hassled lifestyle, that puts us at risk for stress disease.

Testing Your Child's Cholesterol Level

I am convinced that over the next few years we will be reading and hearing a lot more about the child-cholesterol connection than hitherto. It is inevitable, therefore, and just good common sense, that we must address the problem of premature heart disease at its starting point—in children.

Does this mean you need to have your child's cholesterol tested? Many physicians are not convinced this is necessary, but I would still recommend discussing the matter with your pediatrician or internist. You may want to have your own level checked as well—both for your own health and as an example for your child.

I doubt if there is much value in having it checked before your child starts school, although a "baseline" test before the stress of school begins may be a helpful reference point. When your physician gives you the results, make sure you copy down the figures and keep them on record. A test every year or two will then help you to spot any changes. Such an ongoing record could be invaluable for pinpointing any significant rise in stress later in the child's life.

If the level of cholesterol seems high (and many stressful life events will temporarily raise cholesterol levels) your physician may suggest a repeat test in a couple of weeks. This is a wise precaution, because what you are trying to establish is a *general base level,* not a spontaneous reaction to one stress event.

If the second test confirms that your child's cholesterol level is elevated, certain changes will be in order. If the cholesterol is only moderately high, relatively simple changes in diet may be sufficient to lower it—although you would not be remiss to pay attention to lowering stress as well. Higher cholesterol will call for more careful attention to the child's diet and stress levels. Very high levels will require the assistance of your physician. You may want to ask for a referral to a nutritionist or psychologist to address your concerns more effectively.

Your Child's Cholesterol: What's Normal?

What levels of cholesterol are acceptable for children? They are certainly not comparable with adult levels. Acceptable levels rise progressively as the child moves toward adulthood—and the acceptable norms are constantly being changed. As a general rule, however, the National Cholesterol Education Program recommends the following:

	Children	Adults
Acceptable	less than 170 mg/dL	less than 200 mg/dL
Borderline	170 to 199 mg/dL	200 to 239 mg/dL
High	above 200 mg/dL	above 240 mg/dL

Many physicians even consider these norms a little high. It is preferable for your physician, who will know all the compounding factors, to advise you on what is an appropriate level for the following components:

- total cholesterol
- HDL cholesterol
- triglycerides

Diet, Cholesterol, and Stress

This is a book on stress, not on nutrition. And as I have shown, stress can be just as important a factor in high cholesterol and heart disease as diet. But that doesn't mean that diet is unimportant. Although stress does stimulate the production of cholesterol, stress in the presence of high dietary cholesterol is more likely to contribute to heart disease than stress in a low-cholesterol diet.

In addition, for most families, food and stress are closely related. Today's hurried kids are far more likely to dine on high-fat fast food. They tend to eat with the stereo blaring or wolf down junk food in front of the TV. They are prompted by the media to beg for the latest variety of "yummy snack"—and their stressed-out parents will more than likely give in. All too often, a high-cholesterol diet and a high-stress lifestyle go together. No wonder today's kids are in danger of developing stress disease.

With that in mind, therefore, I want to present a few very basic nutritional guidelines and a few observations on the relationship between food and stress.

What should guide the design of a child's diet? The National Cholesterol Education Program (NCEP) of the National Heart, Lung and Blood Institute urges that all children above age two follow the same low-cholesterol, low-fat diet recommended for adults.[9] Fat should make up more no more than 30 percent of daily caloric intake. Cholesterol intake should be limited to 300 milligrams per day. A 10 percent lowering of fats would probably be sufficient for most children.

For more specific information, I recommend that you *ask your physician for help* or for a referral to a nutritionist. This is a highly specialized field, so don't just take the advice of your local health-food store. There has been so much misinformation about nutrition given in recent years that it is no surprise that many people are confused and even skeptical about what constitutes a healthy diet. But the basics haven't really changed that much over the years since my grandmother used to tell me to eat my spinach before I could have any of her homemade ice cream.

In a nutshell, foods are classified into the following categories: proteins, carbohydrates, fats, vitamins, minerals, and water. Each has its own function and works in harmony with the others. Your child's food plan should include a balance of all these foods. You will want to keep in mind, however, that most Western diets tend to be *too high* in protein and saturated fat. Stressing whole grains, fruits, and vegetables and cutting back on commercially prepared foods can help restore the balance in your child's (and your own) diet.

Making It Happen

Any parent, of course, knows it's not that easy. What are you supposed to do—deny your child an ice cream or take away the double cheeseburgers, fries, and chocolate milk shakes? It sounds downright un-American. More important, it sounds almost impossible! Children just seem to be drawn by instinct to junk food. They don't want to eat their broccoli, spinach, or oat-bran cereals. They crave sugars and artificial flavorings.

The battle over getting children to eat the right food is about as vicious as any parent-child battle can get. I know many frustrated mothers and fathers who raise the white flag (or dishtowel) and surrender. "It's just not worth the time and trouble it takes," one told me, "I'll trust nature. If junk food is what they crave, then perhaps it's because their bodies need what it provides."

That's a myth, of course. Children are drawn to what tastes good, and "tasting good" is simply not an adequate criterion for what is healthy. That has always been true, but I believe it is more of a problem in our commercially dominated, high-stimulation society. Something has been slowly happening to the taste buds of our world. Without realizing it, we have become dependent on commercially produced cereals, drinks, and foods and these are intentionally "doctored" to create cravings in those who consume these foods. They are deliberately flavored to enhance sales, not to nourish our children.

My mother's porridge of boiled oats, for instance, simply cannot compare, in terms of taste, with cereals that "snap, crackle, and pop" or are heavily flavored to encourage their sales. I have no doubt now that her porridge was a whole lot healthier for me.

No one can deny that today's children (and their parents) have deplorable eating habits. Depending on age, a child gets between 10 percent and 22 percent of daily calories from commercially prepared snacks and fast foods that are notoriously high in fats and substances designed to tickle the taste buds.

With all this in mind, what can parents do to teach their children healthy eating habits?

First, don't expect your child to eat right if you don't. Most children learn their eating habits from their parents. Switching your child to healthier foods while you stick with junk food just isn't going to work. You may have to take the double-cheese, double-meat hamburger out of your mouth before you can expect your child to listen to what you're saying about a healthy diet.

Second, remember that *how* you teach is as important as *what* you teach. Being too rigid can lead your child to resent your efforts and rebel—perhaps sneaking food behind your back. Try to take the long-term view. Make changes gradually and explain the reasons for what you are doing. Establish some basic rules and be firm about sticking to them, but be willing to "wiggle" on less important points.

It is not necessary to cut out all treats, or even all junk food. Instead, substitute a healthier snack when possible (an apple instead of a candy bar, and unbuttered popcorn instead of potato chips). And when you do allow junk food, make sure it is balanced with nutritional foods.

One strategy is to use a "treat" to reward the eating of a healthy food. The rule is simple: "You eat your fish (chicken, or whatever) and your vegetables, *and then* you can have your treat."

Is it that easy? No, of course not. But it is essential that once you have made your rules, you follow them *consistently*. Your child will not die of starvation if allowed to go to bed hungry because of refusing to eat something healthy. Believe me, if you have ever seen a hungry child you will learn one very important lesson: *A starving child will eat anything.* If your children will forego a treat because they do not want to eat real food, they are probably overfed, anyway. They may not show it yet by being fat; their high energy levels and quick metabolism may keep the weight off. But many an overfed child has become an obese adult.

We are so overindulged as a society that a regular "fast" would probably do us all a lot of good. Fasting, or just going hungry for a while, can also be useful to break some of the cravings that certain foods and food additives create. "Cold turkey" is not only good for nicotine or drugs; it also works for breaking addictions to caffeine, sugar, and salt.

Use your ingenuity to get your children to eat foods you want them to. Don't overfill their plates; smaller portions are less intimidating. Introduce new foods as "experiments" and try new recipes. Let children make out their own menu (with your guidance, of course) and help prepare the food. Not only will they learn valuable skills for the future; they are more likely to "buy into" the meal. Remember that children's taste buds are more sensitive than your own, so hold back on the spices and exotic flavorings.

Finally, don't argue with your children over food. Don't yell or become angry. When they are hungry, they will eat. When they do eat, make sure that the food available is balanced, varied, and healthy. And you will give your child the best chance of beating stress disease.

The Right Setting

No matter how nutritious and tasty a child's meal may be, the setting in which it is served can make or break its value. A child who must eat at a dinner table where there is a lot of bickering or even a silent "cold war" between parents is going to be under a lot of stress, producing too much stomach acid and struggling to maintain an appetite. Anger and anxiety can take away all desire for food.

I recall many a mealtime during my childhood when the "atmosphere" between my parents was charged with hostility. My stomach would knot up, my palms would sweat, and my appetite would vanish as soon as I heard an angry response from either of my parents. How can this help but disturb the normal digestive process? I suspect that such a stressful eating situation could turn even water to cholesterol!

Another "setting" that is problematic is watching television while you are eating. Many children get into this habit because their parents do it. But TV watching and high cholesterol tend to go hand in hand.

A recent report from the University of California says that the more your children watch TV, the higher their cholesterol levels are likely to be.[10] The report warns, in fact, that excessive TV watching at any time—not just during meals—may increase the risk of cardiovascular disease in later life. Surveying 1,077 children at a family clinic, the researchers found that watching TV at least two hours a day raised cholesterol levels above the 200 milligram limit.

Obviously, it isn't the TV set that is raising the cholesterol, but the "TV atmosphere." Kids who stay in front of a TV are less likely to be physically active and more likely to snack on junk foods. (Commercials encourage this). In addition, TV creates stimulation and can arouse the adrenal system. TV time is not the right time to be ingesting food.

Spiritual Food for Healthy Hearts

I cannot resist this opportunity, while discussing food and nutrition, to point out the importance of "spiritual food" for a child. To be truly healthy, children need more than good nutrition and stress management. They also need healthy values and a balanced view of life. They need to know what life's ultimate purpose is and how to feed their need for the meaningful. And I know no better and more effective way to do this than to "feed" them a balanced menu of spiritual values and moral development.

Even if you are not particularly religious or "spiritually oriented," I urge you to at least give your child the option of choosing. Find a way to expose your child to the spiritual dimension of life. Take your children to church or synagogue—or send them with a friend. Have them read the Bible and other classic religious texts. And try to keep an open mind as you talk together—you may find help for your own stress as well.

I have a bias toward the Christian faith because for more than forty years it has provided me with a way of living that cannot be equaled. I can honestly say that I know what it means to be happy—really, deeply, and satisfyingly happy. I doubt if many people these days can make such an honest claim to happiness.

In order to cope effectively with stress, children need to know the value of honesty. They must learn to be loving, forgiving, patient, and kind. They need to be able to feed on the spiritual dimensions of life, to learn to use faith to face their troubles with courage. This is nutritious fare indeed—a dependable prescription for healthy hearts.

Summary

Heart disease begins in childhood. High cholesterol levels in children need to be monitored and modified by giving attention both to proper diet and healthy stress management. The preponderance of commercially prepared foods that are deliberately flavored to induce sales can be a problem for busy parents. Nevertheless, fresh foods, vegetables, and fruits must be offered. Parents should use ingenuity, firmness, and good sense to encourage healthy eating habits in their children.

Discussion Questions

1. Review your family's eating habits. Write down the foods eaten this past week and review the list for its nutritious content.

2. Discuss with other parents any problems you are having in getting your child to eat a balanced diet. Share ways of preparing food to make it more palatable and strategies for developing healthy eating habits.

3. What changes do you feel you should make in your family's eating habits? Write these down so that you can keep track of the progress you are making.

Worksheet 1: Your Child and Stress

Child's name _____

Having looked at the factors that may make a child uniquely stress-prone—personality, physiology, and stress history—take a minute to consider your own child. What aspects of his or her personality, physical health or makeup, or life experience affect his or her response to stress? This worksheet is designed to guide you in putting together what you have learned about stress with your own observations in order to gain an accurate picture of your own child's stress levels. As this book proceeds, we will explore what you can do to make your child less susceptible to stress.

1. List any stress symptoms from chapters 3 and 4 (physical or psychological) that your child has displayed over the past year:

   _____
   _____
   _____
   _____

2. Would you say your child is a "hot reactor" (responds to events with great intensity)?

   Yes _____   No _____

3. Are there any aspects of your child's overall health that suggest an excess of stress in your child's life? Has he or she been sick a lot recently?

   _____
   _____
   _____

   What elements of your child's health could be contributing to your child's stress-proneness (include both recent minor illnesses and chronic illnesses or disabilities)?

   _____
   _____
   _____

4. Have you ever had your child's cholesterol checked? If so, list the readings here:

   _____
   _____
   _____

5. List major life changes (positive or negative) that have occurred in your child's life over the past few years. How has your child responded to those changes?

_____

_____

_____

6. Briefly construct a "stress history" for your child, listing major events in his or her life that you think caused him or her distress.

_____

_____

_____

7. List recent traumatic events in your community or the world that your child has been aware of through the media (a sensational murder, a rape trial, a war).

_____

_____

_____

How do you think that awareness has affected your child?

_____

_____

_____

8. List elements in your child's home environment (home or neighborhood) that could be causing him/her stress. Include people (siblings, friends, parents), threats (dangerous dogs, street gangs, heavy traffic), and events (friend moving away, grandmother coming to live in the home), etc.

_____

_____

_____

9. List elements in your child's home environment that could be depriving him/her of his/her normal support system (tension between parents, parents under unusual stress, loss of a significant person, etc.)

_____

_____

_____

10. How old is your child? _____ What particular challenges are facing your child at his or her current stage of development? (If you wish, refer to the list on pp. 62–63 or ask your pediatrician to recommend a good book on childhood development.)

_____

_____

_____

11. How do you think your child's place in the family affects his stress levels? Does the child get along with his siblings?

_____

_____

_____

12. If your child is in day care, how would you rate your particular child-care situation in terms of stress? What are some particular stress points (for you and your child) related to your child-care situation?

_____

_____

_____

13. If your child is in school, how does he or she react to normal school pressures? Are there any aspects of the current school situation that are causing him or her problems?

_____

_____

_____

14. How does your child get along with his or her peers? Any significant sources of stress here?

_____

_____

_____

15. How are spiritual matters handled in your home? How would you assess your child's spiritual responsiveness and spiritual resources? Are spiritual issues a source of stress in your family?

_____

_____

_____

16. Based on the personality profiles in chapter 5, what four words would you use to describe your child's basic personality?

_____

_____

_____

17. List some aspects of your child's personality you think may make him or her more susceptible to stress:

_____

_____

_____

18. List three specific character traits of your child that you think help him or her cope with stress:

(1) _____

(2) _____

(3) _____

19. List three character traits you would like to see your child develop:

(1) _____

(2) _____

(3) _____

20. How easy is it for your child to talk to you and/or your spouse? (If you don't know, try asking.)

_____

_____

_____

Part 2

Stressproofing
Your Child

Whether or not your child is at high risk for stress problems, there is much you can do to help your child manage stress better. Coping with stress is a skill that can be taught. In this section I want to examine how you as a parent can produce a less stressful environment for your child—and for yourself.

Up to a point, of course, children cause their own stress. They choose to get into arguments. They give in to peer pressure or allow themselves to become fatigued. They won't listen or take advice. They don't believe that you are not only older but wiser and that you've been around the block a few times. You may have times when you muttered under your breath, "I'm going to kill this kid."

Nevertheless, with a little help you might just be able to create an environment that will help your child to be more responsive and less stressed.

7

Stressproofing Strategies

I can remember when I got my first raincoat. I was probably six or seven years old and had to walk a mile or so to school. The rainy season had just started in South Africa, where we lived, so my mother thought I should have a raincoat to keep me dry.

Of course, I wanted a "real" raincoat like my dad's, not a plastic or rubberized one. So my mother found me a cloth one, but I still wasn't satisfied. Daddy's raincoat looked a little like the TV detective Columbo's— a little crumpled. I thought my new raincoat looked too new, too stiff for comfort. So I decided to "dirty up" the raincoat a bit and make it look a bit more like Dad's. On the first rainy day when I was required to wear the coat, I made a few detours through muddy puddles, just to get some wear on it.

Unfortunately, I overdid the "breaking in," and half the raincoat was covered in mud by the time I got home. So I sneaked the raincoat into the bathroom and tried to wash out the mud in the bathtub.

Well the raincoat really did look like Columbo's after that, but to my dismay I discovered it was no longer waterproof. My father explained to me (not exactly in a quiet tone of voice) that in washing out the mud with soap and hot water, I had also washed out the water-repellent coating. "But never mind," he told me, "I'll send it to the cleaners to be waterproofed."

Amazing, I thought. They can put the "waterproof" back into a coat! And I like that idea of waterproofing when it comes to children and stress.

Stress, after all, is inevitable. Life marches on relentlessly; it doesn't wait for people to get their acts together or even to catch their breath. And that is true for children as well as adults. No sooner has one examination passed than the next one waits to greet your daughter. No sooner has your son faced up to one bully than another takes his place. No one ever gets to a point in life where problems stop coming.

We cannot protect our children from all stressors, nor would we do them a favor if we did. Children need to learn how to cope with pressure, handle conflict, and reject peer pressure. They will find it stressful to become educated, build their own confidence, manage money, and find a job. They must learn to get along with other people, especially those of the opposite sex. They must gain experience in managing themselves—their personalities, their gifts, their sexuality. And they must do it all in a context of a highly competitive and often threatening world.

So kids today may be under more stress than ever before—and there is not a lot you can do about it. But there *is* a lot you can do to keep that inevitable stress from damaging your children—and that is what stressproofing is all about. Stressproofing means helping your child become stress resistant. Just as water runs off a coat that has been treated appropriately with repellent, stress can "run off" your child's life. So join me as I help you put on your child's "stress raincoat." Children who learn to deal with stress in a positive way grow up to become adults who can deal positively and effectively with their lives.

In this chapter I will focus on a number of effective stressproofing strategies. I examine the underappreciated (in our culture) contribution of sleep. I look at the need for physical fitness and show the effectiveness of deliberate relaxation. I then suggest some ideas for "inoculating" your child against stress. Just as you can inoculate your children against diseases like polio or smallpox, you can "inoculate" them against excessive stress, gradually increasing their resistance to the inevitable pressures of life. Finally, I will show how a child's level of self-esteem protects against stress and give some pointers on how to build your child's self-esteem in the midst of stress.

Stressproofing Strategy #1: Make Sure Your Child Gets Adequate Sleep

In consulting a variety of scientific resources on childhood stress in preparation for this book, I was amazed at how little attention is paid to the role of sleep in preventing and alleviating overstress. Many fine books and articles on stress management make no mention of it at all. Yet both my experience as a clinician and my reading in the area of sleep research convinces me that sleep is an essential element of stress control. Adequate sleep is necessary if you are going to deal with even ordinary stress; extraordinary stress calls for extra sleep.

Sleep serves two extremely important functions that are essential to coping well with stress: (1) It provides the body with an opportunity to rejuvenate. (2) It serves to restore mental balance and acuity. We neglect these functions to our peril. If you want to stressproof your child, therefore, I suggest that you pay very careful attention to your child's sleeping habits.

An Underslept Society

Most people would agree, of course—if they think about it—that sleep is necessary for all living animals, including human beings. As a culture, however, we have come to depreciate sleep—to consider it one of the "extras" we can cut out of our busy lives or even to see it as synonymous with laziness. We "complain" about our long hours and our late nights with almost a sense of pride—as if losing sleep somehow makes us more virtuous or more productive. When we want to take on a new activity, we are more likely to shave an hour off our sleeping time than to drop another activity. Many of us even feel a little guilty if we nap in the daytime or sleep for more than seven or eight hours. And we pass these attitudes along to our children as well.

"Of course, babies need naps," one mother of a twelve-year-old said to me recently, "but a child of Alex's age should be able to survive without all that sleep." I think she was wrong—and her child was paying the price in terms of stress.

In fact, I believe it is precisely because we, who are among the world's most work-driven and guilt-ridden people, have looked down our noses at sleep that we are also the world's most stressed-out and probably least happy people. We worship work and high-energy play; we despise rest and sleep. But we pay for this imbalance with more headaches, ulcers, heart disease, and depression than most other cultures.

The truth is *we are an underslept society*. I would venture to guess that most, if not all, of us need more sleep than we are getting. This shortfall in sleep is currently being called a "sleep debt" by researchers. They suggest that this debt builds up, just like a bank deficit, and you pay the debt later in increased stress.

Sadly, children as well as adults are suffering from this stressful "national debt." The prevailing present-day attitude—and many parents subscribe to it—is that sleeping is wasted time. "You can do better things with your life than sleep it away" is the common idea which we pass on to our children. True, we grant babies the privilege of sleeping a lot. But by the time the child is five or six years of age, many parents deliberately begin to reduce their child's sleep time. By the time the child reaches adolescence, the attitude that sleep is at best an irritating necessity is often firmly ingrained. Experts are now saying, for instance, that most teenagers carry a "sleep debt" of at least one hour, possibly two.

How Does Sleep Work?

How does sleep help us to cope with stress? Sleep prevents fatigue and helps to restore energy when we are fatigued. Sleep provides the body with an opportunity for healing and rejuvenation. These are all *physical* functions, and they take place during the nondream stages of sleep. Most of these functions are fulfilled even when we are not actually asleep but are quietly resting.

The dream stage of sleep has a different function. About every ninety minutes during sleep, we go into a dream state. (This happens whether or not we remember the dream.) Dream sleep's function is mainly *psychological*. It helps clear out unnecessary memory. The tapes of irrelevant information, gathered during the daytime, are disposed of so that new information can be absorbed the next day. Useful memories are also consolidated by transferring them from short-term to long-term memory. If we did not dream so that our memories can be cleared of unnecessary data, we would quickly run out of brain memory—and probably go crazy. In other words, we dream in order to forget—so we can then remember more.

Dreaming, then, is important to the learning process and therefore especially vital for children. In order to learn well, a child must sleep long enough to have plenty of dream time. This alone makes a case for providing enough time for sleep.

What are the effects of insufficient sleep? They include:

- general lethargy,
- inability to concentrate,
- slowed reaction time,
- mental bewilderment,
- frequent distraction,
- loss of self-confidence,
- forgetfulness,
- headaches and stomach problems,
- irritability,
- dizziness,
- susceptibility to depression and anxiety.

Insufficient sleep, in other words, robs a person of the ability to cope with normal pressure, let alone any extraordinary stress.

Children who do not get enough sleep find it difficult to cope with all the demands placed upon them. They worry excessively. Frustration comes quickly, and they readily resort to aggression and yelling. Sleep-deprived children cry easily, panic quickly, become angry at the drop of a hat. Some have fits, bite their nails, and generally "go to pieces" under pressure. Problems seem overwhelming and they give up easily.

These inadequate coping styles, in turn, cause underslept children more stress. Because they are irritable, teachers get upset with them. Because they can't concentrate and easily make mistakes, they have accidents or break things. It's a vicious circle. When you can't cope with stress, you create more stress.

What causes us to sleep too little? The culprit is usually high adrenaline. *Whenever adrenaline goes up, sleep needs come down.* That, of course, is another reason that insufficient sleep and stress are related. It is no accident that our underslept society is also an overstimulated, adrenaline-addicted society.

If your child is one of those children who just can't settle down and sleep, therefore, consider that he or she may be overstimulated. A child who is highly excited or stimulated by some challenge or activity will not want to sleep, and for a brief period of time the adrenaline masks the need for sleep. A child who is "buzzed" on adrenaline has plenty of energy—but he or she will pay the penalty later in terms of fatigue, irritability, and diminished effectiveness.

How Much Is Enough?

How much sleep do children need? As much as they can get—at least, as much as they want. Here are some strategies for making sure your child gets the amount of sleep that he or she needs.

(1) *If your child does not wake up naturally, consider that he or she may need more sleep.* Try putting your child to bed earlier if he or she is sleeping the whole time while in bed. If you really have a night-owl on your hands— one who just lies there wide awake, remember that resting is also important and meets a part of the child's nondream sleep needs. For some, however, staying awake is just a habit. If your child tends to be sluggish in the morning, then increase sleep time gradually. Add half-hour increments of sleep, wait a few days, and see if natural awakening occurs. No one should have to be awakened in the morning.

Teenagers are notorious abusers of sleep. They stay up late watching TV or listening to music, then feel too tired to get up. Adding up to two hours per night to the average teenager's sleep time can bring about a dramatic improvement in mood and mental acuity.

The solution? Insist that they get to bed earlier, adjust their schedules so that they can sleep later, or take a nap after school. Also, be aware some teenagers stay up just to get some privacy, especially when they share a room with a younger sibling. Providing for your teenager's privacy in some other way could help to get him or her to bed earlier.

(2) If your child is overstimulated and cannot get to sleep (or wakes up and cannot get back to sleep), teach him or her to just relax and stay in bed. (I'll suggest a relaxation exercise later in this chapter.) Physical rejuvenation takes place whenever we lie still and relax, so just resting will be beneficial in itself. In addition, lying quietly will give the adrenaline level a chance to drop so that the child will eventually fall asleep naturally.

(3) Provide an opportunity for daytime naps. A person does not have to meet all his or her sleep needs in one sitting (or "sleeping"). Sleep can be broken into two or three "sessions." A study conducted by the medical school of Athens University found that men who napped at least thirty minutes a day were 30 percent less likely to have heart problems than those who didn't nap.[1] Why? Resting during the day helps to lower adrenaline levels. And this lowering of arousal levels will contribute to better sleep at night as well.

Napping is quite good for one's health. I wish our culture did not see "siestas" as such an indolent habit. We would be better off to take a few more of them.

Let me give one word of caution about extending your child's sleep. A person who sleeps longer than usual one night or takes an unaccustomed nap may have trouble falling asleep the next night. *This is normal.* He or she may even feel more tired after longer sleep than after a shorter sleep. *This is temporary.* Your child's body needs time to readjust, so don't be thrown off by it. In three or four days a new rhythm will be established and your child will feel much better.

Stressproofing Strategy #2: Help Your Child Become Physically Fit

Because many children seem active—even hyperactive—parents don't always think about their needs for physical fitness. A child can be restless, fidgety, and in and out of the house a lot, yet be physically unfit. Stressproofing a child involves developing a balanced program of physical activities that will keep a child healthy and well-toned.

And I'm not just talking about boys. What has alarmed me about American culture generally since coming to the USA nineteen years ago is that it emphasizes physical fitness and sports activities for boys, but almost

Five Ways to Improve Your Child's Sleep

1. Ensure that noise is minimized. A child cannot enjoy restful sleep while everyone else is banging and clanging and lights are shining in his or her eyes.

2. Establish a regular bedtime. Sleep is controlled by a biological clock. Irregular bedtimes confuse this clock and make it more difficult for the child to get to sleep. If you live in a state that makes use of Daylight Savings Time, be aware that the time change in spring and fall can be disruptive to a child's sleep habits. Be prepared to help your child adjust gradually.

3. Try to lower arousal a few hours before bedtime. A child cannot go from a wild game spree or an exciting TV show to restful sleep in just a few minutes. At least one and a half to two hours is needed to slowly reduce arousal. A period of quiet, nonphysical activity—a bath, reading, coloring, or quiet conversation—helps bring on sleep.

4. Avoid caffeine-based foods before bedtime. Colas, coffee, chocolates, and the like are stimulants that will cause sleeplessness, as will high-sugar foods such as candy. Don't serve these foods within the last few hours before bedtime.

5. Create a pleasant ritual around bedtime. In many homes, bedtime is bedlam time. The house echoes with screams: "Get to bed before I brain you." This creates arousal, as does any show of anger and conflict. Children might even act up deliberately because they enjoy the excitement.

Instead of upping the adrenaline levels with conflict, concentrate on settling your children down. Take the time to read an interesting (but not too exciting) story. Create a happy and relaxed atmosphere. This establishes pleasant associations with going to bed and creates memories that your child will cherish the rest of his or her life.

totally neglects it for girls. Most team sports are boy-focused. Our failure to help girls become physically strong has stress implications, but it also shows itself in weak musculature that can cause problems in the child-bearing years.

Teaching children how to exercise and remain physically fit is not only helpful in coping with childhood stress; it establishes the habits that will follow the child into adulthood. A person who has once developed a passion for exercise never forgets it.

The benefits of physical activity are widely recognized, so I'm not going to take a lot of space extolling them. Physical activity strengthens muscles and bones, reduces fatigue, builds a stronger cardiovascular and respiratory system, and helps to release important and natural tranquilizers in the brain. Psychologically, it builds a feeling of confidence, makes a person more resilient, and helps to reduce frustration. Physically fit people usually have improved mood, enhanced self-esteem, and even better work habits. All these benefits can reduce stress as well.

In addition, some forms of exercise help reduce stress by using up surplus adrenaline. But this only happens if—and this is a big if—the exercise is not overly competitive or stimulating. Highly competitive events can end up recruiting more adrenaline than is used up and therefore raise stress levels instead of lowering them.

Anger and frustration should be avoided in physical activity for the same reason. These emotions produce massive discharges of adrenaline that can be damaging in the long run. Some sporting activities are notorious for their tendency to produce anger. The cartoons about golfers breaking and throwing golf clubs are not without some truth. I often joke that golf is a deadly sport—walking eighteen holes is not sufficient exercise to burn off the adrenaline produced by one mistake or fluffed shot. But I'm only partly joking. Any activity—including physical activity—that is too stimulating is not healthy in the long run.

Childhood games have their equivalents to golf. These are games in which activities are complex and difficult to master, so they leave many children frustrated—especially if they have not yet developed the necessary coordination and muscle strength to play properly. If your child gets angry a lot trying to play a game, then it might be time to make a change, even if the game provides good physical exercise. Find a sport or activity that burns up energy but doesn't cause frustration—and you have the prescription for an ideal fitness activity.

Designing a fitness program for children can be tricky. First of all, how can you know if your child is not getting enough exercise? Overweight can be a clue; a child who carries too many pounds probably needs more exercise. The amount of TV a child watches can also be a tip-off; young "couch potatoes" tend to be unfit. But even a thin child who plays outside most of the time could need more of certain kinds of exercise. In our sedentary culture, in fact, unless your child is involved regularly in some sort of exercise program, it is probably safe to assume he or she needs to be.

Unfortunately, the natural activities of children are not enough. Often, these activities exercise only certain parts of the body, usually the arms and legs. Even most chores neglect some parts of the body. Children need to be taught exercises that work the whole body, not just arms, legs, and mouth!

What sort of physical activities will provide overall fitness? Organized team sports—soccer, baseball, football—can provide physical fitness in the context of fun and can also help build cooperation and a team spirit provided (1) safety is made a priority (contact sports can be very hard on growing joints), (2) every child has an opportunity to play and (3) pressure to win is kept to a minimum. Check out the activities available in your community and encourage regular participation. But keep an eye on your attitude. Parents who turn children's team sports into a "win or nothing" contest quickly transform a healthy source of fitness into an adrenaline-recruiting source of stress.

Individual sporting activities such as tennis, track, swimming, and cycling are also excellent sources of fitness, especially for older children. When these sports are engaged in competitively, however, you may need to keep a close eye on your child's frustration. Even when these activities are part of a team effort, they involve individual performance, so the risk of frustration—and excess adrenaline arousal—increases.

Don't overlook the fitness possibilities inherent in "taking classes." Swimming, dance, gymnastics and other programs offered by your local health club or fitness center will increase your child's self-esteem and sense of competence while helping keep him or her in shape.

Then there are family activities. In my opinion, they are the healthiest, because. They build memories and establish the most helpful habits. As a family, you can walk, swim, jog, hike, ride bikes, jump rope, dance, do aerobics, and chase Frisbees. Because these activities are less formal, they are also less frustrating. They are pure fun and sheer, unadulterated exercise.

Work at discovering physical activities that your child finds interesting. If your child hates to jog, for example, you will create a negative mind-set if you insist on jogging together. Karate, t'ai chi, or even jujitsu could be more fun. Then show some interest yourself, in order to reinforce your child's interest.

My oldest grandson has a passion for karate but occasionally gets lazy and doesn't want to practice. Rather than just sitting on the sideline impatiently waiting for the exercise lesson to be over, my daughter, his mother, enrolled herself. She benefits from the exercise, and his interest level has escalated. Now he can't wait for them both to go and "work out." He values the companionship as much as the exercise.

Your goal here is simple: try to develop a lifestyle for you and your child that includes thirty minutes of aerobic-type exercise at least three times a week. Then, when your child seems to be pressured or stressed, suggest that you do something physical to relieve the pent-up tensions. Remember, though, that children's exercise needs are not quite the same as adults' needs. Sustained pounding and some contact sports can be damaging to growing bodies.

Stressproofing Strategy #3:
Teach Your Child to Relax

It sounds contradictory, but it's not: stressproofing requires *both* exercise *and* relaxation. Exercise lowers stress by helping body and mind work more efficiently and by working off excess energy. But relaxation prevents stress damage even more directly, by lowering the level of circulating adrenaline.

In the last twenty or thirty years, Americans have rediscovered the power of relaxation. Unfortunately, many New Age groups have tied purposeful relaxation in with Eastern religions and more amorphous "spiritual" pursuits. This has made more orthodox Christian groups suspicious of yoga, transcendental meditation, and the like. But New Age gurus didn't invent relaxation. It is available to all of us, and it doesn't need to be embellished with quasi-religious notions. It is simply a helpful procedure for turning down our level of stimulation and arousal. Of all the techniques available to us for countering stress, relaxation is the cheapest and easiest.

In order to relax, of course, it is necessary to know when one is *not* relaxed. Each system of the body has its state of arousal and its opposite state of relaxation. And each system displays "symptoms" of arousal that can be helpful in diagnosing high arousal. When my heart beats eighty or ninety times a minute instead of fifty or sixty, for instance, it is aroused. When my muscles become tense or jittery instead of flaccid, they are not relaxed. Monitoring heart rate or muscle tension, then, can be helpful in monitoring stress levels.

More convenient as a stress indicator—and as a tool of relaxation—is the temperature of the hand. This is a fascinating phenomenon that can be used both to help a child recognize that he or she is under a lot of stress and to show him or her how to relax and lower adrenaline levels.

Hand temperature depends largely on the blood supply to the hands. And one of the effects of increased adrenaline is to slow down the blood supply to the hands and feet and to shunt most of the blood to where it is needed for the emergency response—the brain, muscles, and stomach. When the blood supply to the hands is reduced, therefore, the hands get colder.

You have probably noticed that people's hands get cold when they are under stress. Think of times when you have shaken hands with your preacher after a morning service—a time that is quite challenging for the preacher—or with a politician after a big speech. Or have you ever felt your hands turn to ice just before an exam, a job interview, or a meeting with someone important?

Our hands will always cool to some extent whenever we are under stress. For some, the temperature may drop fifteen to twenty degrees Fahrenheit; for others only a few degrees—but it always changes. And understanding the change can be quite helpful not only in telling us that there is stress, but also in pointing us to an effective remedy: *If your hands feel cold, relax so that your hands get warm again.*

Teaching Your Child to Relax

The following exercise is designed to lower your child's adrenaline level and put him or her in a state of low arousal. In the beginning, guide your child through the exercise, but make it clear that you are teaching a skill that he or she can do alone. Practice daily—but if your child wants to do the exercise more than once a day, by all means let him or her do it! Encourage your child to use it whenever he or she feels pressured, tense, angry, anxious, or "wired." Eventually your child should be able to relax consciously while sitting at a desk in a classroom or riding on a bus.

Step 1: Locate a quiet, restful place where your child can regularly relax. The child's own bedroom is ideal—if the child can be alone there. Interruptions—even from siblings who share the bedroom—will disturb the relaxation. You can offer your own bedroom if no other place is available.

Step 2: Make the chair or bed to be used for relaxation as comfortable as you can. A bed is better initially, but the child should eventually progress to relaxing in a chair. (A beanbag chair can be wonderful if it is big enough to support the child fully.) Use pillows to ensure full-body support and total comfort. This helps to turn off the reflex muscle activity of "bridging." If the head and shoulders are supported, for instance, but not the neck, the neck muscles will remain tense to "bridge" between the head and the shoulders. Full-body support will help reduce this "bridging" tension.

Step 3: Emphasize to your child that the whole object of the relaxation exercise is to "play dead." The child is to remain as still as possible for as long as possible. Urge him or her to "scratch all the itchy places now—then try not to move again until the exercise is over." Set a timer for five or more minutes (depending on your child's tolerance) to begin with, then gradually increase it each week until the child is relaxing for twenty or thirty minutes at a time.

Step 4: Now, start the relaxation period with a "progressive tensioning" exercise. Such an exercise involves first tensing the muscles to produce a little fatigue, then relaxing them. You can instruct your child as follows:

"Start at the feet. Tense up your feet muscles, and hold till I count to five. One . . . two . . . three . . . four . . . five . . . Relax your feet and let them rest. Now, tense your calf muscles (show the child where they are) and hold till I count to five (count as before). Relax and let them rest. . . ."

Proceed like this to the knee muscles, the thigh muscles, the buttocks, stomach, chest, hands, arms, shoulders, neck, and finally the face muscles: "Now, try to make a funny face. Hold it tight until I count to five. . . ."

Now, tell your child to try to remain absolutely still with all muscles still relaxed. "Imagine that you are floating on a cloud. Feel your arms and legs lifting you and carrying you away." You can leave the room if you like. The timer should signal when time is up.

Make it fun. Give lots of praise for trying, not just succeeding. If your child falls asleep, you probably need to increase his or her sleep time. For now, let your child use the time for an extra nap.

Deal with any resistance right away. Many children find it hard to relax. They naturally want to fidget or jump up. Reduce the initial starting period to five minutes if necessary, then work up slowly from there.

Step 5: At the end of the allotted time for relaxing, tell your child, "Now, try to move as slowly as you can for a while." Your goal is to create a state of lowered arousal. Perhaps this is the time for your child to quietly read a book or take a leisurely walk with you.

To aid in measuring this cooling of the hand, a useful tool called a "temperature dot" (known under a variety of commercial names) has been devised. This small, temperature-sensitive plastic dot is worn on the back of your hand. Its color changes with temperature, and the range of colors has been specifically designed to cover the range of normal hand temperatures. (For further information on temperature dots, consult my book, *The Hidden Link between Adrenaline and Stress.*[2])

A simpler way of evaluating hand temperature and stress level—one that the child can learn to do for himself or herself—is to place the hands on the face. Although the hands get colder when we are under stress, the face stays the same temperature. Placing the hands on the face, therefore, makes it quite easy to tell if the hands are colder. If they are, then adrenaline arousal triggered by stress may well be the cause.

While not as accurate as the temperature dot, this "hands on face" technique can be very helpful in monitoring a child's stress. Teach your child to "take a temperature" and test for adrenaline arousal. Cold hands will often precede the onset of other physical symptoms such as a headache or stomach distress, so it can be an effective warning to your child.

What comes next? Relaxation. Relaxation helps to lower the adrenaline and warm the hands. It is helpful not only in lowering adrenaline but also in lowering muscle tension. In fact, it generalizes to all the arousal systems of the body.

There are several ways you can teach relaxation to your children. Providing a restful atmosphere—without TV, loud music, or conflict—can do a lot. So can a gentle massage or a warm bath. But teaching your child a relaxation exercise may be the most effective way of helping your child lower his or her adrenaline. The sidebar on page 119-120 outlines such an exercise.

However it is achieved, effective relaxation *does* lower adrenaline and helps to warm the hands and reduce muscle tension. The heart rate slows, and the stomach stops churning. These benefits make the trouble it takes to teach relaxation to your child well worth the while. You might even benefit from learning it yourself.

Stressproofing Strategy #4:
Inoculate Your Child against Stress

Life is full of stressors, just as it is full of germs and viruses. We cannot completely protect our children from either—nor should we want to. If we kept our children in a germ-free "bubble," they would die of disease the moment they stepped outside because they had not built up their resistance to disease through gradual exposure. Children need to build resistance to stress as well. Gradually, and with increasing confidence, they need to be exposed to life's problems so that they can learn what to do about them. And just as we can inoculate our children against deadly diseases like polio or smallpox, we can "inoculate" them against excessive stress.

Stress inoculation works much like disease inoculation. To help the body fight major infectious diseases, we give small doses of a mild virus or disease organism. This weakened form of the disease triggers the body's wonderfully intricate immune system, provoking the body to build "antibodies" that fight the disease in its stronger form.

When we inoculate our children against stress, we expose them gradually, under controlled conditions, to more and more stress, while at the same time showing them how to cope with the stress. Over time, this process helps to build strength of character, a healthy and positive outlook, a sense of personal competence, and a willingness to take on challenges and not avoid risks. When we inoculate our children against stress, in other words, we teach them how to be healthier, more effective adults.

Stress inoculation encompasses five important principles:

(1) *Gradually expose children to problems.* Parents who really love their children are often in danger of overprotecting them. This is a really perplexing problem for many of us. We cannot bear to see them hurt, so we shield them as much as possible. But children need to be gradually exposed to real problems if they are going to be healthy as adults.

This doesn't mean, of course, that you will deliberately expose your child to all the ugly realities of life at an early age. A three-year-old doesn't really need to see bloody war footage on the news, for instance, or to be told in gory detail about what can happen to a child who wanders away from home. An eight-year-old doesn't need to become her single mother's confidante or a small boy the "man around the house" simply because "they need to know how life is." It most certainly doesn't mean "toughening a child" up through physical or verbal abuse.

But exposing children to problems does mean telling them the truth—perhaps at a simplified level—about family tensions and needs. It means letting them share in crises—say, helping hold down expenses during a lean times or helping take care of a sick grandparent. It means letting them know about real problems in the world and allowing them to help meet those needs. Helping serve Thanksgiving dinner at a rescue mission or buying toys for the child whose father is in prison are excellent ways of teaching your children both some of the problems and some of the solutions in the world.

In some cases, exposing children to problems means, in a sense, *making* problems for them—by giving them responsibility and expecting them to follow through. Age-appropriate (and parent-enforced) chores are one of the best ways I know to teach children to face problems and begin to solve them.

As your children mature, try to match their exposure to stress to their level of development. By gradually increasing this exposure and teaching them how to cope, you will slowly be building their resistance to stress "infections."

(2) Resist the rescuing urge. Smart parents do not rush in to rescue children the moment there is a problem. When they are very young, of course, they will need a lot of rescuing. But as children grow older, parents should gradually back off, leaving them to solve their own problems.

I confess that as a parent I did do a lot of rescuing. I jumped in and solved my children's problems too quickly. When something broke I fixed it before the day was out, just so that my children didn't have to feel too disappointed for too long. Even today, now that they are grown up, I tend to want to solve all their problems for them—and I should know better. But I'm learning—and so must every parent who wants to raise healthy, competent children who are free from overstress.

Once again, it's a gradual process. The idea is to leave them to solve the simple problems at first, then gradually move to the more complex ones.

If a four-year old throws a tantrum, for instance, and breaks a favorite toy, don't rush out to buy a new one. Gather up the pieces and put them where they can be seen. Talk over what happened. Let your child feel some sadness over the loss. This helps to teach the meaning of grief. Discuss how and when to replace the toy and even if it should be replaced. By being slow to the rescue and by teaching your child to think and talk about the tragedy of the broken toy, you are helping to inoculate him or her against future, more threatening stress.

A nine-year-old daughter may be heartbroken because her dog, who is almost as old as she is, has been run over and killed by a car. The natural tendency would be to rush out and replace the beloved dog with an adorable new puppy, hoping that the replacement would lessen the pain of the loss.

It is sad that we do this—even sadder, perhaps, than the loss itself. Too often we rush to replace our losses instead of learning how to grieve them properly. Divorced husbands hasten to remarry, disappointed friends rush to find new companions, and people with unfulfilled ambitions quickly replace their thwarted dreams with new ones. Why the haste? Because we can't stand the pain and stress of loss. We've never been inoculated with the grieving virus.

Before you rush out to replace your daughter's pet, allow some time for grief. Perhaps you should hold a memorial service and let everyone in the family reminisce about the fun and happiness the dog brought to your lives. Leave room for sadness, even depression—it is important in helping to keep tension down. If we don't grieve our losses thoroughly, we accumulate a lot of unfinished grieving that tends to compound our later losses and causes us more stress than is necessary.

(3) *Teach healthy self-talk.* Stress inoculation also requires children to learn stress-coping skills. And among the most important antistress skills for them to learn is *healthy self-talk.*

Almost every moment of our day we engage in "self-talk." This, essentially, is how we think—we converse with ourselves. Most of the time, if the self-talk is rational, honest, and in touch with reality, we are basically healthy and our stress is normal. If our self-talk is irrational and untrue, we will experience excessive stress and unnecessary emotional turmoil.

Paying attention to your child's self-talk, therefore, is a good way to gain a clue into the stress he or she is feeling. The next time your child is upset about something, listen very carefully to your child's self-conversation. If necessary, ask what the child is thinking, for instance:

> "Karen, please tell me what you are saying to yourself."
> "Mom, I'm not sure. I think I'm blaming myself because Fluffy ran into the street. I know he always did it. Why didn't I make sure the gate was closed? If I had, he wouldn't have got run over."

This process helps to pinpoint the source of Karen's stress. She is not just mourning her dog; she is blaming herself for his death.

Sometimes children are unable to verbalize their self-talk. In such a case, it can help to ask questions like:

> "Honey, are you blaming yourself for Fluffy's getting run over? Are you thinking that if you had closed the gate it wouldn't have happened?"

If you listen to your children's emotional experiences, paying attention to body language and to little slips of the tongue, you will be able to *capture their self-talk.*

And then comes the teaching part. Once you have an idea what your children are thinking or saying, *reframe or rephrase their experience* so that it is more rational and healthy. We humans have been granted the wonderful gift of logic. We can think, reason and change our beliefs if we so choose. And we can help our children use that gift of reason to counteract the stress of irrational self-talk:

> "Honey, you didn't leave the gate open. You are blaming yourself because you feel sad. Just let your sadness be—don't feed it with feeling guilty. Fluffy got out many times; he could even jump the fence. The traffic in the street was just too fascinating for him. Let's just be sad about what has happened and leave it at that."

By rephrasing the self-talk in a healthy direction and repeating it many times, if necessary, we can teach our children to be more resistant to stress. We will be teaching not denial, but honest facing of the facts—not dishonesty, but truth and reality. Many negative emotions can be counteracted by teaching our children to be honest and logical in their self-talk.

(4) *Teach recovery.* Stress inoculation also includes teaching children to allow adequate time for recovery from periods of overstress. Life is always full of things to do, and there will always be periods of intensified stress or excitement. But such times of high arousal should always be followed with times for recovery. In fact, one of the most glaring deficiencies I find in the most stressed-out patients is their failure to allow for recovery time after a period of overstress.

Let's say that John has been under a lot of stress. He has a great singing voice, so the high-school music club chose him to be the lead in a shortened production of *Fiddler on the Roof.* For some months John has been rehearsing, putting in many hours after school. He enjoys all the attention, but is recruiting more adrenaline than usual.

Finally the play opens and runs for its allotted three days. It's a great success. Everybody says John is destined for glory in show business. But on the Sunday morning following closing night, John wakes up deeply depressed. He won't get out of bed to go to church, and he just wants to be left alone.

What is happening? If you read chapter 3, you probably know that John is suffering from "postadrenaline depression." It's what happens when we've lived on too much excitement for too long—the adrenal system switches off and we feel an enormous letdown. Such a depression is part of nature's design to help us recover. It forces us to rest and not run out to start a new project. That's how we are built. We are not supermen or superwomen, just ordinary mortals with bodies that have their limits and demand recovery time from overuse.

John should be taught to anticipate this "letdown" and to plan for recovery. With some foresight, his parents can realize that the Sunday after the last performance would be needed for recovery. In fact, another week of lethargy and low activity may be necessary for full recovery to be completed. His parents should avoid planning any extra activities for John during that time; they might even excuse him from all but the most necessary activities for a few days, until he begins to get back to normal.

(5) *Teach children to filter their stressors.* Children can also be taught to "filter their stressors." This is another thought strategy in which they learn to ask themselves, when confronted with a problem or crisis, "Is this really important enough for me to get upset about?"

A filter is a device that helps keep out unwanted things. Mind filters keep out unnecessary thoughts and help us to be selective about what bothers us.

Say, for instance, that ten-year-old Joseph is a little too dependent on his peers for affirmation, a little too sensitive to what a particular friend thinks about him. One day Joseph comes home from school looking very upset. Mother asks him what's the matter, and at first he refuses to talk about it. Then finally he blurts it out: "Pete thinks I'm chicken. He wants to go and play in the graveyard near school at night, and because I won't he says I'm scared of graves."

What can you do? You could put your foot down. "Joseph, don't you dare go play in the graveyard at night!" Better still, you can help Joseph to "filter" what Pete is saying and teach him how to deal with other challenges as well:

> "Does Pete know everything?"
> "No."
> "Can he really tell what's going on inside you?"
> "No."

"How can he tell whether you are scared or not? He's just saying that to make you do what he wants you to do. Maybe you are just too respectful of cemeteries and those who are dead to want to go and play on their graves."

> "Yeah, that could be it."

"And if you *are* scared, is there really anything wrong with being afraid of dark, strange places?"

At this point, you can emphasize the *power to make choices*. All "filtering" should ultimately help the child make a choice:

> "So what do you want to do?"
> "I think I'll just tell Pete that I don't want to go with him, and I don't care what he thinks about it."

This element of choice is crucial to helping a child become more stress resistant. Drive home its message to your child:

- If someone criticizes you, *you can choose* whether or not you want it to affect you.

- If someone tries to force you to do something, *you can choose* whether or not you want to do it.

- If something threatens your security, *you can choose* whether you want to be upset about it or not.

Effective filtering, of course, requires a strong ego. In order to filter their stresses, children need to believe in themselves and their right to choose what happens to them. A child who is passive, unsure, unassertive, or self-conscious may be too threatened to filter his or her stresses. In that case, in order to stressproof your child, you may first need to strengthen his or her self-esteem.

Stressproofing Strategy #5:
Build Your Child's Self-Esteem

Self-confidence, self-image, self-love, and self-esteem. These are all phrases that describe how a child feels about himself or herself. And a child with a healthy self-esteem is also more resistant to overstress than one with low self-esteem.

How does healthy self-esteem fight stress? Self-esteem builds confidence; it helps children believe they can handle any challenge. Self-esteem also strengthens children's resiliency—their ability to bounce back when a life problem has knocked them down. Resiliency is one of the qualities that all successful people have; they see failures as opportunities to grow and as challenges to be overcome.

More important, confident and resilient people—people with healthy self-esteem—are less prone to stress. They are less likely to experience the adrenaline-recruiting emotions of anger, fear, and frustration. They are more likely to take steps to cope with their problems rather than worrying about them. One of the most important stressproofing strategies, therefore, is strengthening your child's self-esteem.

What Is Healthy Self-Esteem?

The whole area of self-esteem is a somewhat problematical subject, however. How much self-confidence is healthy, and when does it become cocksureness? How much self-love is healthy, and when does it become self-indulgence or narcissism? How much self-esteem is normal, and when does it become a feeling of self-importance?

Shouldn't we teach our children to be *less* self-conscious, *less* self-pre-occupied, and more "other" centered? I really believe we should. Our "me" culture has caused many people in the West to see themselves as the hub around which the rest of the world revolves. That's hardly a basis for meaningful—stress-free—living.

But even though the concept of self-esteem as it is sometimes inter-preted has some flaws, we all intuitively know that how a child feels and thinks about him or herself is crucial to effective functioning—and that it is important that a child have positive feelings about themselves. Many have a lot of self-hate. They don't like who they are. They would rather be some-one else—someone bigger, smaller, stronger, weaker, smarter, or even less smart. And we know instinctively that this is not healthy.

For some time now, psychologists and popular self-help books have emphasized to parents that the way to make children "feel good about themselves" is to praise their children and help them be successful at what they do. Such a goal focuses too much on making every aspect of the child's life positive and successful—not a very reliable source of healthy self-esteem in an imperfect world where everyone has to fail sometimes!

But even success is not enough to ensure self-esteem, according to a recent publication of the American Psychological Association. This book explores one of the most intriguing quandaries about self-esteem: "Why so many successful, competent people seem to be plagued with problems of chronic low self-esteem."[3] It then goes on to quote one prominent and highly successful person after another as saying that no amount of success has helped them to feel better about themselves. If anything, these highly suc-cessful people found that their external success was always coupled with an increase in internal stress.[4]

This finding fascinates me because it bears out my experience in working with people who by external standards are outstanding achievers. Quite often, in my experience, self-esteem eludes them. I, too, have asked the question that the APA publication poses:

Why, with 40 or 50 years of reasonably successful and responsible life experi-ence completed, do so many people fail to acquire an enduring and realistic sense of self-appreciation?[5]

The answer is to be found, I believe, partly in what I will discuss at the end of this part of the stressproofing section—the neglect of the spiri-tual dimensions of life. But there is another factor as well. I believe that in our culture we attach far too much importance to performance—and our children internalize that message. Too often, our acceptance of our children depends too much on whether or not they live up to our expectations.

This way of looking at self-esteem helps explain why many "successful" people are so down on themselves. The child within the adult has been programmed by early experience to depend on his or her performance as evidence of his or her intrinsic worth. They are still trying to be "good enough," "smart enough," "pretty enough," or "strong enough." And because it is impossible to satisfy such an "internal" parent for long, their self-esteem is bound to lag. This is precisely what the APA book on self-esteem predicts.[6]

To put it more positively, healthy self-esteem must be based not on performance, but on *self-acceptance*, being content with oneself. And children learn this attitude, too, from their parent's attitudes toward them. If we base our acceptance on their performance, they will come to base their own self-esteem on the unreachable goal of being "good enough." But if we accept our children unconditionally, they come to accept themselves unconditionally.

Self-Esteem in Success and Failure

Your child's self-image (the image he or she carries of the self in the mind) will slowly be shaped by successes *and* failures. The key to building healthy self-esteem in our children, then is *teaching them to be more self-accepting* of both success and failure. We make children really "feel good about themselves" by showing them that we love and accept them whether or not they succeed or fail.

But that's not as easy as it sounds. There are several points where well-meaning, loving parents can slip up and teach their children self-rejection.

First, parents sometimes teach children not to trust their successes. "Don't rest on your laurels. You've got to keep trying." Perhaps because we are afraid that success will go to their heads, we create an attitude of discomfort with accomplishment. As a result, children learn to reject their own successes and fail to see them as indicators that they are worthwhile.

More commonly, parents teach children to reject themselves because of their failures. No one likes to fail, and no one likes his or her children to fail. It's easy for children to get the message that failure is proof of unworthiness. If we don't teach our children that failure is a fact of life and that we must *all* fail at some things, even small failures can eat away at self-esteem.

Eight Ways to Improve Your Child's Self-Esteem

1. Make sure your children know that they are worthy just because they exist. Make it clear that whether they are competent or outstanding in other ways makes no difference in your love for them.

2. Be alert to evidence of low self-esteem. Remember that healthy self-esteem is not the same as conceit, nor is it the same as pride. It is just an honest acceptance of who one is. A child who needs to revel in his or her accomplishments probably has *low* self-esteem.

3. Help your child build an honest self-image. Ignoring your child's weaknesses is not helpful, but don't judge them. Children must learn to accept their shortcomings but also to value their strengths.

4. Help your child discover his or her unique talents. No two children are alike. Each has something special to contribute to life. Giving your child the opportunity to explore many activities and interests can uncover abilities and gifts that you never thought about.

5. Provide an atmosphere of trust in your home. Children who can trust their emotions to the intimacy of the family and talk about love, disappointments, accomplishments, or failures are rich indeed. They will have few problems with self-esteem.

6. Make sure that the image you mirror back to your child is not distorted by your own desires or disappointments. Remember that to a large extent children see themselves through the "mirror" of how their parents see them. It is easy to give the message that your child doesn't measure up to your standards. Polish those mirrors. Make sure they are not distorted by your own agenda.

7. Cherish everything about your child, not just the special or outstanding things. Emphasize the positive values of every little inadequacy—and lavish praise for your child's strengths.

8. Make it safe for your child to be whoever he or she is. You do this by showing love and forgiveness—no matter what your child does. By all means discipline your child, but never use discipline as a form of revenge. Children are remarkably fair-minded, and they know when you are being unjust. Don't abuse their trust.

To build your child's self-esteem, therefore, you must make a point of attending to a child's successes *and* failures and encouraging self-acceptance in both conditions. Your job is to hold up a light to reality, help your child look at it with courage, and then temper it with massive amounts of unconditional acceptance. Here, then, is a basic strategy for building healthy self-esteem through self-acceptance:

(1) When your child is successful, help him or her to be accepting of this success. Praise it. Celebrate it. Don't rob it of its glory by saying, "Yes, but

you know you have a long way to go." Keeping your child focused on reality does *not* mean you have to continually rain on his or her parade.

(2) When your child fails, nurture him or her with reassurance. Don't criticize, and try not to show disappointment. In fact, it can be extremely helpful to say something like, "In a way I'm pleased you didn't win this time. We've got to learn how to cope with failures and disappointments as well as successes. Come on, now, let's see what we can learn from this."

You cannot prevent your child from failing, but you can "normalize" failure and reduce its capacity to determine self-image. You can teach your child that even the greatest of baseball players only succeeds in hitting the ball *once in a while*—that no one has a perfect score. If you place a high value on failure and emphasize that it teaches you more than success, chances are that your child will adopt the same belief.

If failure comes too often, then perhaps you should encourage activities where the child can experience more success. Notice and comment on small achievements and be alert for feelings of inadequacy. For instance, if a child keeps saying, "I can't" when asked to do something, you may have to move back to easier activities to rebuild your child's confidence.

Above all, work on providing unconditional acceptance. Make it clear to your children that you think they are lovable and worthwhile no matter what they do. Praise them for just being who they are. Their self-esteem will then be able to stand by itself—and your child will much better able to handle any of the stresses that life throws his or her way.

Summary

Stressproofing your child can take many forms. It can involve helping them sleep better, be physically fit, and learn to relax. It can involve "inoculating" them against stress by exposing them to stress gradually and teaching them good coping skills such as healthy self-talk, recovery time, and "filtering stresses." But the greatest stressproofer of all is building a healthy self-esteem.

Discussion Questions

1. Discuss your feelings about sleep—positive and negative. Do you think you need to change your attitude and behavior about sleep? How can you help your child sleep better?

2. Use the "cold hands" test on a regular basis and make a note about what situations cause you or your child to feel stressed.

3. Review these stressful periods. Can you identify any theme or situation that repeatedly causes you or your child stress?

4. How adequate is your own self-esteem? How do your feelings about yourself, as a parent, impact your child's self-esteem?

8

Stress-Free Discipline

Matt is four years of age, the child of affluent, loving, but somewhat indulgent parents. Matt never really lacks for anything; his parents seldom refuse any of his requests. And that is exactly why they are so mystified by Matt's problem.

Matt takes other people's things.

Notice that I didn't say, "Matt *steals* other people's things," because four-year-olds can't really steal anything. At that age they're too young to know what real, criminal-type stealing is.

No, Matt simply takes things—walks off with them in plain sight. When he visits a friend to play, for instance, his mother has to empty his pockets as soon as he comes home and return all the loot to the friend's mother. But it's not just toys. Matt has been known to carry off a valuable piece of jewelry or a prized little antique object. Without fail, wherever he goes, Matt will leave with something "new."

"Why does he do it? Do you think he is being deprived of something?" asks his mother.

"No, I don't think so," I reply.

"But I give him everything he wants," cries the mother, highly frustrated.

"Perhaps that's part of the problem," I suggest. "He has come to believe he can take anything he wants."

"And I've disciplined him severely," mother announces triumphantly. Then dejectedly she admits, "but it doesn't seem to make any difference."

The Number-One Family Stress Producer

If you ask the average parent, "What aspect of parenting gives you the most trouble?" the answer that is bound to predominate is the one that is giving Matt's mother fits: discipline. Most parents find discipline the most stressful of all parenting tasks. It *also* causes their children a lot of stress.

But why is disciplining children so difficult? Why can't you just speak once and have your child listen? Why can't you make a request just one time and have it obediently complied with? Why does discipline have to be such a stress problem?

It doesn't.

I am convinced that it's just not that difficult to set up an effective program of discipline that doesn't stress out your children or send you to an early grave. Granted, I speak as a grandfather whose primary discipline tasks are behind me, but I really don't think I am out of touch with the needs of parents and children. In my years as a therapist I have helped many parents implement an effective discipline program, so I know it can be done.

The prescription is really quite simple (although I'll grant it isn't always easy): *Know what you want to do, mean what you say, and consistently carry through.*

The problem with discipline, of course—as with all parenting problems—is that your children are grown by the time you start to get it right. Most of the stress involved in discipline, for parent and child, arises from the mistakes we make, not the discipline itself. In this chapter, therefore, I want to offer the benefit of experience ahead of time. I want to point out some of the common mistakes parents make when trying to discipline their children and then outline some principles for effective discipline.

Before I launch into these important topics, let me take a minute to discuss *why* discipline is such an important part of stressproofing in the first place.

A Case for Discipline

Children need firm boundaries. And never in our history have so many children had so few boundaries.

Today's kids have been given so much—money to spend and things to spend them on. Nearly all entertainment—tapes, CDs, TV, movies—is targeted at children, especially teenagers and young adults. While there are large segments of our population who are *relatively* deprived, even the poorest today are rich by the standards of previous ages and other countries. And for many children of busy or stressed-out parents, this exposure to more and more is accompanied with the heady but frightening freedom to do more or less as one pleases.

Not surprisingly, the need for parents to set boundaries is often outwardly resented by children and teenagers. They may complain a lot when their parents treat them as if they have no sense. But deep down the average child (and teenager) hungers for firm guidelines. The child who never hears the word no from a parent is most likely to be an unhappy, stressed-out child.

When discipline is fair and logical, even the smallest child can understand that it is a special kind of love. Effective discipline communicates caring. It says, "I cannot allow you to get into trouble. I want you to be the best person you can possibly be. Trust me; my judgment is better than yours, and I can help you to do the right thing."

Again, children won't always think they see it this way, although deep down they feel it. What do they say? "You're just a square. You don't understand. Everyone else is doing it. You just don't care if I'm humiliated."

Many parents make the mistake of actually listening to these gross overstatements. They feel guilty. Or perhaps they are too busy to be bothered. At any rate, they give in to a child's demands. And who loses? The child *and* the parents.

Children don't really want spineless parents. They may think they value your cowardice in the face of their nagging and haranguing because they reap an immediate benefit, but in the long run they will come to despise it.

Good discipline keeps stress at a minimum. It helps protect a child from harm and gives that child the freedom of taking risks within guaranteed limits. It promotes self-esteem by teaching the child to behave in ways that bring positive reactions from others. And good discipline serves another very important function. It establishes that *the child is not the center of the family—or of the world.*

We have recently lived through a period when our society was child-dominated. We allowed our kids to take over the fifties, sixties, seventies, and eighties. We were overly concerned with not making mistakes, and as a result we made more than we should, and an unnatural chain of command became the norm for quite a few years. Parents were afraid to say no, to give orders, or to discipline appropriately because they were frightened by popular psychology into fearing that their children would somehow become stunted or abused. So they knocked themselves out to be "nice," "understanding," and "tolerant."

Well, we now know we went too far. "Show me a family run by children," Ann Landers once said, "and I'll show you a set of embattled parents trying to buy love."[1] She's absolutely right. The experiment with "permissive parenting" produced many disturbed kids; we now call them the "me generation." And guess what? They are now the parents who are struggling to find a workable way to discipline their children.

Effective discipline—which is also stress-free discipline—establishes a clear line of authority. It involves accepting the fact that at times children will hate parents who exert authority. This is quite normal; I'd say it's even necessary for healthy ego development. And it doesn't negate the fact that children still need limits.

Before we examine the basic principles of stress-free discipline, I would urge you: Don't be afraid to put some bite in your discipline. Mean what you say, but never be mean in what you say. Stand up for your rights as a parent. If you can do this without malice, you'll end up being the most respected and loved person in your family. My grandparents were like this—more than my parents. I love them all the more because they took the trouble to discipline me.

What is Discipline?

What, then, is the point of discipline? What are we trying to accomplish when we discipline our children?

When little Matt, whom we met at the beginning of the chapter, comes home with pockets full, his mother takes his "booty" away, sends him to his room, and tells him to wait there until his father comes home—"and he's going to spank you." When Father does come home, Matt is playing in his room quite contentedly, having forgotten the offense. When Father tries to reason with Matt, he gets nowhere. Spanking seems pointless, since it is now hours since the offense was committed. So Mother gets mad at Father for not "carrying through"; she now blames the father for the problem.

Is this technique discipline? Clearly not; it does nothing to change Matt's behavior. So . . . should the mother take Matt to the bedroom and spank him severely for his behavior? Absolutely not. This would be *punishment*, not discipline—a distinction I want to draw out shortly. Discipline is not revenge (the motive behind punishment) nor manipulation. It is not control, nor is it just a demand for obedience.

So what is discipline? *Discipline is the process of teaching self-control and obedience to reasonable social rules.* It is the means by which we correct faulty behavior and teach correct behavior. When we discipline a child, we are shaping behavior *away* from what is not desired *toward* what is desired.

And what kind of parental actions are most likely to achieve this goal? Here are a few basic principles:

(1) Discipline is most effective when there is a connection with the behavior. The best discipline includes a logical consequence that follows from the wrong behavior. Ideally, it should teach the correct behavior as well.

Say, for example, that your son keeps running into your flower bed when he plays games, tramping and destroying your flowers. What logical consequence would teach the child to stop doing this? He could be required to dig out all the damaged plants and replant new ones. Or you could assign him some other yard work that is tailored to his age and abilities. But having him paint the fence for damaging your flower bed is useless as an act of discipline because it has no logical connection with the offending act.

(2) *Discipline is most effective when adequate warning of the consequence for a particular misbehavior is given.* With advance warning, even unrelated consequences become logical consequences. If you have warned your son ahead of time that he will have to paint the fence the next time he tramples your flower bed, painting the fence is a logical consequence—and can be quite effective.

(3) *Discipline is most effective when the circumstances surrounding the undesired behavior are taken into account.* A child who is sick or extremely tired because of disturbed sleep doesn't need discipline; he or she needs understanding and remedial attention. Let's say that Johnny was up half the night with a stomachache and is hassling and sassing you the next day. There is no point in disciplining him; he is tired and physically out of sorts. No, his illness doesn't give license for misbehaving, but the time to deal with Johnny's misbehavior is when he is recovered. First pay attention to his primary need for rest and sleep and then, if necessary, attend to disciplining his behavior. Very often, once the child has recovered, the misbehavior will have stopped and discipline will not be required.

(4) *Discipline is most effective when the age and developmental stage of a child is taken into consideration.* I have known parents (and have been guilty of this myself) who demand adultlike responsibility from five-year-olds—and then try to discipline the children for acting like normal children.

"Carry this bowl of mashed potatoes to the dinner table, please, Kara." Kara takes the bowl, trips over the cat, and smashes the bowl and potatoes against a newly papered wall.

"Why can't you do something normal?" her mother shouts. "Go to your room, and don't come out until I tell you to."

Fair? No way! I wouldn't be surprised if a seed of resentment has been sown. Kara, despite her immaturity and clumsiness, knows the difference between fair and "no fair." She couldn't see the cat; her eyes were fixed on the mashed potatoes. And the potatoes were a little too heavy for her anyway.

Kara learns nothing from being told to go to her room. A child should never be disciplined for failing at an assigned task that is beyond the child's level of maturity or capacity.

Discipline versus Punishment

If I were to single out the most important point that must be grasped about stress-free discipline, it would be this: Discipline is *not* the same as punishment. I believe that if parents could stop punishing and concentrate on discipline, we could revolutionize child rearing in this country.

Now that's not to say there is absolutely no place for punishment in child rearing. In a few cases punishment may indeed be called for. However, punishment *should be rare* and reserved only for very special circumstances. It should never be the primary approach to discipline.

Now, this distinction between punishment and discipline is obviously important, so let me clarify it. By punishment, I generally mean the infliction of pain, suffering, or loss as the penalty for some wrongdoing. We often think in terms of *physical* punishment such as spanking. But parents can punish in many other ways as well: by yelling, withdrawing love, calling a child names, or humiliating him or her in front of friends.

Punishment usually implies retribution rather than correction. A person who is punished pays for his or her sins, whether or not he or she learns anything. The death penalty for crime gives an extreme but clear example of this principle. The state punishes a murderer by giving him a lethal dose of drugs or a surge of electricity. After that, there is no opportunity for the criminal to change his or her behavior. The point is clearly not education, but retaliation.

Punishment of a crime is intended to act as a deterrent both for the perpetrator's future behavior and for the behavior of others. In some cases, this may be effective. But generally speaking, punishment is for criminals, not children. It is better administered by society, not parents.

Why? The most important reason is that punishment easily becomes harsh and unfair. And the evidence is clear and unequivocal that *all* forms of harsh and unfair punishment produce serious psychological problems in later life. One study, conducted in the St. Louis area, found that 56 percent of adult depressives and 43 percent of alcoholics reported severe beatings with a belt or stick. Only 18 percent of a healthy group recalled such treatment. Furthermore, it was the harsh punishment and not parental problems that led to the development of adult psychological disorders.[2]

Now, it is true that punishment can be administered in ways that are neither harsh nor unfair. Obviously, not every child who experiences a spanking turns up with psychological problems.

However—and this is a crucial point—it takes considerable expertise and maturity to use punishment fairly and effectively. You have to know how to match the punishment to the misbehavior, how not to go too far. You have to have your feelings under control. More importantly, unless you are present *at all times* to punish all misbehavior, punishment is just not effective. Most parents and teachers are not competent enough—and are too emotionally involved—to mete out punishment fairly and effectively.

Furthermore, the potential for permanent harm is too great to make this the preferred mode of discipline.

The only exception to this rule is when a child's behavior is dangerous or life threatening. A child who continues to throw sand in the face of another child, despite verbal correction and even physical separation, should probably be physically punished right there and then. The risk of damaging the other child's eyes is too great to wait for more patient discipline to take effect.

Similarly, a child who persists in climbing onto a balcony railing two stories up or who keeps running into a busy street, should be dealt with quickly, firmly, and possibly with some physical consequence. But even then, be careful and watch your reaction. Your fear of what might have happened will tend to make any physical punishment more intense than normal.

Keep An Eye on Your Anger

And this brings up another reason punishment is usually not the best way to handle a child's misbehavior. Too often, punishment has more to do with a parent's feelings than the child's behavior.

The main driving motive for punishment is *revenge*, which is why it is so attractive to humans. Our basic nature craves vengeance: "You hurt me, and I want to hurt you back." This need is often very strong and is learned early in life. Children are quick to hit back when someone hurts them. Often, what starts as self-defense later becomes a way of "evening the score." As children grow up, society reinforces this desire to exact revenge.

Take a moment to think about how often you respond to your child's misbehavior by punishing him or her. It is the end of a long, tiring day. You are reading a book, and you've come to an interesting part. You are deeply engrossed—when suddenly there's a scream from one of the kids' bedrooms. Irritated that your reading has been disturbed, you rush to the bedroom to find your seven-year-old son pulling your four-year-old daughter's hair because she knocked his puzzle off the table. You grab your son and whack him hard four times on his bottom while you scream at the top of your voice. He cries. Your daughter cries. You're mad. Everyone is stressed.

Punishment or discipline? Which is it? Clearly, you were punishing your son. You were angry because he disturbed your peace and intruded into your mind space, so you took your revenge. You may rationalize your action by saying, "Well, at least that will teach him not to do that again." But does it? Not really. Your son is left feeling aggrieved. After all, you never addressed his injustice—a puzzle lying in pieces on the floor.

Anger, then, and a need for revenge are primary components of punishment—which is why it can be so destructive. The punishment is often excessive, delivered when you're out of control, and it is often unjust. How are you to know that your daughter was not deliberately taunting her brother? Yet he got punished? Not fair!

Punishment also tends to be very impulsive; we do it without thinking. We don't stop to reflect: "How best can I teach my son that to pull his sister's hair is not the way to address his grievance?" We just do what comes naturally—and what is natural can prove to be very destructive.

When you discipline, then, you must take a very different approach. You must set aside any need to hurt back or take revenge, and you must act on reflection, not on impulse. Remember, your goal is to teach self-control of undesired behavior or establish new habits of self-control. Your primary focus must be on *changing* and *teaching*, not on hurting when you have been hurt or taking out your frustrations on your children.

But here comes the rub: Most occasions that call for discipline are fraught with frustration, anger, and fear. If your child suddenly runs into the street, your fear reaction will *also* cause you to be angry. Your natural tendency will be to whack your child—to get back at him or her for causing you discomfort. Many acts of discipline, then, will demand the utmost from you in self-control to avoid going too far in the direction of revenge. You will have to balance your sane desire to correct the behavior against the emotional urge to hurt someone who has hurt you.

If you think this doesn't apply to you, I urge you to look again at your attitudes and behaviors. It's a rare parent indeed who hasn't had at least an occasional urge to punish a child in anger. During stressful moments, you feel threatened. You feel helpless. You feel out of control and afraid. So you revert to primitive aggressive tendencies.

This tendency to resort to punishment instead of discipline when you are angry or fearful means that you should use your saner moments to plan out your discipline strategies. Write them down and put them in a prominent place for all to see. Then, when the undesired behavior occurs, *consult your plan and not your feelings*. Bring your anger or fear under control, and then do *only* what your plan calls for. If you do this, I guarantee that you will have fewer problems with discipline.

Rules for Stress-Free Discipline

If you rule out punishment as a primary form of handling misbehavior in children, how do you go about disciplining them? I've already spelled out some basic principles, but here let me share some specific "rules" for stress-free discipline. You may want to use my discussion as an inventory—to check out how many of these guidelines you conscientiously follow at the present time. Then bear with me while I establish some clear steps for designing a discipline plan for specific behavior problems.

Discipline Rule #1: Present a United Front

Obviously, this is not an issue for most single parents, but for married folks it can be a real challenge—and some divorced couples with joint custody face it as well. You come from different backgrounds and understandably see things differently—including discipline. If you are not careful, you could easily undermine each other's disciplining efforts.

Take some time together every week to review your discipline plan, add on to or modify it if necessary, and reinforce your mutual commitment to it. Agree in advance on all the straightforward details such as allowances, curfews, responsibilities, duties, and limits or boundaries, and spell out the consequences of noncompliance. Then commit yourself to backing one another up in following the plan. Don't play the "Wait until your father comes home" or "Go tell it to your mother" games.

Children are smart. They know how to split the ranks and to work one parent against the other. (I think they give each other private lessons after school.) They can even work as a team to see how far they can test the limits. I know siblings who won't even talk to each other on a normal basis, but on cue they can play out a coordinated con job that will make temporary enemies of their parents and make family discipline a lost cause.

If you can't agree on a particular approach to a discipline, stop right there and don't implement that part of your plan. You'll only do more damage if you try to come at discipline from two conflicting directions. Talk the issue over—seeking counsel if necessary—until you can get resolution and agree on an approach. *Make parental unity a high priority.*

Discipline Rule #2: Be Fair

I am amazed at how even very young children can tell whether something is fair or not. They seem to be born with an acute sense of justice, and they *know* when you are overreacting to a particular problem. To be effective, your discipline must be fair.

I am not just saying that the punishment—or, rather, the consequence—should fit the crime. This goes without saying. I mean that there are some behaviors that *don't call for discipline.* They call for love and understanding—a listening ear and a pat on the back, not on the bottom.

Accidents happen, for instance. Children trip and fall. Objects break. Yet many children feel unfairly blamed for actions that they didn't intend and could not really control.

Parents should not only make allowances for accidents but also for developmental lags or fatigue. A child's level of dexterity will improve as he or she gets older. At three or four years of age, clumsiness is not deliberate, but natural. Muscles and nerves are still developing. Teenagers become clumsy again due to their rapid growth. And some children lag behind others in physical development and dexterity—so make allowances and be fair.

Fatigue in children can be a particular problem. Sleeplessness, over-demands, stress, and conflict can all cause your child to make mistakes. And these do not usually call for discipline—they call for rest. When you sense fatigue in your child, avoid confrontations. Try to be understanding—and both of your lives will be less stressful.

Discipline Rule #3: Discipline Positively as Well as Negatively

I recently came across a "Certificate of Award" available for use by parents. It said, "You were caught being good," and it had a blank for the parent to sign. What a great idea! It's a variation of the popular saying, "Don't try to catch your children being bad; catch them being good." And the gist of that saying is true: You get better results by encouraging and reinforcing good behavior than by just correcting bad behavior.

Much of what we try to teach children has a corrective purpose; it is designed to stop destructive behavior. But this isn't enough. A stress-free discipline plan must include *positive* reinforcement as well.

I personally think the ratio of positive to negative should be about ten to one; your child should receive ten responses praising right behavior for every one that corrects wrong behavior. Improving your "score" in this regard may mean ignoring some minor and unimportant bad behaviors, but it will be well worth the effort.

Failure to obey this rule causes stress for you and your child because it's easy to develop the fault-finding habit. It's easy to become a nag, to pester your kids with "No" and "Don't" and "Stop that!" Such constant criticism—and the yelling that often accompanies it—can't help but elevate the tension level.

So make a point of looking for *positive* discipline opportunities. Pay attention to what your child is doing right—*and reinforce it.*

"Billy, I really do appreciate that you wiped your feet when you came in," can work wonders, even if Billy only gave them a token rub on the outside mat. Sure, you could send him back to do it again (a negative discipline), but praising him for what he did do (positive discipline) will go further. Billy will remember the praise more than the criticism and will probably wipe his feet even better next time.

Did Sally only get a C in math this time? Praise the B in Social Science and ignore the C. Did Darrell come in fifth in the swimming race? Focus on the fact that he still beat lots of other swimmers. Better yet, praise him for practicing hard and giving his all. Teach him that *making the effort* is what counts.

Discipline Rule #4: Try to Anticipate Problems and
Prevent Them

There is little point in disciplining your child for behavior that could have been anticipated and avoided. Much of the time, thinking ahead can save both you and your child a lot of stress.

Let us suppose, for instance, that you have two sons aged eight and six (just like my grandsons). The older boy desperately wants a bicycle. His birthday is coming up soon, so you offer to get him one on his birthday.

Now, you know that the younger brother is very jealous of his older brother. Whenever older brother gets something, he wants it, too. Most of the time you try to give the two boys the same thing at the same time. When you buy one shoes, you buy the other shoes. If one gets a toy, the other gets a toy. This way you keep the peace.

But this situation, you think, is different. After all, it is your older son's birthday. Why shouldn't he get a bicycle? So the birthday comes and goes, and a shiny new bicycle takes its place in the garage.

Three days after the birthday the boys start brawling. Younger brother puts his foot through the wheel spokes while trying to grab the bicycle so he can have a turn. Older brother is furious, and a fight ensues. You emerge from the house to find bloody noses and lots of wailing.

What do you do? Did younger brother put his foot through the spokes on purpose, or was it an accident? Did older brother provoke him? Were there clear rules about sharing—or not sharing the bicycle? What are you supposed to discipline?

Does this sound familiar? Most parents face a similar quandary from time to time. In this case, you will simply have to sort out the tangle the best way you can. But with a little foresight you could have avoided the problem entirely.

You knew very well that one bicycle between two boys who are bicycle-ready spells trouble. So what could you have done? If their birthdays were close together, you could have worked out a mutual deal for them both to get bicycles. If you can't afford this, perhaps you should have waited to get the older boy's bicycle—or bought two second-hand bikes. Or at the very least, you could have talked out the situation ahead of time and spelled out clear guidelines for the boys.

My point is just this: You can avoid a lot of stressful discipline problems by thinking ahead. Be prepared for unusual situations where discipline may be a problem—such as a plane trip, a large family gathering, or a visit to the dentist. Carry entertaining items with you and set up the rules ahead of time. Preparation can prevent trouble!

Discipline Rule #5: Deliver Discipline on the Spot
Whenever Possible

There is a psychological law that says people learn best when consequence follows behavior immediately. And this is especially true of disciplining children. If you delay the consequence, the power of the discipline weakens because children have short memories.

Try to devise your discipline so that the consequence can be delivered immediately. For instance, if it is Tuesday and your son misbehaves, it is useless to say, "Now you won't go to the movies on Saturday." The consequence is too late to be effective. It is better to say, "Go to your room now and stay there for the next hour" or, better still, "I want you to fetch a bucket of water and wash off all the mud you have tracked onto the driveway." This consequence is immediate and tied directly to the misbehavior.

There will be times, of course, when your child will be too upset to respond to your discipline. She may have torn a favorite dress while climbing a forbidden fence, or he may be nursing a black eye after a fight with a rival at school. Under these conditions opt for a period of "time out." Tell the child you are unhappy about what has happened and that you will take the matter up later. "In the meantime, go and cool off in the privacy of your bedroom." Then, at the opportune time, continue to do what you have to do to implement your discipline.

The age of a child can also be a factor in how swiftly you discipline. Older teenagers can grasp the reason for delaying a discipline and might even learn something from the delay. Preschoolers, on the other hand, won't understand why they are being disciplined for misbehavior that is two hours (or even ten minutes!) old.

Most times, therefore, an immediate response is both possible and recommended. So don't delay; discipline now.

Discipline Rule #6: Be Consistent

If you discipline your child for a behavior one day and ignore it the next, you will be setting yourself up for trouble. It's hard for a child to learn anything from inconsistent correction. Instead, your child needs you to *say what you mean* and *mean what you say*. In other words, you need to give your child:

(1) Clear communication. How often have I heard, "But Mom, that isn't what you said. You said that if I finish today's homework I can go and play. You said nothing about the project for next week." How easily we get into these word games. Sometimes the child deliberately twists what was said. But a lot of the time we just don't say what we mean to say. We expect our kids to read our minds.

Try to give clear explanations for what you want and—if possible— why you want it. Then, to avoid miscommunication, try asking your child to repeat back to you what you just said. You may be surprised to find that the message received is quite different from the one you meant to send. So correct your statement—and have the child repeat again until he or she gets it right. (Your only alternative is to carry a tape recorder around with you to verify what your instructions were.)

(2) Uniform enforcement. Follow-through is absolutely vital to stress-free discipline. Once a child learns that you will not be manipulated or conned into changing your mind, the battle will be over. This doesn't mean you can't be reasoned with. By all means, listen to reasonable counterpoints. Be flexible in negotiating with your older children and teenagers, and try to see things from their perspective. But once you have made up your mind, stick to your guns. Doing this on a regular basis will slowly reduce the amount of pouting, arguing, comparisons, and other forms of manipulation you need to listen to. More importantly, you will sense a growing respect from your child.

Discipline Rule #7: Involve the Whole Family in Developing a Discipline Policy

Whenever possible, discipline should be a family affair. In developing a general discipline policy (we'll talk about plans for correcting specific behavior next), you should always involve every member of the family, including your spouse, grandparents, and anyone else who lives in the home. After all, everyone suffers from the misbehavior of one child, so why shouldn't everyone participate in designing the discipline policy?

But there's a more important reason for including others. Group participation helps ensure that the policy is fair. It also ensures that everyone understands the rules so that you are not seen as the "bad guy" when it comes to enforcing consequences.

Ask everyone for suggestions about setting rules and the consequences for noncompliance. Be as democratic as you can. Sit down together and discuss the rules you want to set and the consequences for noncompliance. You cannot expect 100 percent agreement, of course—and you and your spouse will have the final say. But if all family members have an opportunity to express their opinion about the rules and consequences, they will be far more likely to "buy into" the completed plan.

Designing a Discipline Plan

With these rules in mind, let me now set out the basics for an effective discipline plan. Worksheet 2 will help you prepare a plan for handling a specific discipline issue. You may want to make several photocopies of this worksheet so that you can pin them up in several places for all to see. That way, you can remind your child of the plan from time to time: "Molly, go and look at the discipline plan stuck to the refrigerator. What I want you to do is spelled out very clearly right there!"

Don't try to have more than three or four plans working at any one time for a particular child. One is best. Two or three is tolerable. You just won't be able to keep up too many.

Tackle the more important problems at first. A misbehavior that occurs once every six months is hardly worth the effort of devising a plan. Try to focus on frequent misbehaviors.

Here is the procedure to follow in devising a plan:

(1) Decide what you want to accomplish. First, fill in your child's name and the date on the worksheet. Then begin by stating an overall *objective*. What is it you want to accomplish? Perhaps your daughter isn't studying enough. Maybe you want your son to stop being disrespectful, to stop fighting with his sister, to come when you call, or to stop climbing the neighbor's tree. Whatever it is, write it in the first blank of the worksheet.

(2) Identify the specific behavior or behaviors you want corrected. There may be several behaviors connected to your objective. For instance, let's suppose you want your child to stop being disrespectful. Ask yourself, "What specific behaviors do I want to discipline?" and then list them. Think about the specific things your child does that bother you. Perhaps she has a smart-aleck comeback for every request you make. Perhaps he throws things. Be as specific as you can in writing down those behaviors: "I want Nathan to stop shouting bad words whenever I tell him he can't have something." "I want Susie to stop biting her nails."

(3) To avoid focusing too much on the negative, specify the positive behavior or behaviors you want to reinforce. Here, too, you should be as distinct as possible. The best behaviors to list would be the *opposites* of the negative ones you just wrote down. To counteract swearing, for instance, you may want to write down, "I want Nathan to use more loving and respectful language." Or you could be even more precise: "I want Nathan to say 'please' and 'thank you' whenever he asks for something and I give it to him."

(4) Spell out the consequences for misbehavior. What would be a fair consequence for bad language and disrespect to you? "Time out" may be appropriate. "I will send Nathan to his bedroom and require him to stay there first for fifteen minutes, then twenty minutes, and so on." Withdrawal of TV privileges for equivalent amounts of time might also fit.

(5) Spell out the consequences for the positive behavior. "Whenever Nathan says 'please' or 'thank you,' I'll stop what I am doing and praise him." You could also set up a point system so that Nathan can accumulate five points toward a total of, say, a hundred points. When he reaches the hundred points he will get a special treat. A classic reinforcement system is to put a self-sticking metallic "star" in a book or on a poster every time Nathan does the right thing. Remember, positive behavior tends to displace negative behavior when it is reinforced.

(6) Review your plan regularly. Make sure you keep a space on your plan to review it regularly. At some point you will look at your discipline plan and realize you have accomplished your objective. Then you can date it and file it away. You will also want to review your successful plans from time to time to reinforce you in your discipline efforts. If, when reviewing the plan, you realize it isn't working, you can devise a new one. Staying ahead of the game will keep both you and your children feeling less stressed.

Enforcing the Discipline Plan

Now we come to the hard part: implementing your discipline plan. Once you have devised your plan and discussed it with the family, explain it to your child and show him or her where you will put it for reference. Then, whenever the misbehavior occurs, proceed as follows:

(1) Give your child a warning. Remind your child of the discipline plan and the consequences you have specified. Many children, especially young ones, are just not aware that they are misbehaving. Your reminder gives them an opportunity to stop their misbehavior and thus increases the learning value of the plan.

(2) Give your child an opportunity to stop the misbehavior. This is very important in good discipline. Having specified the consequences for wrong behavior, you teach your child to be aware of the misbehavior and to *choose whether or not to continue with it.* The child is learning to exercise self-discipline and to be responsible for his or her behavior. Remember, your ultimate goal is not to catch them being naughty, but to change their behavior.

(3) If the child continues the misbehavior, apply the consequence without hesitation. Don't give second chances; they undermine your consistency. Don't allow debates; they encourage manipulation. Don't allow changes in the plan; this weakens your authority. If the plan calls for fifteen minutes of

---

Worksheet 2: A Discipline Plan

Child's name _____ Date _____

1. *Objective* (What do I want to accomplish?)

_____

_____

_____

2. *Negative Behavior* (What behavior do I want to discipline?)

_____

_____

_____

3. *Positive Behavior Desired* (What behavior do I want to encourage?)

_____

_____

_____

4. *Consequences for Misbehavior* (What will I do if the behavior is repeated?)

_____

_____

_____

5. *Reinforcement for correct behavior* (What will I do if the behavior stops?)

_____

_____

_____

6. *Date plan complete:* _____

"time out," sending the child to his or her room for five minutes is useless; you might as well not bother. It's better to do nothing than to do less than you planned.

(4) *Once you have applied the consequence, try to allow a way for your child to be forgiven.* This does not contradict what I have said in step three. Some misbehaviors can be reversed or rectified, and you can reinforce

learning with a "restitution" plan that acknowledges the reversal. A child who refuses to apologize to his sister for a rude remark, for instance, may need to be disciplined by suspending TV privileges, but you can make it clear that TV will be allowed again if he changes his behavior and apologizes. Now it's his choice.

Now I know that some children will abuse this opportunity. There are some kids so smart (or stupid) that they will manipulate you by saying they are sorry when they are not, just to abort the discipline consequences. Smart parents, however, know this game and are not fooled by it.

Some behaviors lend themselves to restitution. If, for instance, your teenage son tears up some new roses you have just planted while running around playing soccer and you have grounded him for the weekend, you could rescind the grounding if he buys new roses and plants them for you. He will learn a lot more from such a restitution plan than from stewing in his room all weekend because you grounded him. But whether or not restitution is possible, the child should be able to ask and receive forgiveness at any point of the discipline process. This does not mean that the consequences will necessarily be lifted; the child may need to go ahead and pay his or her dues. But the child needs to know there is a way to restore your relationship. Once the consequence has been applied or restitution made and forgiveness has been granted, the behavior should then be past history.

(5) Make sure you forget the grievance when the discipline is over. Don't go on harping about what has happened. Doing so will put you over the line into punishment. Once you have imposed the consequences for the misbehavior, let the matter go. Forgetting is absolutely essential to good discipline.

Specific Discipline Strategies

To deal with the many nonpredictable misbehaviors, and perhaps a few predictable ones as well, there are *three specific discipline strategies* you need to have up your sleeve. In discussing them, I will first present the problem and then describe the solution. You will find that the solutions I offer for these specific situations can be applied to a wide variety of other situations as well.

Discipline Problem #1: Your Child Refuses to Obey You

Thirteen-year-old Rebecca's mom was at her wits' end because Rebecca would not do anything she requested. For example, Rebecca is required to make her bed in the morning before coming down to breakfast. When she comes into the dining room, her mother asks, "Did you make your bed?"

Rebecca replies, "No, I'll make it when I get home from school." An argument ensues. Mother keeps asking questions, but gets nowhere.

MOTHER: Why didn't you make it?

REBECCA: Because I'm in a hurry.

MOTHER: "Why didn't you get up earlier so you can make it before you come down?"

REBECCA: Because I was tired and needed to sleep.

Mother's mistake is believing that if Rebecca can *understand* the causes of certain behaviors she can *control* them. Unfortunately, this is not true. Most children haven't the slightest idea why they do what they do, so it is pointless to ask for reasons. All you do is come across as a nag. It is better to be forthright and say what you want than to debate the reasons why your child is not complying.

Discipline Solution #1: "Do it Now"

Two psychologists from George Washington University wrote a book many years ago about how to get your children to do what you want them to do.[3] I've used their simple but effective strategy many times to great effect: *Clearly and firmly demand that your child do what you want him to do right then and there.* Stick with the demand in the face of all grumbling and excuses and insist that it be done immediately. "Do it now!" is all you need on your side of the conversation.

In the case described above, the mother learned to say simply, "Rebecca go and make your bed right now."

REBECCA: But I'll be late for school.

MOTHER: That's too bad. I don't care how late you'll be for school. Just go and make your bed right now.

REBECCA: You're crazy. I'm all dressed and everything.

MOTHER: Do it now!

REBECCA: But . . .

MOTHER: Do it now!

Rebecca ran upstairs and made her bed, grumbling all the way. Despite the short delay, she was still in time for the start of school.

For the next several mornings, Rebecca's mother followed the same strategy. In just a few days the situation was under control. Rebecca got into the habit of making her bed because she knew she couldn't get away from the house without doing it.

You can use this "Do it now" strategy for many other problems: completing homework, establishing a regular bedtime, cleaning bedrooms, and picking up clothes. With smaller children, you can physically take them back to their rooms and insist that they do what you want them to do. Stop what you are doing and maintain your presence while insisting that the behavior you desire be done there and then. Repeat the demand over and over again like a broken record until you get compliance. My wife has discovered that this tactic even works on me!

Discipline Problem #2: "Your Child Demands an Explanation"

Say, for example, that Edith wants you to drive her across town to pick up a friend so they can go to a movie.

"No, Edith, you can't go today."

"Why not?"

"Because . . . well, because I'm busy. I've got the church sale Saturday, and I've got to bake."

"But it's not fair. You can bake tomorrow, or when you get back. Why can't you take me now??"

There is no productive end to such arguments. They usually end with the parent resentfully complying and being stressed out as a result. Parents, unfortunately, have been conditioned to give their children explanations, on demand, for every conceivable situation. The trouble is, children rarely agree with the explanation. Can you really imagine Edith's saying, "OK, Mom, you're right. I'll catch a bus"? She simply asked for an explanation so she could knock it down.

Explanations, then, serve little purpose except to feed the child's need to argue. If you have the time, by all means allow the debate. But don't expect to win.

Discipline Solution #2: "Because I Said So."

John Rosemond a family psychologist and syndicated newspaper columnist, points out that there are two types of explanations. First, there are explanations that help us understand how things work—like sewing machines and nuclear power plants. Second, there are explanations that try to justify decisions.[4]

Children need as many of the first kind of explanation as they can tolerate. They don't really want to listen to the second. Explanations of the first sort are always appropriate. But explanations of the second sort are appropriate *when you want to give them*, not when your child demands them.

Dr. Rosemond suggests a very helpful rule of thumb concerning the giving of explanations. He calls it the "Save Your Breath Principle." He says that unless a child really wants to know the reason why you say no, there's no point in explaining.

Most children are just not mature enough to understand why going to an X-rated movie or consorting with kids who are known drug users is not a good idea. They also can't understand why riding a bicycle down a busy street or walking downtown at two in the morning is hazardous. And even if they do understand, they may just be trying to wear down a parent's resistance by asking for explanations.

Bottom line, children usually know exactly why you make these rules. They just don't agree with them because they haven't lived long enough to see why your rules are helpful.

So in circumstances like these—and many others—save your breath. Explain all you want about nuclear power plants, but don't be afraid to justify your decisions with "Because I said so," especially on issues of safety, responsibility, values, and priorities. Since many of your decisions are probably arbitrary, anyway, you're being a lot more honest as well.

Now don't misunderstand. Sometimes you should explain your decisions. These are times when the heat isn't on you to change your mind. They are the times when you sit quietly around the kitchen table or on the porch in the evening and you tell your kids what you think about life—including the fact that you want the best for them. These are the times when your children will want to hear, so that's when you explain! These are also times when you should listen, so that they can feel heard.

Discipline Problem #3: "Everyone Else Is Doing It"

This is one of the more favored cries one hears from children, especially teenagers. The scene is the living room. Your thirteen-year-old daughter is pleading with you. "Please, please, can I go? It only happens once in a lifetime."

Where does she want to go? To a rock concert. Some group you've never heard of before is playing in a rather sleazy hall in a sleazy part of the city. In fact, the group itself seems sleazy. And most of the people your daughter wants to go with are older than she is—she and her closest friend want to go with the friend's sixteen-year-old sister and the sister's friends.

You feel uneasy. You know there'll be drugs on the premises. You know you must refuse.

"But everyone else is going; it's no big deal. They'll all think I'm overprotected. And besides, don't you trust me?"

Daughter has just recently learned to use the idea of "trust" and "overprotection." The other kids say it usually throws and unsettles parents. They don't like being accused of coddling their children and they hate the thought of not being trusting parents!

Discipline Solution #3: "I Say No."

The simple but effective response in this situation is, "I don't care what other kids are allowed to do. I say no." You could also add, "I don't care if your friends think I'm overprotective." Or, if you feel so inclined, you could comment that those parents are responsible for their children, while you are responsible for yours. Case closed.

While you know that the "everyone is doing it" ploy is a gross exaggeration, getting into a discussion about this pulls you once more into the explanations trap. The simple phrase, "I say no," is all that is necessary. Your child knows exactly why you are saying it.

The matter of overprotection raises a very important discipline issue: How much freedom should you give your child? When and how should you let go? By how much?

Some children at thirteen are quite mature and can fend for themselves. Other thirteen-year-olds still need a babysitter. And the same is true of twelve-year-olds and fourteen-year-olds. So how much freedom you allow really depends on the maturity of your child. There are no simple rules.

To assess how well your child or teenager is likely to handle the freedom he or she is requesting, examine your child's record of performance. Does he or she share chores, manage money well, come home at a reasonable time, and maintain respectable grades? If so, by all means give him or her more freedom. But a record of irresponsible behavior says you're giving too much freedom as it is—so cut back.

Make it clear to children that freedom is a privilege that must be earned. It is to be granted in direct proportion to a child's ability to show that he or she can handle it responsibly. Until then, *just say no.*

Model As Well As Discipline

Discipline is a vast and complicated topic, and much more can be said about it. But adherence to the principles I have outlined here should help you to live through the parenting phase of your life without too much stress—for you or your child. If you keep your goals clearly before you, you can develop a discipline plan that is not punitive and damaging to children.

Parents owe their children consistency in discipline as well as firm, clear guidelines. But they also owe their children a set of solid values that will inform the boundaries set by discipline. Arbitrary or capricious rules do not really help to discipline children.

Values are caught as well as taught. If you lie to your child, you will teach your child to lie, and no amount of discipline or even punishment will teach him or her to tell the truth. If you break your promises, it is grossly unfair to discipline your child for breaking a promise.

Consistency, then, is the key. And this means not only following through on what you say, but also modeling the behaviors you are trying to instill in your children. There's just no way around this. Unless you practice what you preach, your discipline will be to no avail.

Summary

Discipline is a common source of stress for both parents and children, but effective, stress-free discipline doesn't have to be that difficult. The purpose of discipline is to teach self-control and obedience to reasonable social rules. This goal is best met not through punishment (which is usually motivated by anger and a desire for revenge), but by a carefully thought-out plan of logical consequences for misbehavior. Parents should present a united front, try to be fair, use positive reinforcement, anticipate problems, discipline promptly, aim for consistency, and involve the whole family in designing the discipline plan. If the child misbehaves, the parent should give a warning, apply consequences promptly, then put the matter behind them. With such an approach, even such problem situations as a child's refusal to obey, demand for explanations, and insisting that "everybody's doing it" can be handled with a minimum of stress.

Discussion Questions

1. Think about a time when you have punished your child rather than disciplined him or her. How could you have changed the punishment into effective discipline?

2. What do you think are the most important differences between punishment and discipline?

3. Discipline must be fair, and it must be consistent. Can you always trust yourself to be fair and consistent? How can you ensure that you are being fair and consistent?

4. What are some logical consequences you could impose for the following misbehaviors:

- clowning at the dinner table and knocking over a pitcher of water,
- removing a sibling's belongings without asking for permission,
- writing on walls,
- sneaking out at night to meet friends.

9

Creating a Stress-Free Environment

Eight-year-old Trina sat on the porch, chin on her knees, and watched the sky turn from blue to orange to purple. Behind her, through the open door, she could hear her parents fighting again. It was getting dark, and she thought she should probably go in. For now, though, she wanted a few minutes out here where it was peaceful—no fighting, no brothers picking on her, no little sister getting into her things. She loved her family, but sometimes she wished she didn't have to come home at all.

"Come on over to my house," shouted Brett as the game broke up. And as usual the whole gang raced down the street toward Brett's. Brett's parents looked up from their dinner preparation as the five boys crowded into the kitchen and asked for a drink. "OK, guys, you know the rules," said Brett's father. "The paper cups are over there, the water cooler is there—and one kid at a time. Then you can go into the basement and play video games if you want to—but only until we're finished here. Then it's time for everyone to go home." Brett's parents grinned at each other as the boys drained their cups and pounded down the stairs.

Parents, by and large, set the "tone" of the home. They organize the physical environment—whether making it cheerful and well organized or cluttered and chaotic. They make the rules and either enforce them or let them slide. And to a large extent they determine whether or not there will be a loving atmosphere and a forgiving spirit.

For all these reasons, parents create a child's "stress environment." They determine whether the home environment is a *source* of added stress or a *resource* for stress relief.

This is a big responsibility, but an important one for parents to recognize. In this chapter, therefore, I want to suggest some ways parents can build an environment that helps to stressproof children.

A Stress-Relieving Home

There are several ways that the home environment can help relieve children's stress and avoiding adding to it. One of the most basic—and often overlooked—factors is the *physical* layout—how the home looks and how it is organized.

A cheerful, attractive, well-organized home can be a haven from stress. One that is drab, cluttered, or chaotic can add significantly to stress levels.

This doesn't mean that a house must be in perfect order at all times in order to be welcoming and relaxing. Sterile perfection and rigid organization can be as stressful as environmental chaos. Still, it's hard to be relaxed and stress-free when you are constantly stumbling over items in the floor or when the simplest activity entails an all-out search for the tools to do it with.

Numerous studies have revealed that children are quite sensitive to their physical environment. They may be masters at reducing their rooms to rubble in five minutes, but they still feel less stressed in a serene and organized home. The sidebar on page 158 suggests some ways you can organize your home so that the physical environment becomes a stress reliever rather than a stress producer.

In addition to managing the physical environment, however, parents can manage the *emotional environment* of the home to help relieve their children's stress. A fascinating study carried out at Ohio State University's School of Nursing points to some practical ways this can happen.

After interviewing more than a hundred children of both sexes about how they cope with stress, Dr. Nancy Ryan-Wegner grouped more than five hundred different methods for reducing stress into thirteen categories and had the children rate them for effectiveness.

The children agreed quite unanimously that the *least* effective ways to relieve stress were:

- *aggression*—yelling, screaming, swearing, tattling, talking back, insulting people,

- *acting out emotionally*—crying, pouting, moping, punching, getting angry, feeling sorry, having a fit,
- *habitual behaviors*—cracking knuckles, twisting hair, biting nails, chewing gum, and compulsive eating.

So what behaviors did these children rate as *most* effective in fighting stress? The three stress-relievers that emerged with top ratings were:

- *social support*—talking to a parent, asking for hugs and help from parents, friends, and siblings,
- *cognitive behaviors*—thinking about a problem, talking to oneself, writing about it, working on a model and planning what to do. Thinking positively was very important here,
- *avoidance behaviors*—ignoring problems, changing the subject, not worrying about it.[1]

To me, the striking thing about this study was the way it emphasized the importance of the child's environment in teaching both the effective and the noneffective ways of coping with stress. Let me highlight some important ways parents can help relieve their children's stress and give them effective coping skills:

Stress Reliever #1: Offer Support. One of the best ways that parents can help their kids cope with stress is to make the time to talk with them. And I don't mean lecture or preach. Listen. Find out what bothers your children. Ask them how they might handle various situations. Work through problems with them. Don't tell them what to do—children, especially teenagers, resent being ordered about—but do "brainstorm" ideas with them.

Bedtime is usually a good time for parent-child talks. Once the TV is off, the toys are packed away, and everyone is relaxed, kids are more likely to be open and receptive.

What do you talk about? One way to start is to tell your child something that you like about him or her. (Pick something you can be sincere about; kids can spot a phony answer a mile away!): "You know what I like about you? You always want to know how I'm feeling. You make me feel very special just because you are interested in whether I'm happy or sad." From there, it should be easy to move into, "What are you feeling these days . . . ?"

Try telling some things about yourself and inviting your son to do the same. Talk about something you are looking forward to the next day and ask what your daughter is anticipating. Confess something that scares you, and then leave room for your child to talk about what scares him. There are

Organizing Your Child's Physical Environment

Here are some practical ways you can organize your home to make it a source of stress relief for your children:

1. Make sure your child has some personal space. Whether children enjoy a private bedroom or share a cubbyhole with three siblings, they should have at least one area to call their own—a place where they can retreat, relax, and recover from stress. If space is limited, consider putting a "tent" over the child's bed or even putting a beanbag chair and a light in the closet.

2. Help your child organize. Many children live in physical chaos because they don't know how to organize their belongings. Provide shelves, boxes, pegboards, and hooks. Help your child sort through belongings and establish a "home" for everything. Periodically weed out toys and clothes that have been outgrown or in which the child has lost interest so as to reduce clutter.

3. Tailor the physical environment to your child's size. Is there a hook in the bathroom low enough for his or her robe? Is there a stepstool next to the sink? Can he or she reach the pole in the closet. A child learns to feel competent (and less stressed) when he or she is able to handle simple chores alone. Organize your home environment to make this possible.

4. Make and enforce rules about keeping the house physically stress-free. Establish an acceptable level—a stress threshold—of dirt and clutter and see that the family works together to keep the home below that level. The specifics will vary from family to family—or even room to room—but be sure everyone has a say in the decision. Establish standards that everyone can live with.

5. Lower the noise level. Noise can contribute significantly to a stressful environment. Take a minute to monitor the decibel level in the house. Are the dishwasher, the stereo, the TV, and Dad's hand drill blasting at the same time? If you can bring the volume down, everyone in the family will be less stressed.

6. Establish comfortable traffic patterns. Is the furniture arranged in such a way that people feel comfortable and don't get in each other's way? It is possible to become so used to a certain arrangement that we are not aware of how much stress it causes.

7. Try to make your home visually appealing. Again, the specifics will vary with taste. But you don't have to be an interior decorator to make a room cheerful, appealing, and restful. When choosing colors, be aware that certain colors are more stimulating than others. If the stress levels in your home are high, you might want to choose soothing colors such as soft blue instead of arousing colors such as red or orange, at least for the bedrooms.

no rules here; the point is just to keep the communication lines open and to give your child a sense of support.

On a larger scale, try to help your family to be more communicative and cooperative. Deliberately create a "let's help each other" atmosphere. Building a "team" spirit in the home goes a long way to help a child feel supported. Here are some ways you can build a cooperative, supportive atmosphere:

(1) *Hold regular family conferences.* Once a month, try to bring the whole family together to discuss how chores are handled and identify what problems exist in the general day-to-day running of the home. During these meetings, don't just say what must be done; let your family suggest solutions. This will provide an opportunity for the family to "let off steam."

(2) *Plan regular family outings.* On a regular basis (preferably once a week), do something fun as a family. Visit the park, a museum, an art gallery, or the zoo—some place where you can talk together. Try to avoid passive activities like the movies, and make sure the whole family is involved. Such regular fun time together will foster dialogue and interaction.

(3) *Develop family projects you can work on together.* Again, the rule is to involve everyone in the family. Your project can be gardening, for instance—putting in a backyard vegetable garden or, if you live in an apartment, a hydroponics garden. Hobbies make great projects for developing family togetherness. Stamp or coin collecting, photography, gourmet cooking, or reading together (either reading aloud, or reading the same book and then discussing it) make great family projects. Tailor the activity to the age of your children and don't stick to one project too long. As soon as interest wanes, move to another.

Stress Reliever #2: Check Out Your Child's Thinking. Since clear and honest thinking is essential both to maturity and to stressproofing, periodically check out what—and how—your child is thinking. What kind of self-talk does he or she engage in? How logical and rational are his or her thought processes?

Granted, you cannot expect adult logic from a child, but it is in childhood that adult logic is formed. It is normal for children at certain stages of development to engage in "magical" thinking or fantasy. By careful listening, however, you can gently steer a child toward clearer thinking patterns. When you talk to your child, try to be alert for faulty or negative thinking and gently correct misconceptions.

Having your child write out his or her thoughts is one way to check logic and reasoning and also teach a time-tested strategy for problem solving. Help your kids understand that thinking about problems in one's head *never solves them.* They just go round and round, confined to one part of the brain. Writing down one's thoughts (or talking them out) objectifies them and makes them clearer. It's easier to know whether your thoughts are accurate when you can see or hear what you are thinking.

Writing about thoughts, feelings, and experiences is an extremely valuable exercise for children who are old enough. It's one of the reasons many people find it helpful to keep a journal in which they record their thoughts and experiences. You can give your child a lifelong gift by presenting him or her with a journal or diary and some guidance in how to use it.

Stress Reliever #3: Distinguish between Healthy and Unhealthy Avoidance. As the children in the Ohio State study indicated, avoidant behaviors can be very effective in relieving stress. But this is a tricky topic, because not all avoidant behaviors are helpful. Some only make matters worse. You can reduce the stress in your children's lives by helping them know the difference.

Distraction, for instance, can be helpful. A child who has a lot to think about or is anxious about an upcoming event may find it very beneficial to build a model airplane, sew a dress, or even go to a good movie. By providing relief from persistent or disturbing thoughts, such distracting activities can relieve a lot of stress and even clear the mind for better problem solving. As long as they don't prevent the child from eventually facing his or her problems, they are not unhealthy.

Denial, on the other hand, is clearly damaging. Denial means minimizing problems or turning a blind eye to reality. People who are in denial are so persistent in looking the other way that they are often not even conscious of what they are refusing to see.

Twelve-year-old Nancy has a problem with denial. That's why her mother brought her in for help. Petite for her age and a little shy, Nancy is a really nice person—too nice. Even at her young age, Nancy has the makings of a great "rescuer." Her friends all know that if anyone is in trouble, Nancy will bail her out. If anyone is a little short of cash, Nancy will loan her money. If someone is needed to help with a dirty chore—Nancy is always willing to pitch in.

Nancy's friends are taking advantage of her—but she doesn't see it that way.

"No, my friends would do the same for me, I'm sure," she tells me.

"Have you ever tried asking them to help you sometimes?"

"Not really. But they would if I asked."

Nancy goes way beyond what even a good friend should do. Then she suffers from the stress that follows—stress caused by not finishing her own chores or homework, or by having used up all her spending money on trying to please others. And she consistently blinds herself to what is going on. That's denial. And it's not healthy.

Children need to know the difference between healthy distraction and dangerous denial. They need to be taught—and shown—the value of facing up to reality.

That doesn't mean being chronically negative and taking no risks; it just means being honest with oneself. You will help your children be more stress-resistant if you help them be courageous, to face up to their obligations. Teach them not to dwell on problems, but not to run away from them, either. A person who can face reality and plan a course of action for facing it won't need to worry all the time. Such a person will be far more resilient when faced with stress.

A Home That Builds Resilience

During the latter stages of World War II, we could not buy toys in South Africa, where I grew up. Every factory had focused its production on the war effort; toys just were not being made. So we kids found alternatives. We fashioned toys from boxwood, string, and cotton reels.

It was during this time that I discovered a bamboo grove in the veld nearby. The jointed hollow stems were hard but springy. I knew that this special type of tropical grass was used for making cane furniture, so I became quite intrigued with its toy-making possibilities. I learned to cut the hollow stalks into strips. I built kites and a rough basket or two. Some of the stalks were even large enough to fashion a raft.

What impressed me most about the bamboo was the fact that you could bend it quite far without breaking it. And even if you put it under tremendous stress, it would snap right back. What made that bamboo especially useful for play was its *resilience*.

My days of playing with bamboo came back to me quite clearly a few years back when I read a book called *Vulnerable But Invincible*.[2] In it, Professor Emmy Werner of the University of California at Davis, shares some insights acquired in an ongoing study of children and their stress-coping abilities.

In 1955, Professor Werner targeted the rural island of Kauai in the Hawaiian islands for a lifelong study. All the children born that year were carefully studied and followed for more than twenty years. Of these seven hundred children, Professor Werner classified seventy-two as "resilient."

These children had a tremendous amount of stress in their lives, but they were able to "bounce back" quickly from any emotional blow. They took charge of their lives. They refused to be victims of their circumstances and turned bad experiences into good ones.

What parent wouldn't want their children to be like that—tough and flexible, like bamboo? Developing resilience in children should be a major goal in shaping a home environment.

Factors in Shaping Resilience

But what makes children resilient? Professor Werner believes that both internal and external factors come into play.

Internal factors—characteristics displayed by the children themselves—include:

- an affectionate nature,
- a tendency to respond to people,
- an ability to work autonomously,
- an ability to focus attention,
- an ability to control impulses,
- a positive self-concept, and
- special interests and hobbies.

As a child, I believe I developed many of these internal characteristics out of necessity. Growing up in a dysfunctional and eventually a divorced family, I often felt like I had to "bounce back"—like a piece of bamboo—in order to survive. And to do this I believe I had to learn to be affectionate, responsive, independent, and self-controlled—and to nurture a variety of interests.

Now, I would never wish a dysfunctional family on a child just so he or she could learn to be resilient. An unhealthy family is more likely to work against resilience than to foster it. I'm just thankful that I was somehow able to develop these inner resources and develop the strength to bounce back in the face of adversity. Even then, I was lucky, because being resilient has its risks.

Bamboo, after all, does have a breaking point, no matter how flexible it is. As a child, I used to see how far I could go in forming circles with my strips of bamboo. I broke many pieces of tough bamboo by going too far.

Resilient children, too, have their breaking point—and some parents "bend" their resilient children too far. Instead of using the home environment to reinforce their children's natural resilience, these parents take their kids' "bounce back" ability for granted. By forcing them to take on responsibilities that are unreasonable for their age or to live in a pressured atmosphere for too long, they run the risk of "snapping" the child. And when a resilient child finally snaps, the consequences may be far more serious than in a child with a weaker constitution—simply because more energy and pressure has become involved.

Parents, then, need to work at developing their child's strong internal resilience without placing too much strain on their child. Don't think because your child is strong, that he or she can survive anything. During times of extraordinary stress, you need to make an extra effort to provide a supportive environment for your child—whether naturally resilient or not.

And this brings us to the *external factors* that contribute to making a child more resilient. These factors stem even more directly from the child's environment. They include:

- a lot of attention during the first year of life,
- a positive relationship between parent and child in the early childhood years,
- additional caretakers besides the mother,
- structures and rules in the household,
- close peer friends, and
- required responsibility.

How Parents Can Build Resilience in Children

Parents, by and large, are the key to establishing these external factors that make a child more resilient. They both model it *and* teach it. They provide the environment of "good things" that make for resilience. Allow me to elaborate briefly on two of these factors that I believe are especially important:

(1) *Additional caretakers besides the mother*. When a child only has a mother to depend on, not only is the mother-child relationship more likely to be strained, but the child has no additional source of support when the mother is under stress and unable to focus attention on the child. This can be a real problem for single mothers. And single fathers, while less common, face a similar difficulty.

Additional caretakers help to broaden the base of support and provide the child with additional role models. This variety of resources instills the idea that there is more than one place to go for help—and more than one way of solving a problem. Such a situation naturally builds in resilience.

The most obvious source of additional support, of course, is the father. Children who are actively cared for by *both* parents almost always have an edge when it comes to resilience. But other members of the family, close friends, and even trusted teachers can be valuable members of the child's support network.

Grandparents can be a particularly valuable part of a child's support environment. This role is especially important to me because I am now a grandparent—and because my grandparents were so important and influential to me. I want to help my own grandchildren as much as my grandparents helped me. I want to be part of the environment that helps them grow strong and resilient.

Often, however, there is tension between parents and grandparents. Grandparents are known for "spoiling" the grandchildren. We tend to waive the rules, be too generous, and be lax on discipline. After all, we don't have primary responsibility for the children; surely we can indulge them a little without undermining their characters! But parents often resent this "bend the rules" attitude.

One single parent I know tried to fight her parents over these issues. Finally she decided to just let grandparents be grandparents. She told her kids, "I know that Gramma spoils you when you go over to her house. That's OK because going to Gramma's is a special treat. It's like a vacation. But when you come home again, all rules are back in place. The vacation is over. Understood?"

Everyone understood. And everyone was a lot happier.

The grandparents enjoyed giving to their grandchildren. The mother benefited from the additional support. Everyone enjoyed the reduced tension. And the kids, especially, were granted the resilience-building gift of additional caretakers in their lives.

(2) Structures and rules in the household. These are important in building a child's resilience because they establish clear boundaries—letting the child know just how far he or she will be expected to "stretch." A child whose environment is structured and organized learns to build internal structures into his or her own life—and becomes less susceptible to outside influences that bring stress.

Structures include routines, schedules, organizational schemes, and traditions. Such established ways of doing things are comforting to a child; they reduce stress by adding a sameness and predictability in an often-chaotic world. Children thrive on routine; they gain in confidence and self-esteem when they know what to expect and how to respond.

Structures can range from the way a drawer is organized ("Put the socks on the left—rolled up in little balls") to the way bedtime is handled ("You start getting to bed at eight-thirty") to the way a family celebrates a holiday ("We always open presents on Christmas Eve"). Structures can even include the way space is defined in the home.

For instance, we always made our bedroom off-limits to our daughters when they became teenagers; we structured our home so that physical boundaries were clear. (They would happily have used our room, TV, and stereo for their fun.) We also made our closets off-limits (especially my wife's). Our girls hung their clothes in their closets, not ours. My wife's clothes were not theirs to use. Her shoes were not their shoes—not until they were officially retired from duty and handed down! At the same time, we tried to respect our daughters' rooms and belongings. I never borrowed anything of theirs without *first* asking permission, even though I had bought it for them.

Rules can serve the same important function. A child who knows there are rules is granted great freedom to learn resilience—*within* boundaries.

Rules can be both negative ("You mustn't do such and such") and positive ("You must do . . .").

Negative rules make the limits of behavior clear. One "negative" rule should always be a part of every family: No one in the family can verbally abuse another. In moments of anger it is so easy to shout and call others by derogatory names. Disrespect should never be tolerated because it quickly becomes a habit and can come to characterize an entire home environment.

Positive rules, on the other hand, reinforce healthy behavior and can point the way back to healing. A good positive rule, for instance, is that the one who is at fault must be the one to apologize.

It should go without saying, of course, that rules must be applied consistently and fairly to all. When they are, they become effective tools for building resilience.

A Happy and Humorous Home

A sense of humor not only builds happiness but is a helpful if not essential stressproofing tool. Evidence for this comes from the University of Minnesota, where Drs. Masten and Garmezy have studied the development of several groups of children. In a very detailed study of children from a working-class neighborhood in Minneapolis, they followed 205 children for more than a decade, beginning in third grade. Of these children, 28 percent were minority children, and 38 percent had single parents.[3]

These researchers were particularly interested in the role of humor in helping children cope with stress. They enlisted the help of a cartoonist to provide a number of cartoons and asked the children to add their own humorous captions. By rating the captions for how funny they were and the children for how hard they laughed, they came up with some fascinating conclusions!

The results showed that children who laughed and smiled a lot were generally more popular with their classmates and did better at school, even when they were under greater stress than other children. Because the ability to laugh at funny cartoons is related to intelligence, the smarter children tended to do better. But for a given intelligence level, the better a child's sense of humor, the happier that child seemed to be, and the better he or she was able to deal with stress in their world.

Now there's a lot more to happiness than a sense of humor. And certain forms of "humor" can serve as masks for bitterness and cruelty. At the same time, I don't know many unhappy people who laugh a lot! There is an unmistakable connection between being happy and being able to express that happiness through laughter.

And why are humor and happiness so important to a stress-free environment? For one thing, our bodies are healthiest when we are happiest. As I point out in my book, *Fifteen Principles for Achieving Happiness*, profound changes occur in our immune systems when we are unhappy.[4] Important "killer cells" are diminished, and we become more prone to immune deficiency diseases. The late Norman Cousins made an eloquent statement on the impact of humor and happiness on our bodies. Having recovered from a bout with cancer, he wrote his book, *Anatomy of an Illness: Reflections on Healing and Regeneration*, from a patient's point of view. In it, he argues that the capacity for self-healing and the will to live are important factors in overcoming serious illness. For more than a decade since his book appeared in 1979, he preached the message that humor heals. We need to heed this message today, more than ever before.

But humor is also important from a psychological point of view because it helps us put the stressors of life into better perspective. Sigmund Freud believed that humor was a way of gaining control over a situation that you don't really have control over. I think this is quite accurate. Humor forces us to step back, to look at our troubled situation a different way and perhaps to say, "Maybe it's not really that bad."

So teach your children how to laugh—and enjoy a good laugh yourself on a regular basis. Create a happy, humorous environment. Happiness is not elusive and mysterious. It is a "habit of the heart" that *can be learned*. Once learned, you cannot easily forget it.

A Spiritual Home

As I draw this section to a close, I want to emphasize again the value of creating a spiritual environment. I am convinced it helps to make a home more stress-free.

I make no apologies for my emphasis here. My perspective is clearly Christian, and I cannot separate who I am as a spiritual person from who I am physically or psychologically. To take one part of me away from the other would be to violate my very existence. So I speak to you as a Christian. If this is not your perspective, I can only ask you to give me a fair hearing and serious consideration. My object here is not to present an apologetic for the Christian faith but to emphasize its healthy aspects.

Now, when I speak of a spiritual environment, I am not just talking about a set of values. Values are indeed important. We internalize many of our values from our earliest years. Because they have to do with those aspects of our thinking and behavior that we consider important, they define who we are as persons. They influence our actions, our motives, and even our feelings, even when we hardly ever think about them.

But there is more to one's spiritual being than values. And creating a spiritual home is *more* than just laying out a set of values for your children to assimilate.

A person may have strong values—freedom, honesty, hard work, and love of family—but still not have any idea where to turn in times of disaster. Values are simply not enough in moments of grief, failure, or disappointment. They can't really support you, for instance, when your child has been killed in an accident or your business has gone bankrupt.

In times like these, you need to be able to reach out to a resource outside of yourself. You need a perspective on life to help you see beyond it, and you need a set of beliefs that can give you hope and speak peace to your troubled mind.

What am I referring to? I am pointing to *faith*, to *spiritual awareness*. It is not enough to create the stress-free environment in which your child can grow and develop. It is not enough to instill positive values and healthy habits. If you neglect to give your child spiritual resources, you will leave him or her without resources for overcoming hopelessness or emptiness.

It is possible for children to enter adulthood free of stress and capable of overcoming all problems—but without any *purpose or reason for living*. A spiritual environment provides the foundation of this purpose. In fact, I doubt whether any parent can provide a child with a purpose for living that is not founded in spiritual values.

But let me be even more specific. I strongly believe that the Christian faith is the healthiest, most effective, and essential spiritual base that any child can have. It provides a total solution for all of life's problems because it addresses human need at the core of its problem: It unites us again with our Creator. More specifically, it fulfills four essential human needs that we must all address sooner or later if we are going to live full lives:

- the need to be relieved of guilt,
- the need to feel that life has meaning,
- the need to love and be loved, and
- the need to forgive and be forgiven.

These needs are so absolutely fundamental that I would like to conclude this chapter with a brief discussion of each need as it applies to children. In

Hints for a Humorous Home

The family that can laugh together really will be less stressed. Here are some ideas for making laughter an integral part of your home:

- Share funny stories about things that happened to you at work, school, or at church. Encourage your kids to do the same.

- Read the "funnies" together on Sunday afternoon. See if you can improve on them and make them funnier. (This is a game I often play with myself.)

- Take advantage of your child's "joke" phase—that period around eight or nine years of age when many kids develop a passion for riddles and puns. Have patience with the "knock knock" jokes and determine to enjoy them.

- Don't be afraid to clown around. Occasionally make funny faces at each other or make up undignified walks just for laughs.

- Have a "family funny film festival" with popcorn, Cokes, and a set of videos ranging from the Marx Brothers to the latest cartoons.

- Teach your kids the difference between "happy humor" and humor at someone else's expense. Teach them to laugh with, not at people.

- Buy your children books with humorous themes. If you can, read them as a family and share the laughs.

- Don't overlook opportunities to poke fun at yourself when you have made a mistake or acted foolishly. Your kids will learn to do the same.

so doing, I hope to show how you can provide the right spiritual environment to foster the spiritual growth of your child.

(1) The need to be relieved of guilt. Guilt has fascinated me ever since I became a psychologist. Perhaps it's because I felt so guilty as a child. I remember that from my earliest years I was aware of a strong inner voice that told me when something was wrong. I have no idea where it came from. My parents were certainly not zealots of any kind. They were honest people, but never do I recall any extraordinary pressure to "be good" or any criticism for negative behavior. I think I was just naturally aware of right and wrong and felt so uncomfortable when I tried to do something bad that I avoided wrongdoing like the plague.

The neighborhood where I grew up, in a suburb of a small South African town, had many children. The homes had been built before water-borne sewerage was available, so behind every row of houses there was a lane down which "night carts" used to go to collect the sewage. Later, sewers were installed, and the lanes were hardly used—which made them perfect play areas for us kids.

Nighttime was especially fun. The lanes were dark and unlit. "Hide and seek" was exciting because the dark made it scary. But the lanes also gave access to neighbors' fruit trees. So in the summer the neighborhood kids loved to scale walls in the dead of night to steal a few peaches, grapes, or apricots from other people's gardens. Of course, you did this even if you had fruit trees in your own garden. The point was to take someone else's fruit. Stolen fruit always tasted better.

But guilt was my bugaboo. I just could not bring myself to steal. I climbed the walls so as not to be a bad sport. I wanted to be with my buddies. But I could not take any of the fruit. We never did any damage, and my buddies never took more than a few items of fruit, often picking it up off the ground where the ripest fruit had fallen. Most of it would go rotten anyway. But I felt guilty—for all the right reasons. So I feigned stomachaches or said I would "keep cavey," so that they could steal fruit. I could not take what wasn't mine.

Guilt tenderness followed me into my teenage years. I could never cheat on my homework or on an examination. I could never tell a bald-faced lie without losing sleep and finally confessing the truth.

Slowly my guilt began to be a little neurotic. I started feeling guilty even when I wasn't guilty. I began to feel anxious when I knew others were being dishonest. So by the time I graduated from high school my guilt-sensitivity had started to become a bit of a handicap, and I began to feel I needed to be relieved of it. I even contemplated doing something really bad just to break the power that my guilt seemed to have over me.

It was at this time, at the tender age of seventeen, that I came under the influence of a group of young people at our local church. This group of young people seemed vitally alive to me. They were full of joy—outwardly happy and inwardly peaceful. And they were all deeply committed Christians. These new friends gave me a book to read—Charles M. Sheldon's classic, *In His Steps*[5]—and I was deeply moved. Finally, at a youth rally in May 1950, I committed myself to Christ and discovered that it was through him "we have redemption through his blood, the forgiveness of sins, according to the riches of his grace."[6] I had learned that there was a place where I could dispose of all my guilt feelings, founded or unfounded: at the cross.

Slowly my guiltiness was healed. When I *was* guilty, I could confess it and be cleansed. When I *wasn't* guilty, but just felt guilt feelings, I could ignore the feelings and still believe I was forgiven. My healing had begun. I had found relief for my guilt.

All children need to know what to do about guilt feelings because every normal child develops a measure of it in our culture. Every day a child feels guilty about something or other. Outwardly there may be bravado; inwardly there is anxiety over wrongdoing. Psychologically, we can teach forgiveness by modeling it to our children through our attitudes and through the way we discipline them. Spiritually—and this goes down to a much deeper part of us than our minds—I believe there is *only one place* to find relief from guilt: at the cross.

No child is too young to discover the forgiveness of God. The earlier the better. Life is so much less stressful for a person who isn't carrying around a load of guilt.

(2) The need to feel that life has meaning. I can't fully explain it—but I know it for a fact. When at age seventeen I gave myself in commitment to God and claimed his forgiveness, I also found a new purpose for my life.

Up to that point I had seriously begun to think that I would probably not live past my twenties. Several people I knew had died. Polio had taken a terrible toll on my friends, and some had been killed in the Korean War. Life seemed very fragile—and pointless.

Years later I recall reading Bertrand Russell, the famous agnostic philosopher. In his book, *Conquest of Happiness*, he describes how at age five he had figured out that life was one long drudgery and probably not worth all the hassle.[7] I can remember similar feelings at age fifteen. I craved meaning and longed to know that life has a purpose. I was appalled at the idea that one gets born, lives, and then dies—with nothing else beyond. Self-pity began to take root, and I felt alone in my pain.

Then I became a Christian and everything changed. God became real to me. Scripture was a rich resource for my life and understanding. I wasn't alone in my pain anymore. People became important, and friends took on a new preciousness.

What particularly stands out during that first year of being a Christian was how very special all religious holidays became—especially Easter, the celebration of Jesus' death and resurrection. Our young people's group went camping in the kloofs (mountains) outside a nearby town. I recall rising before sunrise on Easter Sunday and climbing to the top of a kloof by myself to watch the sunrise and experience again the wonder of the resurrection story. I sat there as the sun broke over the horizon, awed by the meaning of it all. Life seemed so full of beautiful things and wonderful people.

Now, my conversion certainly didn't change the facts about the world, but it had changed the way I saw those facts. In Rabbi Harold Kushner's eloquent phrase, God had given me "new eyes" with which to see the world.[8] And that new perspective made all the difference.

How do you, as a parent, impart a sense of meaning about life to your child? By exposing him or her to the story about God and how Christ came to redeem us. I don't mean ram religion down a child's throat. And I certainly don't mean portraying God as resident policeman and executioner— ever vigilant to punish errant children. Many a parent has crippled children with such an unbalanced picture.

I do mean teaching your child (or letting someone else teach him or her) about God and about his wonderful plan for the universe—and especially his plan for your child. Your child needs to know about God's glorious plan of salvation and about the grandeur of God's creation. Your child needs to know that God is personal, and that while he doesn't make everything easy for us, he can give meaning to the bad things that happen in our lives.

Expose your child to the reality that life is beautiful when lived in harmony with God's plan, and your child will come to believe that life, even with its tragedies and disappointments, is essentially meaningful.

(3) The need to love and be loved. This need is so basic that it has become a cliché. It's the theme of 75 percent of the pop songs on the charts. But even if the phrase is hackneyed, the need is still real. We all need a meaningful human connection. Without it we are doomed to loneliness and despair.

Quite often I see patients whose problem is basically the absence of any human connection. Oh, they have friends at work. Some are even married and even have children. But the people at work stay in their own worlds, their marriages are emotional wildernesses, and their children have either moved away or don't want to be bothered by an aging parent.

I can diagnose the problem quite easily. "Chronic loneliness because of insufficient human contact." Often the sufferer has never learned how to give or receive love. They've been lonely people since their earliest years, and have never learned how to connect.

But what do I tell these people? What advice can I give them? Where can they go to be loved?

As I have looked around our society for places where people can find and give love, I have usually been disappointed. I have referred many lonely people to hiking clubs, sailing clubs, secular singles groups, dance clubs, and theater groups, and they have all reported the same story: These people seem to be so much into themselves there's hardly any room or time for anyone else. They don't feel loved in these places.

There are very few places of community to which people can go for connectedness—except the church. Despite its weaknesses, despite the fact that it is full of imperfect people, the church is unsurpassed as a place where children and adults, singles and families can learn to love and be loved.

I willingly refer my love-starved patients to church-based support groups which are generally different from other groups, because the people are different. They are motivated by a desire to reflect the love of their Creator, who loved them so much that he gave the supreme sacrifice for their salvation. Generally speaking (and in this imperfect world there are always exceptions), they don't exist for selfish reasons.

But in the final analysis, we cannot rely entirely on the church groups to meet our love needs or those of our children and to teach them about love. Church people, no matter how committed to their faith, are still imperfect and only amateurs at love. With the best intentions in the world, they will still fall far short of the ideal.

So we cannot just look to the church to teach our children love; we must teach it in our homes. Our families are safer and more reliable places to learn love—or at least they should be. It's no secret, however, that many homes are not reliable teachers of love, either. Many homes are deficient in love. And yes, I mean Christian homes, where Mom plays the organ and Dad is a deacon, or where Moms and Dads are fine, honest, hardworking, churchgoers. "Emotional ice chest" is how one client once described his Christian home. "I never learned a thing about love in my family, even though they preached it every Sunday."

Even families that are basically functional and healthy can fall down on the job of teaching and sharing love—because they, too, are made up of imperfect human beings. We can care more for our children than for our own lives and still let them down in terms of love.

Our children, then, need a more solid foundation for their love than any human can provide, and God in Christ must be that essential foundation. Only God's love is secure, unchanging, and pure in motive. Only God's love can transcend human frailties.

My three daughters have found this love. Now, above everything else, I desire my four young grandchildren to experience this same love in their hearts and know it deep within their minds. If they do, loneliness will be a stranger to them and happiness their lifelong companion. I know this with all my being. After all, I've lived it.

(4) *The need to forgive and be forgiven.* What does forgiveness have to do with stress? And where does it help children to be less stressed? My answers are simple. Forgiveness has everything to do with stress. And a person who feels deeply forgiven is a person at peace with him or herself. When you are at peace with yourself, deep down at the very center of your being, you are in the best possible place to withstand life's stresses.

Think for a moment about the ocean. A storm may rage on the surface. Winds may blow fiercely, and waves may roll high enough to dash even the largest ship. But no matter how vicious the storm on the surface, a mere one hundred feet below the surface, the ocean is quite calm. The deeper you go, the calmer it becomes.

To be at peace in the deepest part of your being is like having a deep ocean inside you. It is strong and stable, not easily swayed. Life's storms only touch your surface. But without knowing the forgiveness of God, you cannot be at peace in the deep parts of your being.

Jesus once said, "Peace I leave with you, my peace I give unto you: not as the world giveth, give I unto you."[9] How does Jesus give this peace? Primarily through the forgiveness and reconciliation with God he made possible through his death on the cross. This is the foundation of all forgiveness, even the forgiveness we give one another. And every child needs to experience this forgiveness.

Every child, in addition, needs to experience human forgiveness on a regular basis in order to be normal and to become skilled in coping with stress. In my discussion on discipline in a previous chapter I emphasized how important it was for a child to be able to ask for and receive forgiveness, even at the height of whatever discipline is taking place. There should *always* be room for repentance and an opportunity to be forgiven. Deprive a child of forgiveness, and you will create a neurotic wretch of a person. Give a child plenty of forgiveness, and you will help to build a deep, stress-free ocean of peace within.

But experiencing forgiveness isn't enough. Every child must *also* know what it is to be the forgiver. What happens to a person who can't forgive? People who cannot forgive store up memories of hurts done to them and conjure up fantasies of revenge. Sooner or later, they become angry, resentful, and bitter—prime candidates for stress disease.

Most people find it *harder to forgive than to be forgiven*. That is why Jesus told the parable of the unmerciful servant.[10] It is the story of a king who discovers that a servant owes him millions of dollars. He can't pay, so the king threatens to sell his wife, children, and possessions. The servant falls down on his face, pleads for mercy, and promises to pay everything he owes. But the king, moved with compassion, forgives the debt—totally!

The same servant, just after leaving the king's chamber, encounters another servant who owes him a few dollars and demands payment. This servant now pleads for mercy, but it falls on deaf ears. The first servant has him cast into prison.

When the king hears about this, he calls for the first servant. "You are a wicked man," he says. "I forgave you all your debt because you asked it of me. Could you not have had some compassion on your fellow servant, who owed you so little?" The king orders the servant to be punished.

The parable ends with these words from Jesus: "So likewise shall my heavenly father do also unto you, if ye from your hearts forgive not every one his brother their trespasses."

These are astonishing words. I think of them as the "fine print" of the Bible because many Christians fail to pay attention to them. The message is very clear: If you want God's forgiveness, you must be willing to forgive others. Nothing is simpler. It is perfectly logical and absolutely fair.

To be able to forgive others for the hurts they cause you is a sign of spiritual and emotional maturity; children must learn it in order to be stress-free. And they must also learn that God does not require us to do something we cannot do. Forgiveness is within our power because God makes us able to forgive. Or, to put it another way, we must do the forgiving even if our natural urge is not to forgive. God will help us overcome our resistance, but only if we take the first step of being *willing* to forgive.

A child who learns to forgive is like a child who learns to say, "I am sorry." Such a child is blessed indeed.

The Benefits of a Stress-Free Environment

There is no doubt in my mind that when parents work at providing a stress-free environment for their children, they produce the healthiest, happiest, and most successful children of all. And I really mean it when I say "*work.*" You don't have to be a highly successful parent, and you certainly don't have to be perfect. But you *must* be committed to providing the best environment you can. If you maintain that commitment, your mistakes will then wash out—in fact, they might even turn out to be blessings. When parents surround their children with an atmosphere of love, freedom, consistent but nonpunitive discipline, and spiritual resources, their children will be a lot freer of stress and stress disease. They will also show:

- fewer signs of rebellious and aggressive behaviors,
- less anxiety, worry, depression, and fear,
- less guilt, shame, and humiliation,
- less illness and other physical problems,
- more love and affection to others
- higher self-esteem, self-acceptance, and self-confidence,
- better social and relating skills,
- the ability to be self-disciplining,
- more effective problem-solving skills,
- higher motivation to succeed for the right reasons,
- greater respect for the needs and rights of others,
- greater openness to the love of God, and
- greater freedom to express their spirituality,

I am convinced of these results by the many families I have worked with over the years, but above all by my own family. I have learned by trial and error—and by many mistakes. I hope my children have benefited from these mistakes and that we will see in successive generations of our family not just a continuation of these benefits, but a greater degree of healthiness in body, mind, and spirit. This is my prayer for you also.

Summary

Parents create a child's "stress environment." They determine whether the home environment is a *source* of added stress or a *resource* for stress relief. Parents help provide a stress-free environment for a child by providing (1) a home where stress is relieved (2) a home where resilience is fostered, (3) a home full of humor, and (4) a spiritual home. Stress relief can come both from the physical environment and from emotional support. Resilience is fostered by many factors, both internal and external, but the presence of caretakers besides the mother and the presence of structures and rules in the home can be especially productive. Humor, which is related to happiness, has both physical and psychological benefits; it helps relieve stress because it puts troubles in perspective. Spiritual values and faith help build a stress-free environment by providing relief from guilt, a sense of meaning and purpose, love, and forgiveness.

Discussion Questions

1. Review the ways in which parents can build an environment that helps a child to be less stressed. How does your family measure up? Affirm those things you do that clearly make for positive experiences for your child.

2. Discuss the concept of "resilience" as it relates to children. Think of some examples in your own life when you were beaten down but were able to "bounce back."

3. How important are spiritual issues to you? Can you be forgiving without help from God? What does God give us that helps us to forgive?

Part 3
Stressproofing At-Risk Children

For a variety of reasons some children are at greater risk than others for developing stress problems. In this section of the book I want to look at some of these high-stress situations and suggest some special helping strategies.

What puts these kids at greater risk? Sometimes it's how parents treat them. Sometimes it's what children do to themselves. Sometimes it's just the special circumstances of their lives. But whatever the cause of the stress, the solution begins with listening to the child—to his or her spoken or unspoken pleas for help or relief—and then taking positive steps to reduce the stress.

Our children are the future of our world. But that future is not static, nor fixed, nor cast in any final form. As caring parents we can be shapers of their future lives. We can steer them away from high-risk life-patterns and teach them the skills they need to flourish in today's high-stress world.

10

When Parents Are Part
of the Problem

"You kids will drive me crazy."

"Look at the gray hairs you're causing."

"You're going to send me to an early grave."

These were my mother's favorite lines whenever she became frustrated with us kids. No doubt you can recall your own mother's expressions of frustration—and you've probably used a few yourself.

I'm the first to admit that child raising is stressful business. Children can be so demanding. They are by definition immature, unpredictable, self-ish, and self-serving, and they can put a strain upon even the most patient, resilient, and mature adults. When they are very young, they disturb your sleep, get into everything, and break all the rules. When they start school they get into fights, cause trouble with the neighbors, knock out teeth, and break all the rules. When they reach adolescence they pout, criticize you, threaten to run away, and break all the rules. When they get old enough to drive they command the family car and demand one of their own. When you ask them to telephone and let you know they will be late, they think you are being overprotective. They can't understand why you can't get to sleep until you finally hear them return home and go to bed, no matter how late it is. And, oh yes, they like breaking the rules.

Kids cause stress—no doubt about it. But is it all one way? Are parents always the innocent victims of their child's misbehaviors? No. Parents can be a source of stress for their children, too.

Remember, first of all, that parents have the real power in a family. We're bigger, at least until our children reach adolescence. We control the purse strings. We determine to a large extent whether a child is going to have a healthy feeling about himself or herself. And we can start or stop love—a powerful force that can either encourage or devastate a child. All of these factors put parents in a position to cause their children considerable stress.

Some parent-caused stress is unavoidable, of course. Parents get sick and even die. Mothers and fathers lose their jobs. Families move. Grandparents grow frail and need to be cared for, sometimes at the expense of the children. Such occurrences are more or less beyond a parent's control, although much can be done to lessen the stress they cause in a family.

But many other parent-caused stress *can* be avoided. Parental attitudes, discipline methods, and even the timing of divorce *can* be adjusted to lessen the stress they cause. It is all a matter of choice and of priority.

In this chapter, then, I want to look at the most common kinds of parent-caused stress and explore some strategies parents can adopt to put less pressure on their children. I will then conclude with my "Ten Commandments for Stress-Free Parenting."

The "Tone" of the Home

Every home has a "personality." It is a corporate personality; everyone in the household contributes something to the overall temperament and style of functioning. But it is the *parents,* primarily, who determine the tone and character of a family. When this tone is disruptive, overly sensitive, repressive, inconsistent, unsupportive, and conflicted, the stress level in that family escalates.

This is probably self-evident, but let me cite one study to support what I am saying. In 1988, more than two hundred German children participated in a study that examined how child-rearing patterns affected children's stress levels (as measured by anxiety in the child). Two dimensions of child-rearing which reflect the home atmosphere or personality were found to be central in causing high levels of anxiety: *restriction* and *inconsistency.*[1] Children whose parents used an overly restrictive parenting style—granting them little freedom to meet new friends, go places, and explore new activities—were more anxious and stressed than other children. And the same was true of children whose parents were inconsistent, unreliable, unpredictable, and overly reactive (shouting, quick to punish).

Parents, therefore, should carefully review their family patterns to see how they contribute to stress in their children. The tone you set can make all the difference in how much stress a child feels.

How can you tell whether the tone of your home is stressful? Check yourself out on the following list:

- Are you very strict; do you demand absolute obedience?
- Do you or others in your family shout a lot or overreact to situations?
- Do you or others tend to get angry a lot, or do you pout or blame others for your problems?
- Are you a person of your word? Do you keep your promises? Are you reliable?
- Do you, as parents, accept others as different and allow them just to be themselves?
- Can your children get their dependency needs met with the family because there is an atmosphere of love and unconditional acceptance?
- Do you or your spouse look to your children for your "completion," or do you try to live out your dreams through your children?
- Is there someone in your family or in your extended family (aunt, uncle, or cousin) who humiliates, manipulates, intimidates, or exploits your children?
- Does your family have the "no talk" rule—you cannot talk openly about feelings, thoughts, or experiences that focus on pain or other negatives?

There are many more signs of family stress patterns, but if your family has any of these you need to do something about it. Begin by talking with your spouse about your concerns and then planning a strategy for change along the lines outlined in this book. If the tone of your home is really stressful—or if you really have difficulty determining whether or not it is—then consider getting professional help.

No One on the Home Front

Living in a household where both parents work outside the home can be stressful for a child. So can growing up in a single-parent family where the mother or father has to work to support the family. And it's no secret that these two situations are rapidly becoming the norm in our society. Relatively few families can manage on just one paycheck—even if they wanted to—and single parents usually have no choice but to work for a living.

In either case, however, the result is the same—the child has no full-time parent at home.

What effect does this have on a child's stress? Most studies have produced contradictory findings. So much depends on other factors—such as the personality of the child, the quality of child care, and the flexibility of the parents' jobs. But most experts agree that it is preferable, at least during the early stages of childhood, to have at least one parent (usually the mother) available full time to nurture the child. When this is not possible, the child may feel the stress of:

- General time pressure—lack of both "quality time" and "quantity time,"
- Long hours in day care or alone time as a "latchkey kid,"
- Frequent turnover of caregivers,
- Distracted, fatigued, or guilty parents,
- Parents' inability to take off time during working hours to attend school functions and athletic events,
- Being sent to school or day care when sick or slightly under the weather because the parent cannot take time off,
- Lack of predictable care during holidays.

This is not to say that two-job and single-parent families inevitably produce stressed-out children. With careful planning and perhaps some good counseling, working parents can minimize the stress a child feels by providing ample support, love, and care.

It's not easy, of course. When you've been on the job all day and then must spend the rest of your time doing household chores and caring for your children, life can become pretty hectic. But take heart. It is only "for a season." Sooner or later children get older and the task becomes less burdensome. Maintaining a long-term perspective will help reduce your own stress and therefore cut back on the stress you pass on to your children. Meanwhile, here are some stress-reducing ideas for two-paycheck parents and single parents:

(1) Try not to bring your work home. Put a little space between your work life and your home life by playing a relaxing tape in the car, taking a short walk before picking up the kids, or just closing your eyes and relaxing at your desk. Try to unwind a little before coming home to the kids so that you don't unload your work frustrations onto them.

(2) Consider other job options. Research job situations that offer flexible options such as flex time, job sharing, permanent part time. And explore the possibilities of working at home. You may be able to earn a paycheck while being available to your kids.

(3) Keep your priorities straight. Decide ahead of time what you will need to let go in the interest of giving your children what they need. When time is limited, time spent with your kids must take top priority over other pursuits—even housework.

(4) Take shortcuts when you can. Your kids would rather have your attention over peanut butter sandwiches than a three-course meal that took you hours to prepare.

(5) Enlist your children's help. Including your children, at levels appropriate to their stage of development, in the everyday workings of the household will increase your togetherness, make more free time for fun activities, and teach your children self-confidence. But be patient.

(6) Seek help for your own stress. Talk to other parents in the same boat, try to eat healthfully and exercise regularly, and seek counseling if necessary. Try to avoid passing your stress (from job, from guilt, from feeling "pulled apart") to your children,

Daddy Loves You Best!

"You were always Mommy's favorite," Kari says to her younger sister Karen, during one of their regular arguments. "Yeah, well, you're 'Daddy's little girl,'" retorts Karen. Kari and Karen keep close tabs on who is getting the most from which parent.

Among the primary causes of stress in children is the rivalry that inevitably arises between siblings. If they are close together in age, they have endless fights over toys, food, TV, closet space, who sits on Mommy's lap, who sits in the front seat of the car, who is served first, who gets the bigger slice of cake, or who goes to bed last—any of a trillion minor issues. If children are separated by a few years, the rivalry may take a different form. Because younger children require more protection and care, an older child may feel neglected or rejected. And because the younger child is unable to do as much as the older one, he or she may come to feel inferior.

All these frictions between siblings are common and probably inevitable to a certain extent. So what's so bad about sibling rivalry? Simply put, the bickering and fighting is stressful both to the children involved and to everyone else in the family. Sibling rivalry triggers anger and resentment. The fighting, competing, pushing, pulling, screaming, and sulking all contribute to a stressful atmosphere in the family. Remember also that the rivalry and conflict can carry over into adulthood. Many children continue to fight, compete, push, and pull long after they have become adults.

It is natural for children to be rivals. It is a universal phenomenon that probably started with Cain and Abel. I saw it at work between my father and his brother and between myself and my brother. And even as a child, I didn't like it, although I didn't know how to stop it. I know now, however, that it was really my parents' responsibility to do something about it. Sharing is not natural; it must be learned. And it is the parents' responsibility to discourage rivalry and encourage harmony between siblings.

Many parents, unfortunately, do just the opposite. By playing favorites with their children, they feed sibling rivalry. It is hard as a parent not to feel more warmly toward one child than another. When they are of the same sex it's a little easier to handle, but how can a father favor a daughter over a son, or a mother a son over a daughter, without its becoming a source of stress?

When parents carry over their own rivalries and favoritism from their own childhood, these tensions are easily communicated to their children. In this way it gets passed on from generation to generation. When unchecked it becomes the basis for major splits and ongoing warfare in families.

Parents who have lots of problems, who fight and cause tension in the home, will inevitably feed the rivalry between children. Children will take sides, thus feeding favoritism and causing conflicts.

The right handling of sibling rivalry begins by parents adjusting their feelings about who is their favorite child. You cannot change your feelings about a child just by deciding to change it. But you *can* begin changing your behavior toward all your children. If you change your behavior, the feelings will follow.

One father I counseled had two sons aged eight and six. He had clearly come to favor Bill, the younger, because the older son's personality was too much like his own. Soon his preference became very noticeable. He punished the older boy more often and criticized him more. He touched and held his younger son more often. The older boy was neither blind nor stupid; he knew he was being treated unfairly—and he took his frustration out on his younger brother. Soon the rivalry between the two boys was intense, and their life together became one continuous round of fighting and bickering.

One day, the older son finally got up the courage to say to his father, "You just hate me. You only love Billy." The father was flabbergasted. He had never realized that others could notice his favoritism. In therapy, he learned how to put his feelings aside and *behave* toward his older son *as if he loved him more*.

"But if I don't *feel* love for him, how will it work?" the father protested. "Trust me! Your feelings will change," I assured him. So he began to behave more lovingly. Here are some of the things he did:

- He touched his older son more.
- He held his son more.
- He complimented him more.
- He spent more time with him.
- Instead of jumping to Billy's defense, he helped him talk things out with his older brother.

In just a matter of a few weeks, the father reported a dramatic change *in his feelings* toward his older son. Slowly but surely, the emotional bond was strengthened between the father and older son.

Feelings respond quite miraculously to behavior. I believe that's why that wonderful love chapter in the Bible, 1 Corinthians 13, talks of love not as a feeling, but as a *behavior:*

> Love is patient, love is kind. It does not envy, it does not boast, it is not proud. It is not rude, it is not self-seeking, it is not easily angered, it keeps no record of wrongs."[2]

These are all behaviors, not feelings. In addition, parents should try to turn sibling rivalry into a positive experience for all involved. Here are some ideas.

(1) Set up boundaries. No name calling. Give "time out" for hitting or fighting. If your children fight, then separate them for a period of time to teach them that they must learn to cooperate.

(2) Set up rules. Favors should always be rotated. "Your turn now, his turn next. Let's keep a record." This helps to reduce competition.

(3) Teach children to talk out conflicts. Every child should be free to express feelings (including anger), although aggression should be a "no-no." Bad feelings don't go away because you enforce silence. Let children talk these feelings out.

(4) Teach (and model) civility and respect. Courtesy to others is a behavior that must be learned and practiced. So insist that your children show respect to one another: "Please say you are sorry and give the toy back to your sister." And remember that your own behavior is your most effective teaching tool. Teach respect by showing it toward your children, your spouse, and others you meet.

(5) Don't show favoritism—even if you feel it. Share your love equally and be absolutely fair. This keeps jealousy at a minimum.

Great Expectations—and Children Who Fail

Parents don't always equate their own high expectations and overly ambitious tendencies with their children's stress, but there is an undeniable connection. Children of overly ambitious parents typically respond in one of two extreme ways:

- *They become overly ambitious themselves,* causing stress by putting too much emphasis on achievement and expecting too much from themselves, or

- *They become aimless and drift along without ambition,* causing stress by creating tension in the family and setting themselves up for failure and rejection.

The middle road, where parents are *balanced* in their ambition, not only produces minimal stress in the family, but prepares children best for their own success.

I will discuss the problems of the overly ambitious child in chapter 11, so my comments here will be confined to the aimless child. And it is surprising how many of these there are. It is far from uncommon for a child of hardworking, successful, and ambitious parents not to follow the pattern set by the parents. Sometimes it is only one of the pack who falls back—and this is even more puzzling to the parents. This child seems to drift along in life, reaching adulthood without self-discipline, goals, or ambition.

Outwardly it may seem—and these children might even believe—that their life is *less* stressed this way. But because most children do internalize their parents' expectations, the aimless drifter usually feels the stress of being a "failure" in the parents' eyes and often in his or her eyes as well.

Parents of such failure-prone children are often bewildered and disappointed, and they may blame themselves for their children's failures. But they may or may not be responsible for what has happened. It is certainly possible to give one's children every opportunity to succeed and model the right behaviors—and still have children drop out of the race. Some children, for example, simply rebel against the values of the parents. Times change and values change, and children may simply develop a different value system.

But in many cases, the parents *are* directly responsible for the fact that their children have grown up without direction or motivation. How?

- *They may have allowed the rat race to put too much stress on themselves and the family*—so that their children simply decide not to put that kind of pressure on themselves.

- *They may have set their values down as conditions for love:* "Do it my way and I will love you. Do it your way and I will reject you." Such messages always undermine motivation.

- *They may have indulged their children* to the point that they have never learned to postpone gratification or to work for something they want.

- *They may have overprotected their children* so that they are emotionally stunted and naive and never develop the skills and confidence in themselves to be successful adults.

You may not fully understand why your child as a teenager or young adult is so disappointing. But if you are guilty of any of the above, now is the time to take steps to change your parenting style.

I have seen many youngsters who have started down the "failure" road do a complete turnaround in adulthood. Once they were on their own and accountable only to themselves, they moved on to greater responsibility and even success—although they may be doing something different from what their parents wanted them to do. One son of a physician became a park ranger. A daughter of a journalist became a policewoman. Yet a third refused to become manager of her father's store, but set up a competing business that did very well. All were very successful—but not complying with their parents' expectations. I sincerely hope that each of these parents will eventually come around to affirming their children for "doing it their own way."

When Families Don't Work Right

Over the past decade we have made tremendous progress in understanding how dysfunctional families impose stress on children. We have come to understand that the family is a "system"—that all the members of a family are "connected" in some way to each other, and that disruption in one part of the system affects all the other parts. This means that when one member of the family has difficulty functioning, *all* family members are affected—and the family system fails to operate the way it should.

All families go through periods of above-average stress and strain. Sickness, a death in the family, financial problems, and interpersonal conflicts are inevitable. But dysfunctional families suffer more during such times of stress. Because the family is not operating the way it should, family members have difficulty pulling together and rallying their resources to cope with their problems. In addition, the strains set up in the family make the dysfunction worse.

What are the more common dysfunctional patterns? Some families experience dysfunctional *communication:*

- Family members frequently misunderstand one another.
- Children are used to carry messages between parents.
- Silence is used to express disapproval or to punish misbehavior.
- Discussions always lead to verbal fights.
- Family members nag each other incessantly.

Other families display dysfunctional *relating:*

- Children are used as scapegoats (often one child more than others).
- Parents become too enmeshed in the lives of their children.
- Family members find fault with one another on a regular basis.
- Bickering is constant.
- Parents see children as extensions of themselves instead of separate persons.
- Members are excessively disengaged from each other.

A family can be dysfunctional when it comes to *expressing love:*

- Love is seldom expressed verbally.
- There is little touching, hugging, or other physical show of affection.
- Parents do not show respect toward their children.
- Family members fear emotional intimacy.

And *discipline* can also be a dysfunctional area in a family's life:

- Parents punish rather than discipline.
- Anger is the primary emotion during punishment.
- Forgiveness is withheld after discipline.
- Parents use fear to frighten children into compliance.

Let me give an example of a dysfunctional family pattern. Jim and Charlene are both low in self-esteem. Both grew up in families where love was seldom expressed openly, so Jim and Charlene looked to each other for the fulfillment their childhoods had deprived them of. They saw each other as extensions of themselves, and this made them very controlling of each other. Their disappointments stopped them from affirming each other and kept them focusing on each other's weaknesses. So when children came along, Jim and Charlene turned to the children to meet their self-esteem needs. Their kids had to be the best—not because their success would help them get ahead in life but because it would boost Jim and Charlene's self-esteem.

Whenever parents see their children as an extension of themselves, you will find a dysfunctional pattern. Instead of being free to develop their natural talents, the children are coerced into fulfilling parental dreams. This not only puts too much pressure on the children and deprives them of the acceptance they need; it also sets the parents up for disappointment. Stress is the inevitable result.

Other dysfunctional patterns are even more serious and not only produce intense stress but can retard a child's development. Parents who can't control their hostility are particularly dangerous to the well-being of everyone in the family. They create fear, double binds (where a parent says, "I love you" but does things to hurt the child), and eventual hate for the parents.

The starting point for repairing a dysfunctional family is yourself, no matter how sick everyone else is. After all, you are the only person you can change directly. So start by taking a close look at ways you can modify your own reaction and behavior patterns. Since family systems are interconnected, the changes you make in yourself are bound to influence the whole system. Others will begin to change if you do first. By taking the first step toward your own wholeness, you can give others in the family permission to start changing as well.

If your children are old enough, talk with him or her about the way your own family system functions. Ask how they feel and what they would like to see changed—and *listen*. Next, talk with your spouse. Do so calmly, without anger, and at an appropriate time. (During Monday Night Football is probably a bad time.) You might even benefit from planning a weekend trip away from the kids. Spend some time together reviewing dysfunctional behavior patterns that have developed and rehearsing new and healthier ones.

If all else fails, insist on getting family counseling. *Don't* let your bad family habits become permanent. The sooner you interrupt them the better. Once bad patterns of relating become entrenched, your children will pass them on to their children—and stress will be passed on from generation to generation.

When Families Split Up

Whether you like the idea or not, the truth is that separation and divorce is one of the most stressful life-events a child can experience. For many children, divorce spells the end of life as they have known it. Even when a family has been very conflicted, the children rarely welcome a divorce.

More than a million children experience divorce every year in the United States. That's a lot of children! Divorce causes stress for them in many ways:

- They may become victims of a parental game of "tug-of-war."

- Many may suffer a significant drop in their standard of living.

- Some live in an atmosphere of bitterness and hostility.

- Many are uprooted—forced to move and to change schools and friends.

- A significant proportion lose the regular presence of one parent and a male or female role model.

- Even if all their friends' parents are divorced, many still feel humiliated and "different."

- Many have their needs neglected because their divorcing parents are stressed out.

- Money becomes a preoccupation in the families of many.

- Many are torn between love for both parents.

Typically, boys feel the stress of divorce more than girls, at least at first, usually because the father leaves the home and robs his son of a resident male model. Boys also don't show their emotions so easily, so they suffer more internally. Parents also shield girls more than boys, who are often left to fend for themselves emotionally. But divorce is also difficult for girls— it's hard on all children. The worst age for divorce is around puberty—anywhere from eleven to thirteen. At this age, children are most aware of what is going on but least able to cope.

The adjustments forced on children during separation and divorce are major and cause quite a lot of stress. And while it is difficult to separate out preseparation conflicts from the divorce itself, most studies show that children of divorce do have more emotional and scholastic problems than other children.

I am not here to argue that all divorce can be prevented. I certainly work hard to prevent it in my work as a clinical psychologist, because I hold to a high view of marriage. I believe that too many couples throw away good marriages unnecessarily because they don't understand how to change their dysfunctional patterns.

When a divorce is inevitable, however, parents should pay *primary* attention to finding ways to reduce its impact on the children of the marriage. There is much that parents can do to lessen the stress associated with separation and divorce. I cover this topic in detail in my book, *Children and Divorce*,[3] but here is a brief list of the most important strategies:

(1) Provide extended emotional support for these children. Grandparents can be particularly helpful in bridging the gap until a new home is established.

(2) Change things slowly and gradually. Children adjust better to slow change. It is easier to adjust to one change at a time then to many changes. Let the child get used to one parent's absence, for example, before approaching the possibility of a move. If possible, let the children continue to

live in the same neighborhood and go to the same schools as before. Also continue to provide the same support systems, such as church and youth groups. Such a strategy may spread things out a bit and even be more difficult for the parents, but it is easier for the child.

(3) Minimize the display of conflict. This is the most difficult but perhaps the most critical, of all parental strategies. Anger, resentment, and bitterness between separating parents always harm the children. For the kids' sake, keep conflict at a minimum.

(4) Don't take your anger out on the children. It's very easy to blame them for a spouse's leaving you or for making things worse for you. Children do cause conflicts. But a divorce is almost never their fault and—more importantly—your anger only intensifies the conflict. Work at keeping your anger under control.

(5) Give children extra attention. Young children, especially, will often cling desperately to the remaining parent, fearing that he or she will also leave. Reassurance is best given by allowing extra time with you and in doing activities together. This does not mean giving children unlimited access to you or giving up all your privacy. But it does mean understanding that the child is under extra stress and needs you more than usual.

(6) Don't attack your absent spouse in front of or to your child. Attacking the departed parent creates unnecessary loyalty conflicts in the child. A child has a right to love both parents.

(7) Allow the absent parent to still be a parent. Many parents try to prevent the absent parent from having contact with the child as a way of punishing the actions of the other. This is not fair to either parent or child. Remember, a person may be a failure as a husband or wife but still make a very good parent.

(8) Don't allow guilt to dominate your actions. Claim forgiveness for whatever you feel you have done wrong and then focus on doing the right thing. Don't make promises to your children you can't keep just to relieve guilt feelings. Broken promises cause more stress than promises that were never made.

(9) Work at healing yourself quickly. Research here is very clear. The healthiest and least stressed divorced children are those whose parents have made a quick and healthy adjustment to their own divorce. Health breeds health. Wholeness seeds wholeness. The best protection any parent can give a child is to be emotionally healthy yourself.

"Blended" but Not Stress-Free

Fifty percent of divorced parents remarry and create "blended" or "reconstituted" families. For the parent this may auger a new and exciting period of life—a second chance at making a success of marriage and finding happiness. For the children involved, however, a parent's remarriage may be the beginning of a nightmare. At the very least, it will be a challenge that demands a lot of adjustment. Stress is inevitable. And about 60 percent of these stepfamilies will divorce again—bringing even more stress. Ghosts from marriages past will haunt the new couple (like jealousy and insecurity) and raising two sets of kids will become a special challenge.

I cannot provide a complete guide here on how to build a reconstituted family. I have several chapters on this topic in my book *Children and Divorce*. But I do want to provide some suggestions on how to minimize your children's stress levels:

(1) Don't force your new spouse to be the substitute parent for your child unless circumstances warrant. Children have a right to maintain some allegiance to their absent natural parent.

(2) Don't expect your new spouse to instantly develop an emotional attachment to your child. Love takes time to develop.

(3) Don't expect to feel the same way toward both your children and your stepchildren. Your relationships and feelings *must* be different, and to deny this will just cause more conflict.

(4) Don't compare your children with your stepchildren. Both you and your new partner may have a tendency to be blind to the defects of your own children but see your stepchildren's faults in a glaring light. Agree to stop comparing and just accept that your children are different.

(5) Make lots of allowances for mistakes and imperfections in the new family. No one is perfect, and the pressures of "blending" a new family is likely to bring out the worst in all.

(6) Always be the one to discipline your natural children. Making sure that the stepparent is *not* to be the discipliner prevents resentment from building up against the stepparent.

(7) Avoid creating or keeping secrets. Members of stepfamilies easily form conspiracies and keep secrets to build alliances. Insist that everything be in the open. Don't allow your children to exclude the stepparent by secretiveness or withholding information important to the family.

(8) Use humor as much as you can to diffuse tensions and to build mutual acceptance. Humor is a great healer. But don't make fun of someone just for a laugh. Keep the humor fair—and neutral.

(9) Try not to take things too seriously. Too much seriousness builds anxiety and fear. These emotions breed mistrust and suspicion.

Ten Commandments for Stress-Free Parenting

Allow me to end this chapter on a positive note. Parents *can* be a major cause of stress for children, but they can also prevent a lot of stress. Parents are not perfect. We fail all the time. We can only do our best—no more. Here are my Ten Commandments for minimizing parental stress:

(1) Don't fight unnecessary battles. Parents tend to argue unnecessarily over hair, clothes, chores, boyfriends, girlfriends, going to church, choice of music, untidy rooms, and on and on. Instead of majoring on minor issues, choose your battles. Confine your areas of conflict to the important things of life. Make sure the issue is worth fighting over. Then pull out all your guns and make sure you win the battle!

(2) Talk out your conflicts. I have yet to meet a child or teenager who has good communication with his or her parents but is overly stressed. Overstress and good communication don't coexist. Talking out issues *reduces* stress, even if it does not give the child (or teenager) everything he or she desires.

(3) Never criticize your child. Name calling (like, "You're really stupid, do you know it?") damages self-esteem. And criticism never motivates a child to try harder; it only invites the child to throw in the towel.

(4) Give honest feedback. When a child asks you, "How did I do?" affirm that which was good and be honest with the bad. A child will come to trust your feedback more if it is genuine.

(5) Give your child lots of room to grow. If you draw the lines too close or set out your blueprints for your child's life, your child will feel stifled. Let him or her determine the general direction for life inside the boundaries you establish. You *cannot* tell a child, "You will be a lawyer—like it or not." You *can* tell a child, however, "I want you to try your best and I will give you every encouragement to become whatever you want to be."

(6) Have someone to talk to. Sharing with others is essential to understanding yourself. No one can think with complete clarity. We need to hear ourselves talk. When we do, issues become clearer and we understand our problems better, even if those we trust do nothing but listen.

(7) Dispense love generously. Say you love your child. Show you love your child. But don't be possessive or set conditions for your love. Love must be free and unconditional.

(8) Dispense forgiveness generously. Model forgiving attitudes and a willingness to accept your responsibility for any failure. Show your child that you forgive yourself and encourage him or her to do the same.

(9) Affirm your child generously. Positive affirmation is a powerful shaper of behavior. The child who hears, "I think you are great!" is a child who not only tries harder, but succeeds with less stress.

(10) Give spiritual guidance to your child. Children need spiritual nourishment. They need to know that there is a God who loves them. Many children live in poverty, but there is no child more poor than the child deprived of a spiritual heritage.

Summary

Parents can cause unnecessary stress in children in several ways. The "tone" parents set in the home, the absence of an "at home" parent, parental favoritism, unreasonable expectations, dysfunctional family patterns, separation, divorce, and remarriage can impose extraordinary stress on a child. Of all these stressors, divorce and remarriage are probably the most serious. But even in these high-stress situations, careful thought and consideration for the well-being of all the children in the family can prevent or alleviate much stress—particularly the long-term damaging consequences of childhood stress.

Discussion Questions

1. Review the various ways in which parents can cause stress for children. Examine each cause with respect to your own family. Make a list of the more serious parent-caused stresses in your family.

2. Dysfunctional family patterns are often passed on from generation to generation. As you look at the relating styles you and your spouse have brought to the marriage, which can you trace back to your families of origin?

3. Using the "Ten Commandments for Stress-Free Parenting" as a guide, write down a plan for yourself to follow in reducing the stress you place on your children.

11

Slowing Down the Fast-Track Child

The Hofmeyers, Lena and Larry, are typical of a new breed of parents. They both have successful, demanding careers. Lena is a sales manager and Larry a business executive. Together, they earn a good income. Apart, they could barely pay their rent. But they fully expect to keep on moving up. And they want nothing but the best for their two boys—eight-year-old Hunter and six-year-old Troy. They are "fast-track" parents in a "fast-track" household.

What is a typical day in a fast-track household? Both Lena and Larry have to leave by eight in the morning to get to work on time. Both work long days, seldom getting home before seven o'clock at night. Because they work long hours, they have a live-in nanny five days a week, and several babysitters are on call to cover for their frequent weekend business trips.

But Larry and Lena are not uncaring parents. They really want the best of both worlds for themselves and their kids: successful, fulfilling, and lucrative careers . . . and a rich, warm, fulfilling family life. They have worked hard to get their kids in just the right schools and to enrich their lives with exposure to science and the arts. They spend a fortune on lessons of various kinds (although they must count on the nanny and the babysitters to get the boys to the lessons). And they make a special point of reading stories to their children and tucking them in at night.

But life on the fast track is not easy. Because Larry is away more, the kids demand his attention when he is home. But he is often so exhausted that he falls asleep on their beds while playing with them. "We have great difficulty giving our children quality time," explains Lena. "Some nights Larry and I are so exhausted that all we want to do is go to bed. We haven't had sex for ages. There's just no energy for it." To compensate, Lena and Larry try to plan a family vacation at least twice a year. Sometimes they are successful in getting away; often they are not.

Stress is taking its toll—and not just on Lena and Larry, but on the children as well. The boys' manners are atrocious, and they have developed a "wild" style of relating. Hunter uses pushing and bullying to get the better of his younger brother. In response, Troy whines and "tattles." Lena and Larry increasingly spend their "quality time" as referees.

These parents want the best of two worlds but are barely getting one—and it's the wrong one. To make matters worse, as they have begun to realize that things are not working out as well as they had hoped, they have turned up the heat on their children, demanding more of them by way of performance. Like many fast-track parents, they are transmitting their highly competitive and performance-driven attitudes to their children just as surely as they have passed on their genes. And the whole family is paying the price in terms of stress.

Who Are Fast-Track Parents?

Over the last fifteen years a new set of family issues has emerged and brought with it a new style of parenting and a new breed of children—"fast-track kids." The most visible of these are in relatively high income brackets. In 1980 there were about 370,000 two-career households with joint incomes over $75,000. Today there are more than 3.5 million of these households.

But not all fast-track parents are big-shot business or professional people, earning large salaries so they can have live-in nannies. Many are juggling two jobs or trying to go to graduate school and work for a living at the same time. Some are single parents trying to be breadwinners, mothers, and dads—all at the same time.

So what is a "fast-track" parent? He or she is typically a high-driving, go-getting type of person. (Obviously, there is a strong Type A personality tendency underlying this behavior.) Many fast-track parents are money oriented; they consider possessions to be the mark of success. But some pursue more high-minded goals; they are primarily concerned with maintaining high standards or pursuing meaningful endeavors. Whatever their aspirations, fast-track parents tend to be single minded. Success is very important to them. So is having the right car, living in the right neighborhood, or having the right friends.

And if you think that fast-track parents are only well-to-do, think again. For an affluent fast-track parent, the goals may include a luxury car and a live-in maid. But those a little further down the money scale may be determined to own their own house or buy their first new car. Even further down the affluence scale, the "good life" means living in a nice apartment and owning any sort of car.

Success is all relative! It is the fact that you are deeply invested in climbing that scale that determines whether you are on a fast track or not.

To some extent, of course, we all have the potential to get caught up in the fast track—to push ourselves and our children too hard in our desire to get everything done. And that potential is aggravated by the fact that we live in a fast-track society—a culture of sports cars and microwaves, quick fixes and instant answers. It's hard to resist the lure of "do more, and do it faster."

But when we surrender to the fast track, we inevitably up the stress levels for ourselves and our children. The human body was designed for camel travel. For many of us, stress is the consequence of trying to live at supersonic speeds and pressures.

What Happens to Fast-Track Kids?

How does the fast track affect children's stress? In several ways:

(1) Fast-track parents give their kids too little attention. As a result, fast-track kids often grow up both coddled and neglected. This is not a contradiction in terms, but two sides of the same coin. Even well-meaning fast-track parents have difficulty giving adequate attention to raising their kids, so these children often grow up showing signs of neglect. At the same time, they tend to be overindulged—given too many things and too little discipline. As a result, some lack solid values or the feeling that life has any real meaning. Some suffer from emotional neediness. And still others lack training in basic skills and responsibility.

Childcare workers report children who show up for kindergarten expecting to be dressed and served because parents don't have time to teach them how to care for themselves. They never learn to fend for themselves. It's easier, when a parent is in a hurry, to tie a child's shoelaces than to teach that child how to do it. It's easier (and quicker) to pick up toys behind a child than to take the time to supervise the child's doing it. It is simply less of a hassle to indulge a child's every whim than to redirect his or her desires to healthier activities. Many fast-track parents take this path of least resistance.

(2) Fast-track parents pressure their kids. These parents usually demand more from their kids, so the kids constantly feel scrutinized and judged.

Because so many fast-track children have difficulty living up to their parents' expectations, they often develop a pervasive sense of failure.

Sometimes parents have differing ideas about what their child should be achieving. The resulting conflict between the parents can push and pull the child into extraordinarily high stress.

As a result of these pressures, many fast-track children exhibit stress symptoms at an early age. Increasingly we are seeing the damaging consequences of this fast-track lifestyle in our therapy consulting rooms. Reports are becoming more frequent about how children are being damaged by it. According to a 1990 news story, nursery school teachers were finding that three- and four-year-olds were coming to school with trembling hands or facial tremors from too much pressure at home.[1] No matter how much these children achieved, they never felt they were able to measure up to their parents' accomplishments or expectations.

(3) Fast-track parents overprogram their kids. Some experts feel that fast-track children aren't even allowed to be children. Because of their need to be supervised while their parents are away and because of their parents' desire to give them every opportunity, they go through a variety of "programs" and lessons—gymnastics, piano, dance, art, computer camps, basketball workshops, Little League, and the like. They are hurried through childhood without an opportunity to just play and be kids. This stifles the development of creativity.

Tim Mauldin, a psychologist and director of a learning center in Los Angeles, reports that whereas there was a time you could put five regular kids around ten pebbles and they'd invent a game, overprogrammed children only notice the pebbles and complain about nothing to do.[2] They cannot use their imagination to be creative because they never get an opportunity to be creative.

(4) Most importantly, fast-track parents raise fast-track kids. Fast-track parents tend to transmit their attitudes to their children, influencing many of them to stay on the fast track also. Many children of fast-track parents easily become driven and ambitious, determined to live up to their parents' (and their own) high expectations. Too often, unfortunately, they pay the price in terms of stress disease.

Fast-track kids are characteristically driven and competitive—not always for their own good. They don't know how to be good losers. "I only got a B. How is this possible? I always get an A. I demand you give me an A." I've heard this complaint many times as a graduate school professor. But most of the time it's a fast-track trait learned in kindergarten—from fast-track parents.

What characterizes the children of fast-track parents then? Too often, they are: overprogrammed, overly coddled, overly competitive, overindulged, overentertained, easily bored, and easily frustrated. They quit too easily when a project gets hard, they lack endurance, and their development is out of balance. I will enlarge on several of these themes in the remainder of this chapter.

But I would be misleading if I implied that all fast-track children are created by fast-track parents. I know some ordinary parents who program their children for the fast track even though they may not be on it themselves. Sometimes they push their children as a way of compensating for their own lack of accomplishments. And others just want the best for their kids, so they push them into extra lessons and accelerated programs. Sadly, many of the stress consequences are the same.

Hothouse Homes

A hothouse is an artificial environment in which plants are encouraged to speed up their growth. Under such conditions, plants grow big and beautiful, but lack endurance, because root systems are superficial and weak and because the plant has not been "hardened" to normal weather conditions.

Fast-track parents often create such "hothouses" for their children. They try to speed up their children's development with an "enriched" environment and a pressured curriculum, hoping to create more intelligent and competent children. At the same time, they try to protect their children from the pressures of everyday living.

Unfortunately, normal human development just doesn't always work out this way. Intellectual development can sometimes be accelerated, just as a plant can be pushed to grow. But full maturity cannot be accelerated; it requires time and experience.

When children are given too much, too fast, and too soon, two serious risks are incurred:

(1) *The child's development can become unbalanced and uneven.* For instance, the "hothouse" effect may accelerate a child's reading skills without the comprehension skills' keeping pace. A child, then, may be able to recognize words and can read them aloud, but may not understand what is being read. This can be very frustrating to a child and can even disturb a child's emotional development.

A very common example of unbalanced development is the child who is intellectually advanced but emotionally immature. Such a child inevitably feels the stress of not fitting anywhere—being "too smart" for younger kids but "too young" for his or her intellectual peers.

(2) *The child's development may have no substance.* Hothouse plants grow fast, but they quickly wither if they are taken out of the hothouse and placed

in the outside world. The same is true for children. Many do well when they are young because they are given a lot of attention and help, but they never develop good learning skills for themselves. Their fast-track learning doesn't instill stamina or self-discipline. They never learn to fend for themselves in the real world.

Where Is the Balance?

Clearly, the fast-track, hothouse approach is stressful for children. But I realize that in avoiding the trap of pushing children too hard, parents may fall into an opposite trap—not expecting enough of their kids. In choosing how much to push their kids, parents risk two errors:

- *They can expect too much*, demanding that a child "deliver the goods" and stressing the child out in the process (this is obviously the "fast-track" or "hothouse" error), or

- *They can expect too little* and allow their child to waste his or her gifts.

I am certainly not advocating this latter error. Children need to be challenged. They need guidance and help and even an occasional hard push to achieve their full potential. The wise parent, therefore, applies him or herself to the task of walking the fine line between being too demanding and leaving children to their own haphazard development.

How can you know if you are pushing too hard—if the heat in the hothouse is too high? Usually it shows itself in distress symptoms. Children who are pushed too hard complain of headaches, stomachaches, and nightmares. They cry a lot and become self-critical. Their anxiety level escalates. They may start biting their nails and become restless, fidgety, and worried. Or their anger level may increase; they may become unstable, frustrated, and quick tempered. Finally, they may just throw in the towel and refuse to be pushed any further.

Any of these signs need to be carefully monitored. If they persist, consider that you may need to take the heat off your child. Stop demanding as much as you do. Let up on activities and allow more free time for relaxation and fun activities.

Highly successful parents can't always understand how important idle moments are for children. "Down time" gives kids badly needed opportunities for reflection and self-rejuvenation. Many fast-track parents have become so accustomed to continuous work that they forget that children don't yet have the same capacity for sustained output.

Chances are, of course, that the habits parents are teaching to their children are putting *the parents* at high risk for stress disease—not to mention setting the children up for stress damage. Instead of pushing their kids more, most fast-track parents need to learn to push *themselves* less!

How can you tell if you are not expecting enough from your children? Usually this is self-evident. Your children are not succeeding at anything. They may have become self-satisfied and overly confident. Their efforts are at best sporadic and half-hearted, and they may even tend to be arrogant and boastful about not succeeding. (This may be a cover for self-esteem problems; children who enjoy few successes often feel bad about themselves.)

A teacher's feedback may be extremely helpful here. When you hear several teachers say that your child is "not trying hard enough," it may be time to "turn the heat up" and demand some attention.

Why Children Underachieve

Most children who underachieve do so either because their motivation is stifled either by not having enough reinforcement for achieving or because they are being pushed into achieving in an area they don't feel competent to master. Let me illustrate each of these:

(*1*) *Inadequate reinforcement kills motivation.* We humans are designed to respond to rewards. If there is no "pay-off" for our efforts, we tend to become demoralized and lose interest. And this is especially true of children. Underachievers often see no reward for positive behavior.

Now, a payoff for effort need not take the form of money or gifts. In fact, these are probably the least effective of all reinforcers. "Paying" for effort and positive behavior is actually a form of bribery, and it carries the same risk as other forms of bribery: The one who is being bribed keeps "upping the ante." So a child who at first is content to put in an extra hour on math in return for an ice cream eventually finds that the treat is not enough to sustain his interest. Instead, he wants a trip to the movies . . . or a video game . . . or a bicycle. Kids are born extortionists. Their ingenuity and craftiness at "working a deal" knows no bounds.

A much more effective "reward" for motivating a child is "social reinforcement"—a fancy term for simple love and affirmation. A child wants to feel valued and appreciated. He or she wants to hear compliments, especially if they are true. In fact, most children will sustain *any* sort of grind to hear a parent say, "I think you're the greatest!" When this sort of reinforcement is lacking, children quickly become underachievers.

(*2*) *Inadequate competence quickly discourages children and leads to under-achieving.* Many fast-track parents fear two things: The first is that their child is not normal, the second is that their child is merely normal. Anything less than superior throws them. "How can we, who are so capable and brilliant, have a child who doesn't match our talents?"

Instead of facing the possibility that their child's gifts and abilities may be different from what they want, they turn up the heat in the hothouse, expecting to see their child "improve" into what they want him or her to be. Such parents invariably have no idea what is "normal" for children. And they rarely take enough time to find out what the child's real interests and abilities are.

Many children, then, find themselves being pressured into studies, activities, sports, and the like, where they are *below* average, or at least don't stand out as stars. As a result, motivation drops. They quickly lose interest, and they may even resist the activity or deliberately fail so they don't have to try again. A series of such deliberate failures can cause a child to begin believing he or she *is a failure*. Such a belief quickly becomes a self-fulfilling prophecy.

Parents should try to be more realistic about their child's potential. *Listen* to your child. Pay attention to his or her innate talents and areas of interest and encourage activities that will allow him or her to shine. Reinforce (with love and affirmation, of course) your child's *efforts* and *willingness to learn* instead of getting hung up on whether he or she wins the prize or gets the award. Help your child develop the ability to enjoy the learning experience just for the pleasure of learning itself, rather than for the high grade or even for the thrill of competing.

Hurried Kids and Hurried Households

A variant of the fast-track child is the "hurried" child. It's the childhood version of "hurry sickness," a pervasive sense of urgency that is concerned solely with goals and the completion of tasks. Hurriedness is a major cause of premature heart disease and anxiety because of the adrenaline it releases. Every adult I know who suffers from "hurry sickness" started to act this way much earlier in life—usually in childhood.

People with hurry sickness have a preoccupation with time. They do everything as quickly as possible, hurrying from one task to another. At home, at the office, socializing with friends—no matter where or what is being done, such a person is in a tremendous hurry. All day, every day, he or she lives like the White Rabbit in *Alice in Wonderland*: "I'm late! I'm late, for a very important date."

Preoccupation with time or time urgency is not the only symptom of this form of fast-track living. The other component is the preoccupation with task completion and unappreciation of the process of doing the task. People with hurry sickness take trips to exotic places and focus all their attention on *getting there* and then *getting home*; they don't really enjoy the journey or savor the experience. They hide behind cameras without appreciating the wonderful vistas before them, thinking, "Let's hurry up and get it done. I can always enjoy the pictures when we get home."

Fast-track children develop these characteristics quite early. They are usually hurried by their parents, and they quickly learn to hurry themselves. They don't learn to enjoy the *process* of writing a paper, playing the violin, or playing volleyball; they want the grade, the applause, or the trophy. They want to be "excellent" even if that means hating what they are doing. Their focus is always on the *goal* rather than the process.

Most hurried children, of course, have hurried parents and live in hurried households. Because hurried parents "speed up" everything, like walking up the "up" escalator and down the "down" side just to save a few seconds (I'm guilty of this), their children learn to do the same. Because they tend to finish the sentences of people who talk too slowly, their children learn to interrupt conversations. Because they prefer to do something while doing something else at the same time, their children learn to "multitask" also.

There is rarely time for fun or relaxing in such homes, and family members rarely have time to listen to one another. Parents who are in a hurry themselves don't have time for this. So the family seldom spends time together talking, learning, questioning, listening, sharing, or interacting, even over meals. Instead, they watch television and eat "fast-track" food. Parents are often too tired or distracted to really get involved in their children's lives, or they quickly become frustrated with the "pointlessness" of much childhood activity. When children report experiences to them, for instance, they tend to withdraw, forget, or simply doze off.

I heard recently that a major greeting card publisher (no names please) now markets a line of greeting cards for hurried parents to tuck under their kids' bowl of Cheerios (or other high-energy cereal) in the morning. I haven't seen one yet, but I believe one reads, "Have a super day at school. See you when I get home!" That's a hurried parent for you. Another one, placed under the pillow at night, reads, "I wish I were there to tuck you in, but have pleasant dreams."

I feel like writing to the publisher and suggesting a line of cards that hurried kids could leave their parents. They could post them on the car's dashboard or slip them into a briefcase. And one could read, "Remember me? I'd appreciate an appointment to talk."

Preventing Hurry Sickness

Hurry, like the fast track, is hard to avoid in our society. I used to think that farmers had a more leisurely life, but I've seen farmers who are more hurried than bank presidents. And some stages of life are unavoidably hectic. Parenting young children, for instance, can be about as hassled a time in life as anything I know. There are simply too many demands and not enough time in the day to take care of them.

Nevertheless, if you want the best for your children, there is no substitute for spending quality—*unhurried*—time with them. That means slowing down enough to sit down and talk with your children. A celebrated study some years ago showed that the only common denominator among National Merit Award semifinalists was that all came from families that always sat down to dinner together.[3] Eating together—that's all. And their children became superstars.

What can parents do to slow down their pace and prevent their children from developing hurry sickness? Here are some suggestions.

(1) *Remind yourself and your child to slow down.* Our culture encourages hurry, but you can *choose* to slow down. And you can help your child to make the same choices.

(2) *Plan activities that involve the whole family and that help you to focus on process, not goals.* In other words, if you like hiking, don't just rush to the top of the trail; enjoy the hike. Slow your pace. Search for birds and animals. Stop and take in the scenery. Smell the air. If you choose to make Christmas cookies, concentrate on the fun of mixing, rolling, and decorating—not producing a gourmet result.

(3) *Create "quiet times" for both yourself and other family members.* Try to find a time when you can relax, pray, and meditate—sometimes individually, sometimes as a family. Quiet times can help you all get in touch with deeper feelings and restore perspective on your busy lives. Leisurely walks, watching a sunrise or sunset, or sitting together in a quiet chapel as a family can all help you slow down your rushing.

(4) *Above everything else, protect your family's free time.* Resolve not to dream up activities just because you can't stand seeing your family idle. Unstructured time is not necessarily wasted time.

(5) *Give absolute priority to your family commitments.* If you have promised your kids an outing on a particular day, keep your promise, no matter how pressing your other engagements are. If your family expects to take a quiet evening walk together, don't disappoint them. Not only should your children be able to trust your promises; keeping your commitments will remind you and teach them that the process of living together is as important as the goal of growing up.

In summary, teach your child how to enjoy the little pleasures of life. Every child deserves some long ice-creamy afternoons. Every child should know the smell of new-mown grass and feel the dew on naked feet. Every child should hear stories of your childhood adventures or your travels, about your parents and grandparents and times gone by. Every child should know the comfort of lounging with the family by the fireplace (or heating grate) on a cold winter's night.

These are my most cherished memories. I wouldn't exchange them for anything. They are the memories that make me appreciate what real life is all about. And these kinds of memories just cannot be hurried.

Keeping Your Family Off the Fast Track

Fast-track living is hard on both parents and children. But fast-track parents can still be excellent parents *if* they devote time and attention to meeting their child's needs. But this may mean some dramatic changes in both attitudes and behavior.

If you want to protect your child from fast-track stress, you may have to stop getting upset when your child only gets a B on a test or if he or she doesn't win the top prize. You may have to cut back on some of your outside activities in order to devote more time and energy to family. You may even need to make some hard decisions about your goals and your lifestyle. You will almost certainly have to remind yourself on a regular basis that *life is for living, not winning.*

Getting your family off the fast track may also involve bringing your guilt feelings under control. *All* parents feel guilty. No parent feels that he or she is perfect. In fact, you will probably always feel that you're not doing or giving enough. I still feel this way myself, even though my children are grownup.

These twangs of guilt are *only feelings*. They may or may not have any basis in reality—and often they don't. And they may put you in risk of pampering your child to alleviate your guilt—a far greater parenting failure. It is easy to overentertain, overindulge, or overcompensate your child to appease your bad feelings surrounding your imagined neglect or failure to be a good parent.

If you are guilty of fast-track parenting, don't wallow in guilt. Instead, confess your guilt, get help if you need it, *and change.* Wallowing in or indulging your guilt feelings is never constructive. Do what you can, to the best of your ability, and then leave it be. You will make fewer mistakes than if you try too hard.

Finally, keep in mind that you are a part of a *fast-track world*. We are all cogs in a vast machine that is moving too fast. We can't get off permanently, but we can occasionally jump off to relax and slow down.

We can also refuse to be preoccupied with where the machine is headed. Our world holds up success as the ultimate goal, but it doesn't know how to enjoy the process of moving toward success. When success is the ultimate and only goal, the "good life" becomes a joy ride with no real purpose.

Success that is separated from the real values of a good life inevitably fails to satisfy. But you can instill the values that can make success more fulfilling. Pointing your children toward the values, beliefs, and attitudes of a deep faith in God and showing them how this faith sustains you in success or in failure will prepare them for a far more satisfying life than our fast-track world can offer.

You can teach your child that the future is rich with promise and full of deeply satisfying meaning if, in addition to living it with God, you live it one day at a time, tackling one task at a time, and solving one problem at a time. This may put you at variance with your fast-track world, but the improved quality of your life and your child's life will make it all worthwhile.

Summary

The pace of life in modern-day society has increased to such an extent that many parents are living a "fast-track" existence and creating "fast-track" children. Not only does this rob children of their childhoods, but it also disturbs their normal development and leads to overstress.

The challenge for all parents is to challenge children to reach their full potential without pushing them too fast or too far. This balance can only be achieved if parents are clear about the deeper issues of life and if your values are centered on more abiding values. Success just for success' sake is simply not satisfying. Unless one is able to enjoy the journey toward success, the achievement of success will be hollow, unrewarding . . . and stressful.

Discussion Questions

1. You may not be a stereotypical "fast-track" parent, but to some extent you may be pushing your child too fast. Review the characteristics of a "fast-track" parent and discuss how strongly you evidence these characteristics.

2. Fast-track children also tend to be hurried children. Plan a series of activities for your family that will help you all to slow down and enjoy the process of living.

3. What does success mean for you? Write down some achievements that you believe would make you feel successful. Now, write a short list of what you value in life. Discuss whether these values are compatible with your idea of success. How can you make them more compatible?

12

Calming the
Angry Child

Nine-year-old Matthew had always had a quick temper. Even as a tiny boy, he flared up at the slightest provocation. At first, however, he only got angry when he was frustrated. When Matthew was about four, he would become furious when he couldn't open a box or a drawer. If he was given a toy in a box for his birthday, for instance, and could not get the box open in just a few seconds, he would throw it down and jump on it as if to destroy it, screaming at the top of his lungs. He broke several new toys even before they were out of their protective containers.

When Matthew was six, his parents enrolled him in junior soccer, thinking (and hoping) that learning to play a team sport and having a physical outlet for his energy would help bring his anger under control. But soccer only gave Matthew some new opportunities to vent his frustration and rage. If he was dribbling the ball up the sideline, making some progress for his team, and an opposing player got the ball away, Matthew would drop to the ground, beat the turf with his fists, and scream at the top of his lungs. His father would run onto the field, pick him up, and try to calm him. In an average twenty-minute game Matthew would have at least three such temper outbursts.

Teaching Matthew any new skill was extremely difficult because he became furious if he was not able to master the skill immediately. Teaching him to ride a bicycle was a real challenge. Matthew would get on his small bicycle while his father held the saddle and Matthew began to pedal. "Leave me; don't hold me," Matthew would shout. But as soon as his father let go, Matthew would fall over and go into a rage.

Now, at nine, Matthew is about the angriest person I have ever seen. The anger is damaging him in several ways:

(1) *Matthew's anger is damaging him socially.* He has few friends, because his angry outbursts are frequently directed at his playmates. If he loses his turn while playing a game, for instance, he accuses the other players of cheating—in a very loud and derogatory tone of voice. As a result of his anger, Matthew is slowly being ostracized. No one wants to play with him.

(2) *Matthew's anger is damaging him psychologically.* He has come to believe that getting angry not only gets him whatever he wants, but that he will be rescued whenever his anger gets him in trouble. He literally controls his world. His family is always jumping to his anger, soothing his fury and placating his irritations.

(3) *Matthew's anger is damaging him physically.* He now reports frequent headaches. His blood pressure is high for his age. His body is constantly bathed in adrenaline, which over time will work its damage in his arteries. And whenever he gets over a bout of fury, he throws up, gets a nosebleed, and feels dizzy.

(4) *Perhaps most importantly, Matthew's anger is shaping his personality.* He is becoming sulky, irritable, and argumentative. When asked to do something he becomes infuriated. He scorns people in authority (like his schoolteacher) because they are not as easily intimidated as his parents by his rage reactions. In many ways, Matthew's anger is becoming a permanent part of him. He is well on his way to becoming an angry person—and he will pay the price in years to come.

When Anger Is Out of Control

Every child gets angry sometimes. He spits, swears, rants, and raves. She bites, scratches, pouts, and throws things. He kicks and screams; she collapses on the floor in tears.

Anger is a natural response to threat. Human beings are not born with control over our anger—it is something we must learn. Some children learn it early and well. Others never learn it, or they learn to control their anger in unhealthy ways. These are the children who grow up at risk for developing some manifestation of stress disease at some time in their lives.

In our culture, acts of aggression and the acting out of angry feelings are more readily tolerated in boys than in girls. This is changing, to be sure, but boys are still encouraged to give vent to their anger more often than girls, who are frequently disciplined (formally or informally) for displaying their anger.

"Nice girls don't behave this way," or "Men won't like you if you show you are angry" are still the sorts of messages we send to girls. "Don't be a sissy, stand up for yourself," or "Tell him what you think of him," are the messages we send to boys. Then when it comes to tears, however, girls are told that it's OK to cry, but boys are discouraged.

This double standard is unfortunate. Generally, it leaves males with only one acceptable outlet for built-up tension—the outlet which is the most hazardous from a stress-disease point of view. Girls, on the other hand, learn to repress their anger or adopt sneaky, "passive aggressive" behaviors.

All of us, male and female, ought to be free to express our stresses and tensions through a full range of emotional outlets. We ought to be free to cry when we are sad, laugh when we are happy, and express our keyed-up condition or fears through appropriate anger when called for. Our emotional outlets are channels of human expression that God has given us so as to be fully in touch with ourselves. When they are blocked, the mind and body become disoriented and we are not capable of living our lives to the fullest.

But while we all need to develop a broad repertoire of emotional expression in order to be psychologically healthy, limits must be maintained. We can't laugh all the time. We can't cry forever. And anger, especially, cannot (or should not) exist as a chronic emotion or habitual behavior without causing damage.

While the venting of anger through aggression might be an effective form of release, it is a highly inefficient coping mechanism. More significantly, anger often provokes a counterattack from the person being attacked, thus perpetuating the battle—and the anger. And as we have seen, the angry child (one who has learned anger as a habitual response) is a child at high risk for stress-disease later in life.

For all these reasons, the caring parent must attend to a child's anger responses and try to shape them in a healthy direction. Out-of-control or chronic anger is a sign that *something is wrong.*

Before we look at anger in more detail, you may want to take Stress Test 7, "How Angry Is Your Child?" Don't be too worried if your child seems to score high on this test. Many children go through brief periods when their anger is high; it's all part of learning the limits of what you can and cannot do and discovering alternative ways of getting what you want. In the pages to come, we will be exploring some ways you can help your child handle his or her anger in a healthy way.

Anger—Good or Bad?

We tend to be very ambivalent about anger in our culture. Is anger good for us? Is it bad? And this confusion has been fed by an "anger industry"—

Stress Test 7: How Angry Is Your Child?

Child's name _____

   The following inventory covers the more common signs of anger in children. All children occasionally manifest these signs, but if several of them are persistent or if your child evidences many of them, you may have a problem.
   Rate each statement according to the following scale and enter the rating in the right column:

0 = My child never or rarely does this.
1 = My child occasionally does this (no more than once a month).
2 = My child often (once a week or so) does this.
3 = My child does this frequently—daily or several times a week.

		Rating
1.	My child blames others for his or her troubles.	_____
2.	My child throws or breaks things whenever he or she feels frustrated or irritated.	_____
3.	Whenever my child gets angry, calming him or her down takes a lot of placating.	_____
4.	My child does not like change of any sort and becomes angry when change is forced on him or her.	_____
5.	My child changes the rules of games when playing with other children.	_____
6.	My child says spiteful or hateful things whenever he or she is thwarted.	_____
7.	My child is negative, deliberately slow, and resists doing what he or she is told to do to the point that discipline becomes a stand-off.	_____
8.	My child seeks out arguments or reasons to become upset, even when everything is at peace.	_____
9.	My child ostracizes, scorns, and complains about others.	_____
10.	My child loses control when she or he is angry and shows it with facial expressions or body language.	_____
11.	My child uses foul language whenever he or she gets angry.	_____
12.	When my child is learning something new, he or she easily becomes frustrated and wants to do something else.	_____
13.	My child is stubborn and refuses to do what he or she is told to do unless you use the right tone or voice or approach.	_____
14.	My child's friends don't like to play with him or her because he or she is such a bad sport.	_____
15.	My child gets into fights with other children and has great difficulty controlling his or her temper when teased.	_____

Total Score _____

Test Interpretation

0–5	Your child is remarkably free of anger and is not prone to frustration. If anything, he or she may be a little too passive—but don't try to change this!
6–10	Your child is showing a normal degree of anger and irritation, but the higher score (nearer 10) is more appropriate for younger children (under 6) and the lower score (nearer 6) more appropriate for older children.
11–15	Your child is beginning to show an above-normal degree of anger response. Again, the higher score is more appropriate for younger children. Some attention to your child's response may be needed.
16–20	Clearly your child has a problem with anger and should receive your attention.
Over 20	Your child has a serious problem with anger, especially if he or she is already of school age. Take immediate steps to help your child cope with his or her anger, and seek professional help, if necessary.

---

an approach to counseling and psychotherapy which is based on the belief that anger is a creative energy which must be encouraged and allowed to have free expression. "The angrier you get, the healthier you are," one colleague once said to me. And his own life epitomized this philosophy. He died not long afterwards, in his early fifties, from a heart attack!

As we saw in Part One of this book, stress and anger are close cousins. The "fight" portion of the "fight or flight" response in stress is reflected in anger. The massive discharge of adrenaline that accompanies anger is supposed to help us fight our enemies and preserve our lives. Instead, it often acts as a boomerang and comes back to harm us. Angry people, as we have seen, are prone to ulcers, headaches, and the most serious of all stress-disorders, premature heart disease.

The physiology of anger and rage is quite fascinating in one major respect: It clearly shows that emotions have complex biological underpinnings. As we saw in Part One of this book, the whole body and mind mobilize for survival when we become angry. The brain releases both hormonal and neuronal messengers. The eyes, facial muscles, heart, stomach, spleen, bowel, and bladder all get signals and go into a special emergency mode. Blood vessels of the skin contract, sweat is released on the hands and feet, blood pressure goes up, blood sugar is released, the cholesterol level rises, adrenaline surges, and the brain goes into high gear. When the anger passes, then, one experiences its aftermath as the body systems return to normal. These can include headaches, stomach pains, diarrhea, and exhaustion.

Short lived, as we have seen, an anger response is normal and even helpful, though it is better suited to a more primitive lifestyle than most of us live today. If prolonged, however, this emergency response increases wear and tear in many of our systems and eventually causes permanent damage.

The role of adrenaline in anger is crucial and recognized by many experts in the anger field.[1] In fact, adrenaline is often referred to as the "anger hormone." Adrenaline rushes through our veins every time we are angry, mobilizing us to fight or flee. But as we saw in chapter 2, this same adrenaline gives us a "high," a feeling of well-being. This means that being angry has some secondary benefits. It provides us with feelings of excitement and stimulation—the pleasurable feelings associated with the adrenaline rush. This explains why some people like to pick a fight whenever they feel depressed; for them, it is the quickest way to get out of a funk. Anger, then, can become a key element in an adrenaline addiction.

Even the great church reformer Martin Luther knew how anger could be stimulating. He once wrote: "When I am angry I can write, pray and preach well, for then my whole temperament is quickened, my understanding sharpened and all mundane vexations and temptations gone."[2]

But Luther did not understand how prolonged anger can be damaging to our minds and bodies. If he had known he might not have been so quick to think that his anger was an asset to his preaching.

But Isn't It Bad to Stifle a Child's Anger?

Clearly, anger can be damaging. But isn't anger *more* damaging if you don't "let it out"? Parents are often confused about how they should respond to their child's anger, fearing they may harm their child if they try to suppress the anger but also fearing the harm that uncontrolled anger can do. This confusion is heightened by psychologists who teach that anger should never be "stifled"—that unvented anger causes a variety of physical and psychological problems.

For years I have contended that the free expression of anger is *not* only unpleasant for others, but extremely dangerous to the angry person. In the past decade, I have received reinforcement from one of the best books available on the topic of anger, Carol Tavris's *Anger, the Misunderstood Emotion.*[3] Dr. Tavris's book helps to put some sense back into common psychological thinking, which in past decades has tended to encourage the free expression of anger and to discourage attempts to control it.

After a very careful and thorough review of the anger literature, Dr. Tavris concludes that freely venting anger doesn't relieve the anger, but *increases* it—and that letting yourself rant and rave can actually be harmful to your health. The dangerous aspect of anger, she points out, is not stifling it, but having it in the first place. If you act out your anger, you reinforce it. Eventually, you may establish a hostile habit.[4]

It is better, Tavris argues, to "keep quiet about your momentary irritations and distract yourself with pleasant activity *until* your fury simmers down."[5] Chances are that you will then feel better, and feel better faster, than if you "let yourself go." Furthermore, by controlling your anger in this way you are *less likely* to anger your enemy into further retaliation.

Anger You Feel and Anger You Do

There is a case to be made, therefore, for teaching your children how to control their anger. The uncontrolled expression of anger through aggressive behavior is neither necessary *nor* healthy. Children who learn to control their anger will be not only more at ease with their world, but happier in themselves.

But there is a fine line here. Parents must walk a balance between giving our children license to *act out* their anger and forcing them to *repress* or *deny* their anger.

Children need to be aware of their anger—to acknowledge it and talk about it and even express it in nondestructive ways—in order to handle it in a healthy way. They need to understand that there is a difference between:

- *anger as a feeling* (the emotion you experience in response to threat) and

- *anger as behavior* (what you do with your feeling of anger—usually aggression).

This distinction is extremely important. What we *feel* in anger and what we *do* with that feeling are two separate things and should be kept separate.

Almost two thousand years ago, the apostle Paul wrote, "If you are angry, don't sin by nursing your grudge. Don't let the sun go down with you still angry—get over it quickly." This advice zeroed in on *three important truths* about anger that are consistent with our most up-to-date scientific understanding:

- *Anger, as a feeling, is not necessarily bad.* Paul says, "*If* you are angry." He doesn't say "never get angry." It's almost as if he assumes that feelings of anger are inevitable—which they are. No one can totally avoid feeling angry.

- *Anger, as a feeling, is intended to be temporary.* The idea that you can dispose of it before the sun sets suggests that anger, as a feeling, should be resolved as quickly as possible. Although anger as a feeling is not necessarily bad, you are not to dwell on feelings of anger.

- *The destructiveness of anger is connected with what you do, not with what you feel.*

Five Myths About Anger

Before you can help your child develop a healthier control of his or her anger, you may need to set aside some common myths about anger and develop a clearer and healthier approach to your own anger. After all, most of your child's angry outbursts will be modeled after those of you or your spouse. It makes sense to put your own house in order before you try to train your child in better anger management.

What are some of the myths you should reconsider?

1. *"I need to vent my anger."* Not true. You should always attend to your anger and address the cause of it. "Letting it out" implies acting out anger aggressively. This invariably leads to more trouble.

2. *"If I suppress my anger I will become emotionally or physically sick."* Not true. What makes you sick is not letting your anger in, letting it out, or wrapping it in ribbons and throwing it in the ocean—but simply being angry and doing nothing about it. Holding back your angry behavior may help you to gain better control over your situation. It won't make you ill.

3. *"My anger helps me to be more creative."* Not true. Your anger may release a lot of adrenaline and give you a feeling of exhilaration—but this is not the same as being creative. If anything, anger makes you *less* creative because a highly aroused state makes you less likely to make the new mental connections that are the essence of creativity.

4. *"When I feel all bottled up with anger, I need to just let it all out."* Not true. Something is causing you to bottle your anger. It is better to find out what is causing you to bottle your anger and to deal with this constriction before your anger builds to a high pitch. Exploding in anger only hurts others and makes you enemies when you need allies. It is much better to handle "bottled-up" anger by *slowly* diffusing it.

5. *"Tantrums are healthy expressions of childhood anger."* Not true. Tantrums are a child's attempts to gain control and manipulate a situation to his or her advantage. If you give in to a tantrum, you are teaching the child an unhealthy way of getting what he or she wants in life. A child should gain nothing from a temper tantrum—except the knowledge that a person cannot always get his or her own way.

Another way of understanding this distinction is to ask, "What is the purpose of the feeling of anger?" It is first of all a signal—part of our body's alarm system. Its *primary purpose* is to make known a grievance.[6] Its *secondary purpose* is to help mobilize our emergency system for action. Only then does action come in.

In a sense, anger functions in much the same way that a smoke alarm does. The alarm's function is to warn us of a possible fire and get us moving to do something about the fire. It detects the smoke and clangs or buzzes until we pay attention and put out the fire. As we will see, this is precisely how we ought to deal with anger.

If a child is taught that it is bad to feel angry or is encouraged to avoid or ignore angry feelings, that child could reach the point of not even recognizing his or her own anger. This is called *repression,* and it is never healthy.

Repressing anger is like ignoring a smoke alarm; it undermines the alarm's protective function. If you fail to recognize your angry feelings, you are ignoring a very important warning system and failing to attend to an emergency state. Repressed anger can cause severe internal stress and lead to headaches, fatigue, gastric disturbances, and high blood pressure—all the symptoms associated with prolonged adrenaline arousal.

The danger of repressed anger is one reason we spend so much time in therapy helping people get "in touch" with their feelings. The phrase has become a cliché, but there is no other way to describe the process. Many people today are just not in touch with their angry feelings. They refuse, even when confronted with a video of their angry behavior, to own up to it and take steps to deal with it. And they pay the price in terms of disrupted relationships and stress disease.

A healthy response to anger, then involves *first* recognizing the alarm (what you feel) and, *second*, choosing how to deal with the threat (what to do). Understanding these two distinct steps can help you guide your children toward a healthier way of dealing with anger. When a child behaves angrily, he or she should not be punished for *feeling* anger. The behavior (aggression) can be disciplined, but not the feeling. Everyone has the right to feel anger, talk about it, and hope for a listening ear. Once they recognize the alarm, they can choose to act in constructive ways. They can choose control and positive problem solving rather than adrenaline-recruiting aggression or other unhealthy expressions of anger.

Understanding Your Child's Anger Response

The anger response is necessary for survival. At its most basic level, as I have already mentioned, it serves as a signal to warn us of a violation or threat and then mobilizes our bodies to respond.

But the anger response is far from simple. What begins as a very primitive response to physical threat in an infant becomes far more complex and sophisticated as the child matures. Understanding the development of the anger response can help you guide your child toward a healthy expression of anger at every stage of development.

Anger As an Instinctive Response

Underlying all the different kinds of anger is a very primitive, instinctive, protective response to threat.

This simple protective instinct is also the *first* form of anger human beings experience. Babies have the capacity for it at birth. If they are accidentally smothered by a pillow, they will fight and kick to get the pillow away.

And this instinctive form of anger, triggered whenever we are threatened, continues with us throughout life. Soldiers and policemen know it well. It is reinforced in their training, and it helps them face danger and do their duty. Parents sometimes experience it when their offspring are threatened.

If kept in check, then, the instinctive response is a healthy form of anger. But except in situations of severe abuse or physical threat, there is seldom a call for this kind of anger in our modern society. The threats we face are rarely physical, and an instinctive response is rarely useful.

A growing child learns, for instance, that danger can take many forms. Words can be dangerous. People can hurt with their looks and their laughter. And one can't survive these threats by fighting and kicking; one must learn new, more socially acceptable ways to handle threats.

If your life is in danger, therefore, then welcome the instinctive response and follow its impulses. Children, however, need to slowly give it up in their everyday life as they grow to see that not getting your way is not a matter of life or death.

Anger As a Conditioned or "Useful" Response

The basic, instinctive, protective anger I have just described is what babies first experience. They cry and show anger when they are hurt or hungry. As they grow, however, they begin to learn that they can use their anger to get them what they want and get them out of doing what they don't want to do. This is what I call "conditioned" anger.

My fifteen-month-old granddaughter, Ashley, has a beautiful temperament, by and large. She is a quiet, loving, and peaceful child. She responds well to strangers and is quite friendly. But just this past month she has discovered the power of anger. Her favorite word, at this stage, is *NO*— said with great force and accompanied with a scowl, which is her interpretation of what an angry person looks like.

What is happening here? Ashley's instinctive anger, designed to protect her from danger and starvation, is becoming a "conditioned" response. She is learning to use her anger to get her way—to act angry and to display her anger in order to gain some advantage. All this is quite natural—and cute—for a fifteen-month-old child. But conditioned anger is typically neither cute nor acceptable.

Temper tantrums are classic conditioned anger responses. The anger outburst, the first time it occurs, embarrasses the parent into doing what the child wants (or at least giving the child extra attention), so the child quickly learns to use it to his or her advantage. Later in life the "tantrum" moves beyond lying on the ground, kicking and screaming. It takes the form of silence, pouting, and emotional blackmailing. Many marriages are spoiled by these adult tantrums.

Conditioned anger, in other words, is a form of manipulation. Parents should work hard to avoid reinforcing this misuse of anger.

How do you keep from reinforcing conditioned anger in a child who is throwing a tantrum? *Ignore it!* If you *never* give in to the demands of a child who throws a tantrum, I can guarantee you that the fit will extinguish rapidly.

Ignoring a tantrum will be difficult the first few times. Your kid may go hysterical—even turn blue with rage. He or she may kick and scream. Try to think of this as a healthy ventilation for the lungs. Forget about the embarrassment. Every other parent will take pity on you; you are in good company. Ignore the other shoppers (tantrums occur more often in stores than anywhere else because there needs to be an audience for it to work). If you don't like watching the display, retreat to a safe distance where you can still keep an eye on your child while you go about your business. Keep reminding yourself that temper tantrums *are never fatal!*

Sooner or later, the tantrum will blow over. Then, the moment your child is quiet, give him or her love and attention. Respond to *reasonable* requests—a toy or an ice cream cone may help to reinforce the idea that one gets more by *not* being angry, than by throwing a fit.

You will want to be alert, of course, to the possibility that an organic disturbance or an allergic reaction could cause a loss of self-control. Such attacks, which are rare, usually don't occur in stores or at school. They are likely to occur in private places, because they are not manipulative. If you are in doubt about your child's tantrums, consult your pediatrician to put your mind at rest.

Anger As a Response to Frustration

Not all anger is an instinctive or even a conditioned response. Anger also serves *social* and *psychological* purposes; it helps us interact with our world to get what we need and to overcome our obstacles.

In babies, of course, all anger is instinctive. The baby is not angry *at* anyone when it screams instinctively; it has not yet grasped the independent existence of others. But as soon as the young child begins to grasp that there are "others" that can be blamed for the lack of whatever it needs, anger begins to be directed at people.

The age at which we believe a child fully understands *directed* anger is about three years. After this age a child is capable of "real" anger and his or her outbursts become less physical and more psychological. (At this point anger also becomes more of a stress problem.)

At this point, too, a child begins to develop an understanding of *frustration*. Whenever the child can't get what he or she wants or when a barrier prevents the child from reaching a desired goal, a state of frustration is created that leads to aggression. This is the well-known *frustration-aggression* law, and it holds for all people, of all ages, and in all cultures: When you can't get what you want, you get angry.

The frustration-aggression law is one reason why the overcrowding of children leads to a greater incidence of aggression. Opportunities for frustration proliferate as more children are placed in greater proximity to one another.

Adults as well as children have this tendency to become aggressive whenever their goals are blocked. For the child, this anger may be triggered by having to share a toy or by not being able to master a task. In an adult, it may come from failing to make a sale or from being misunderstood by a mate. In either case, the anger's purpose is to help the child or adult get what he or she wants.

As with instinctive anger, however, frustration anger has limited effectiveness in our society. It may be helpful in overcoming some physical obstacles, such as confronting a bully who won't give a ball back. But anger is seldom helpful in confronting psychological obstacles such as feeling unattractive or being humiliated. And much frustration anger is simply counterproductive because of a basic fact of life: You can't always get what you want *right now*.

Some delay is inevitable in life, even when our purposes are legitimate. I have to wait to get paid, for instance, and I don't get paid every minute I work—not even every day. Becoming angry in response to such delay simply increases my stress level without getting me what I want. Learning to *delay gratification* is an important part of growing up—and an important way to keep anger and stress under control.

How can you help your child to be less angry when frustrated? Here are some ideas:

(1) *Help your child to be more flexible.* A flexible personality is a great aid to peaceful living. Rigidity, which is a symptom of emotional constrictedness, simply leads to useless frustration.

When your children exhibit frustration over blocked goals, talk the situation over with them. Help them make a list of things that will happen if they don't get what they want—usually, the consequences just aren't that bad—and of alternate ways of reaching the goals.

And try to exhibit flexibility yourself. Approaching your blocked goals with maturity and creativity will set a great example for your children.

(2) Help your child learn to delay gratification. Don't give your child what she or he wants immediately. Teach your child to wait (without anger) by slowly delaying the giving.

If your child asks for a cookie, for instance, respond by saying, "I'll give it to you in two minutes." Then help the child understand what two minutes are by saying, "Now, let's wait and see how long two minutes is." Set a timer.

"But I want it *now*," wails your child. "Then you will not get it now," you respond patiently. "As soon as the timer goes ding, you get your cookie. Watch the clock."

Then, when the timer does go off, *do exactly as you promised.* And the same principle holds for other instances of delayed gratification. If you promise your child an outing at the end of the week, carry through. If you promise a basketball game together next season, put the game on your calendar. The reason many parents fail at teaching delayed gratification is simply that they don't follow through on their promises. Children come not to trust them!

(3) Teach your child to live with compromises. Compromise is an inevitable part of learning to live with other people. It doesn't necessarily mean you are lowering your standards or your goals or settling for second best. It simply means you are acknowledging the fact that you can't always have life the way you want it—a fact that every child needs to understand.

Sharing with others is a form of compromise. If children don't learn to share, anger gets out of control.

My oldest grandson had the privilege of bringing home the class pet bird the other weekend. This is an exotic, colorful bird that talks and is very friendly, and each child in Vincent's class periodically gets a turn to take it home.

As soon as Vincent got the bird home, Allen, his younger brother, naturally wanted to hold the bird. Vincent refused. Allen tried persuasion and even wailing, but to no avail.

Finally, we worked out a strategy. Since it was the teacher's intention that the bird be shared with the whole family (smart teacher), it was only right that Allen got a turn at having the bird sit on his shoulder also. So we set the kitchen timer for five minute intervals. As soon as it dinged, the bird changed shoulders.

Everyone, including grandparents who were visiting at the time, got a turn to play with the bird. And amazingly, we got through the weekend without much conflict. We were all learning to compromise—and our stress levels were much lower as a result.

Anger As a Response to Hurt

We now come to the most important and common form of anger. As the child continues to develop, he or she begins to experience anger in yet another way. First, anger is an instinctive, protective response. Then it becomes a conditioned manipulative device and a response to frustration. Eventually, it becomes *a response to symbolic hurt.*

At a certain point of development, in other words, increased cognitive sophistication enables the child to think and reflect more about what happens to him or her. Conscience is more fully developed. Shame becomes powerful as a controller of behavior. Sensitivity increases. All of this means that the child can now interpret the *meaning* of acts done to him or her. And with this sophistication comes a deeper and more painful form of anger—one that results from a feeling of hurt or injury deep within the self.

Now, this doesn't mean that the earlier forms of anger are no longer operative in the child's life. As we have indicated, instinctive anger, conditioned anger, and frustration anger can hit us at any point in life, and each must be handled positively in order to keep stress at a minimum. The majority of anger after age seven or eight, however, is anger in response to hurt.

There are many opportunities for hurt in a child's life. Other children cheat, lie, tease, or reject. Adults lecture, punish, withdraw love, or emphasize ineptness and failure. Children must learn how to deal with these hurts. And anger is a natural part of this learning process because it signals that the hurt has occurred and gives the child a chance to choose a response. If no action is necessary, the child learns to accept the hurt or set it aside.

But the child who learns to feel hurt also has the opportunity to learn some potentially unhealthy ways of handling anger, including:

- *Scapegoating,* in which the anger is displaced onto an innocent other. Children often come home from school and vent their anger on their siblings or parents—or they blame their problems on someone else. This is scapegoating.

- *Sublimating,* in which the child channels the anger in some socially acceptable direction. In sports, for example, anger can be sublimated into a "fighting spirit" and a determination to defeat someone else. Sublimation can be a healthy response to anger— but *only* if a child also is able to acknowledge the underlying anger and the hurts that caused it.

- *Passive anger,* in which the child dawdles, displays negativity, criticizes others, underachieves, pouts, manipulates, or behaves disrespectfully. Such behaviors can be "passive-aggressive" ways of venting unexpressed anger. Passive expressions of anger are never healthy.

- *Repression,* in which the anger is pushed out of consciousness. As we have seen, when anger is repressed, it is literally forgotten—yet lives on in the unconscious or in ways that the angry person doesn't recognize.

How can a parent help a child to deal with hurt anger? Here are the steps you should follow:

(1) Help your child recognize feelings of anger. Remember, the feeling of anger is an important signal that a threat is the problem; it must not be ignored. Help your child put a name to what he or she is feeling. Point out angry body language and other forms of acting out: "I notice you have an angry look on your face, and you slammed three doors on your way to your room. Are you angry about something?"

(2) Try to slow down the acting-out response. This step helps short-circuit angry behavior and gives the child a chance to calm down enough to choose a healthy response to anger. Remember, it is *anger as aggressive behavior, not anger as feeling* that has the potential for so much destruction.

How do you slow down the angry response? Teach the child to take time out before responding. And the traditional "counting to ten" may not be enough. Set a timer for several minutes if necessary. Tell the child, "First, I want you to cool down, and then we'll talk about solving the problem."

(3) Help your child discover the cause of the anger. As soon as your child has become aware of the feeling of anger and has taken time out to cool down, talk about what may be causing the anger. Explore the hurts, insults, rejections, outrages, disrespect, transgressions, or broken promises the child may have experienced.

This step is difficult for many children (and adults). Their anger may be so intense they can't think; they just want to lash out. Or they may not have developed the analytical skills they need to understand their own feelings. Discovering the violation may take a little time, therefore. Don't hurry the process. Encourage your child to *reflect* on what happened and to *talk* about why it made him or her angry.

Your child may find that just talking about the problem is enough to take care of the angry feelings. In fact, he or she may discover that there has been no actual violation—that he or she was imagining or exaggerating the hurt or that the talking itself has allowed the anger to dissipate. A lot of anger can be brought under control just by reasoning with oneself and talking the problem through.

(4) Show your child how to address the violation. Not every hurt is imagined, of course. Children get hurt when they have not harmed anyone else

and are blamed for actions they did not commit or committed by accident. *Sometimes* they will be quite justified in feeling angry. And it is at this point that you can teach your most valuable lessons about handling their hurts.

The Key to Handling Hurts

The critical question when it comes to anger, of course, is: *What do you do when you have been hurt undeservedly?*

How can you handle your anger in a way that "answers the warning" without triggering stress damage?

I can't tell you how often I consult with patients where this is the issue. It takes many forms. A wife who has just discovered that her husband is having an affair. A father who has just received a phone call from the police saying that his fifteen-year-old son has been arrested for possessing cocaine.

But it's not only adults who ask this question. Teenagers ask it also. A boy who has been jilted by his girl in favor of the school football hero, asks it. A girl whose best friend turns on her and aligns herself with a jealous competitor in a school election asks it.

And older children ask this question as well. Once they have the capacity to understand betrayal and deception, broken promises, and ingratitude, they become capable of feeling deep hurt and overwhelming anger. The hurt and the anger can be intense.

The natural impulse in response to hurt, of course, is to lash out and take revenge. Your child's natural inclination, when hurt, is to attack the person (or toy, bicycle, lawn mower, washing machine, or dog) who has hurt them. But retaliation is also the most dangerous and least effective way of resolving anger. Unfortunately, it is also a time-honored response. History is full of anger that has gotten out of control and turned into revenge. Gang warfare, vigilante groups, lynching mobs, family feuds, and lifelong hatred are all manifestations of undeserved hurt and uncontrollable anger.

What must one do to be free of it? What can we teach our children about handling anger that will bring them wholeness rather than stress, hatred, and self-destruction?

The Revised English Bible translates Romans 12:17–19 in a way that makes very clear what the ideal should be:

> Never pay back evil for evil. Let your aims be such as all count honourable. If possible, so far as it lies with you, live at peace with all. My dear friends, do not seek revenge, but leave a place for divine retribution.

This advice makes clear psychological sense because revenge *always* hurts the one who seeks it more than it hurts the one to whom it is directed. A simple study of human history shows this is true. A vengeful spirit leads to bitterness, ongoing anger, and a cycle of retribution. Vengeful people are never happy people—and they are usually unhealthy people as well.

But if revenge doesn't work, what is the best approach to redressing a wrong that has been done to us?

You will recall that I earlier quoted Ephesians 4:26, which encourages us to "Be angry but sin not." The same chapter goes on to say:

> Have done with all spite and bad temper, with rage, insults and slander, with evil of any kind. Be generous to one another, tender-hearted, forgiving one another as God in Christ forgave you."[7]

Can any advice be clearer? Or more healthful? *Forgiveness* is the antidote for revenge. Forgiveness is also the key to handling hurts. In most cases, forgiveness is the only dependable path to healing.

Forgive—and Then What?

What is forgiveness? It is not a feeling, but an action of the will—a voluntary surrendering of your right to hurt back. Forgiveness is saying to yourself, "I don't know what I have done to deserve this hurt or even if I do deserve it, but I choose to forgive the one who has hurt me because I know it is the only way for me to let go of the hurt."

Obviously, forgiveness isn't easy, and it won't be easy for your child. Forgiveness takes courage, and it may need to be an ongoing process. Sometimes the decision to forgive must be made several times for the same hurt, because memories of the incident may trigger more anger. Explain this to your child, and offer him or her support and encouragement. Try to model forgiveness in your own life, and share stories of your own hurts that were healed by forgiveness.

If the child is old enough, help your child to write out a "Bill of Forgiveness" to make the forgiveness process more concrete. It can say:

> I (my name) hereby totally forgive (other's name) for what he/she has done to me. I cannot change what has happened but I will do my best not to hurt back.
>
> Signed   _____

Once the forgiving has been done, several further steps may be in order. *Confronting* the offender—either to ask him or her to stop the hurtful action or to correct a misunderstanding—may be appropriate. This, too, can be difficult, and your child will need a lot of encouragement and support

Teaching Your Child to Handle Anger

These seven helpful principles will help you raise a child who is peaceful instead of angry:

1. *Teach your child to deal with each hurt as it arises.* Allowing hurts to accumulate makes them seem overwhelming—a mountain of hurts that cannot be moved.

2. *Teach your child to take responsibility for his or her own anger.* Your child's anger belongs to him or her; no one else is "making" him or her angry. The anger may or may not be appropriate, but it exists, and it must be reckoned with.

3. *Teach your child to allow other people to have feelings also.* Anger is seldom one-sided. Others have a right to feel angry also. Help your child see *both sides* of the conflict: "If someone has hurt you, it's possible that it's because you have hurt that person yourself."

4. *Listen, receive, and accept your child's anger.* Talking about anger helps to pinpoint its source and also may diffuse some of its intensity. Once your child is aware of where the anger came from, encourage him or her to let the anger go and focus on dealing with the cause of the hurt.

5. *Show your child how to forgive.* Explain why revenge is dangerous. Remind your child of what he or she would want if he or she were in the other person's shoes. And model forgiveness yourself.

6. *Where appropriate, show your child how to face up to the person who is doing the hurting.* This isn't always appropriate or even possible. The person may be too manipulative or reactive, and may even have moved away. But where possible, encourage and support your child in "facing up to the enemy."

7. *Teach your child to seek reconciliation above self-justification.* Reconciliation restores broken relationships. If your child can learn to forgive and be reconciled to those who cause hurt, he or she will have no problem dealing with life's major hurts.

from you in learning how to confront without being aggressive. Helping your child plan a strategy for confronting and rehearsing what to say and do can help build confidence and courage.

Reconciliation, too, can follow forgiveness. Hurt and anger can push apart close friends and family members. A rift in such relationships can cause ongoing pain, but reconciliation restores relationships so that love can continue.

To teach reconciliation, wait till the feelings of anger have subsided. Wait until you feel your child has forgiven as best as he or she can. Then suggest a meeting with the offender and some ideas for initiating reconciliation:

- "May we talk about what happened last night?"
- "May I tell you what I thought you said?"
- "May we be friends again?"

Such an initiative, like forgiveness and confrontation, takes courage. But the rewards are usually so satisfying that your child will probably be encouraged to try it again in future situations.

Confrontation and reconciliation can be powerful tools for dealing with hurt. Without forgiveness, however, even positive confrontation is likely to lead only to a continuation of conflict, and reconciliation will be impossible. Forgiveness, then, is the key to handling anger effectively.

Place a high value on forgiveness in your whole family. Model it for your children, and teach them how to use it as an antidote to anger. If you do, you will be giving your children a great gift.

Summary

Anger is a major cause of stress and can be the primary factor in causing early heart disease because hostility, in all its forms, stimulates adrenaline flooding. However, it is important to distinguish between the *feeling* of anger and aggressive *behavior*. Anger as a feeling should be accepted and talked about. Anger as a behavior should be controlled. Then, attention should be given to addressing the underlying cause of the anger. Anger can be an instinctive response, a conditioned or "useful" response, a response to frustration, and a response to hurt. In any of these situations, parents can help their children handle their anger in a healthy way. And the most effective means to this end is modeling. Parents who serve as models of control, understanding, and forgiveness give their children a great gift.

Parents should pay careful attention to how they can reduce the problems that underlie angry and aggressive behavior. These include feelings of being unloved, humiliated, and shamed. Since forgiveness is the only antidote for undeserved hurt, children need to know how and when to forgive. The most effective way for teaching forgiveness is to model it yourself.

Discussion Questions

1. What instinctive needs are the basis for human anger?

2. A child who is overly angry is also at greater risk both physically and psychologically. Discuss some of the ways that anger can hurt a child.

3. The link between anger and adrenaline is a crucial one. What does anger do to our adrenaline levels, and why is this important for our survival? What can go wrong?

4. The message of this chapter is clear: Anger should be brought under control. What are some practical ways you can teach your children to do this?

13

Unspoiling
the Spoiled Child

All across America, in affluent households or in those not so affluent, parents have one thing in common: They worry about whether or not they spoil their children. And they ought to worry. As a culture, we probably spoil our children more than any people on earth.

Children come into the world demanding very little: warmth, nutrition, security, and love. It's not much, really. But by the time they get to three or four years of age, many children have come to believe they are entitled to a lot more.

This is the essence of "spoiling." Children come to believe that they are entitled to whatever their heart desires. It can be a major source of stress for both parents and children.

Let me tell you about Tim, whose parents recently brought him to see me. Tim is fourteen now—a little overweight, and very obnoxious. When the family has visitors, Tim brings out his portable video game, plugs in a cartridge, and dominates the atmosphere with his antics and comments. He speaks to adults as if they were his buddies, but he treats them the way he treats other children; he plays the role of the big bully and tease.

Tim's parents don't like what they see, but they're baffled.

"We give him everything; we can't understand why Timmy's grades are so poor or why he has no friends."

"It seems the more we give him, the more he wants. He doesn't seem to appreciate anything and tires within minutes of everything from games to outings."

"I've tried and tried to get him to help around the house. I've even offered to pay him, but he says he's entitled to everything anyway, so why should he work? We really can't afford therapy, but he's our only son and we want to give him the best. What have we done wrong?"

How can I break it to them gently? Should I just tell them straight out: "You've spoiled your son. You've failed to teach him how important work is and how to value what he's got"?

I tend to be rather directive as a therapist, and I believe that people are a lot more robust than they make out to be. I know they're trying to be the best parents possible. So I spell it out as clearly and honestly as possible:

"We all love our children very much and desire to give them the very best. We work hard to be able to give them a better start in life than most of us had. We want them to have all the right experiences and opportunities, and we feel anxious whenever we sense that they are being deprived. But there is a bigger mistake than not giving them enough. It is *giving them too much.*"

I then go on to show the parents how they have been denying themselves so their son could have more. They have dutifully deprived themselves of even minor pleasures so their child could be happy. The result? They've lost both ways. They are unhappy, and their son doesn't appreciate what they give him. With the best of intentions, they have created a monster.

Spoiling Causes Stress

But where does stress come into all of this? Tim gets everything he desires. His selfish whims are always being satisfied. He never goes without anything he needs. He doesn't seem to be overstressed—or does he? But Tim is experiencing stress nevertheless.

Being spoiled is stressful for children for several reasons:

(1) *Because spoiled children expect their whims to be satisfied, they never build a tolerance for frustration* nor learn to delay gratification. As a result, they are angry a lot of the time.

(2) *Spoiled children rarely feel fulfilled.* Any sense of satisfaction they may enjoy is momentary and comes from the temporary pleasure of getting what they want. But spoiled children aren't able to experience the real satisfaction of achieving something they've worked for or receiving something they've waited for.

(3) *Spoiled children become dependent on gifts as tangible proof that they are loved.* They never learn the meaning of real love. When life gets hard and they can no longer depend on doting parents to prove their love to them, they discover that a huge void remains unfilled.

(4) *Spoiled children do not live harmoniously with other children.* They become selfish, self-centered, and self-indulgent. Consequently, they are disliked and rejected and become very lonely people.

(5) *Spoiled children are ill prepared to handle stress.* Like the tree protected from the wind, spoiled children put down no roots. They stay near the surface and never develop a strong and stable foundation. And when the storms of real life do come, these trees topple easily.

(6) *The families of spoiled children don't develop real cohesiveness.* Children compete with each other to see who can get the most. There is little sharing and much fighting. Family members don't learn how to support each other through troubled times. As we have seen, stress is far more damaging to children when there is no family cohesiveness.

(7) *Spoiled children live in an "unreal" world.* Spoiling parents create a home environment that is far removed from the real world. Children who grow up comfortably suffer a rude awakening when they leave home. They find they don't have the maturity to deal with real life problems and consequently suffer significant stress.

It is possible to be generous to your child without raising a spoiled—and stressed out—child. All it takes is some careful thought about what you are doing and the courage to be firm with your children. If you really care for your children, you will do what is necessary to raise them unspoiled.

Do You Spoil Your Child?

Many parents spoil their children to some extent, at least in our culture. And spoiling is not just for the wealthy. You don't have to be well off to give your children more than is good for them.

One woman I know, a widow, sacrifices a large part of her tiny pension to indulge her twenty-four-year-old son. She doesn't need to; he is perfectly capable of supporting himself. If she stopped supporting him, he would be forced to get a regular job. He would gain independence and self-esteem, and she would be able to do more for herself. But I have yet to convince her that what she is doing is bad for them both.

Spoiling can be very selective. In some families I know, one child is singled out for spoiling while others are not. Quite often the youngest child is spoiled more. He or she gets special privileges and is not disciplined as the others are. This often occurs when the parents are older and there is a large gap between the youngest and the next youngest child. The feeling that this is "our last child" softens their thinking. Other siblings resent the spoiling—and the spoiled young child is not necessarily the better for it.

Stress Test 8 is designed to help you understand how you treat your children and to alert you to possible spoiling of one or all of them. I could

Stress Test 8: Do You Spoil Your Child?

Child's name _____

Read each question carefully and then place a check in either the yes or no column. If you are in some doubt about how to answer the question, talk it over with your spouse. Try to be absolutely honest.

	Yes	No
1. Do you believe you must help your children keep up with their friends?	___	___
2. Do you sacrifice personal comforts such as food, clothes, and outings, so that your children do not have to go without?	___	___
3. Were your parents very strict, so that you find yourself being lenient with your own children to compensate?	___	___
4. Do you find it easier to give in to your child's demands than to refuse them?	___	___
5. Whenever your child asks you for something, do you find you feel guilty if you refuse?	___	___
6. Do you often feel angry about how much your child demands of you?	___	___
7. Do you call your child's attention to the latest in toys or fashion so that they can want something new?	___	___
8. Are there times when you succumb to your child's demands against your better judgment because your child says, "But everybody has one" or "Everybody does it"?	___	___
9. Do you take your child with you everywhere—to the theater, restaurant, or movies?	___	___
10. Does your child have boxes full of gadgets or toys that he or she never uses or plays with?	___	___
11. Does your child lack a sense of the worth of things or of the value of money?	___	___
12. Does your child have the expectation that you will give him or her everything requested?	___	___
13. Does your child throw temper tantrums or sulk when not getting his or her own way?	___	___
14. Does your child show an obvious disregard for the value of your belongings or the belongings of others?	___	___
15. Do you often throw or give away clothes, toys, shoes, or children's gadgets that have barely been used?	___	___

Total Score _____

Test Interpretation

Add up the total number of "yes" answers. There ought to be a few of them; no parent is perfect. But the more "yes" answers you give, the more you are likely to be a spoiling parent. The following interpretation can be made of your score:

0–3	You are quite normal as a parent. Occasionally you indulge your child, but never to the point of excess.
4–6	You are a bit of a spoiler. You may occasionally see some spoiled behavior and should be a little cautious. Make sure you temper your generosity with instruction about the value of things and the benefit of sometimes doing without.
7–9	You probably spoil your child, but perhaps not too seriously. Be careful, though. If your child is taking advantage of you there will be serious repercussions.
Over 10	You have a serious problem with spoiling. Sit down and take stock of your situation. Plan a strategy for change.

---

have devised a test to measure how spoiled your child is, but I think your first focus ought to be on what you are doing, not what your child is doing.

Once you have completed the test, review it with your child if he or she is old enough. See whether your perception of yourself agrees with your child's. You might be quite surprised by your child's insights here. Children are a lot smarter than we give them credit for. They often know perfectly well what you are doing to them—even though they may not want you to change.

One mother was teasing her six-year-old child who had threatened to run away from home because of some dispute. "What would you use for money?" she asked him.

"I've got money in my drawer. I'd just take that."

"Oh yeah?" she replied. "And how long do you think that will last you?"

Her son responded quite insightfully. "A lot longer than you think it will. I wouldn't spend it like you spend your money on me."

Case closed! Mother went away a lot wiser.

Once you have examined your own behavior, *then* you might want to look to your child's behavior for signs of spoiling. Here are several signs to look for:

- Spoiled children neglect their toys, stereos, bikes, and other expensive objects.
- Spoiled children mistreat valuable objects.
- Spoiled children demand only the best in clothes and toys, just for the sake of spending more or for the status.

- Spoiled children don't show appreciation for what they have.

- Spoiled children refuse to work or make any effort of their own to earn a desired object or some extra money.

- Even though they never use it for themselves, spoiled children refuse to lend a personal object to someone else.

- Spoiled children quickly become bored, show little interest in activities, and persist in keeping up with the latest fad.

- Spoiled children expect to be treated or given a gift whenever they are taken to a store.

- Spoiled children are constantly searching for new stimulation and have a basic discontentment with their lives.

Spoiling versus Indulging

Some experts make a distinction between *indulging* a child and *spoiling* a child.[1]

A *spoiled child* is defined as one who is excessively self-centered, immature, manipulative, inconsiderate of others, prone to temper outbursts, and generally unpleasant to be around. This bratty behavior results from parents who fail to set and enforce boundaries for acceptable behavior.

An *indulged child*, on the other hand, may be showered with parental affection and attention, but is generally well-behaved. Boundaries are clear. Gifts are carefully chosen for their appropriateness, and privileges are often earned. Obedience is valued. Such a child is high on a parent's priority list—but not spoiled. Indulging, then, has a positive connotation.

This may be a useful distinction—although the boundary between indulging and spoiling is difficult for most parents to observe. We know, for instance, that picking up a crying infant doesn't spoil him; it simply provides the comfort and security the child needs. After four or five months, however, crying can turn into an unreasonable demand for attention.

I can see this possibility clearly in the case of my little granddaughter. It is so easy to respond to her every cry by picking her up. Fortunately, my daughter (the mother) knows this and has learned not to rush forward and pick up her child every time she cries. She can tell the difference between different types of cries. She responds to some—and ignores others.

It is this selective responding that makes the difference between indulging a child (which can be healthy) and spoiling a child (which is never healthy). Indulging a child focuses more on giving love than lavishing possessions, more on giving attention than things, more on responding to the child's real needs than on jumping to every call.

By all means, indulge your children if you can. Give them what they need to grow up healthy and happy—and enjoy giving them extras. But keep your eyes on the boundary between indulgence and spoiling. If you concentrate on developing their characters as well as their creativity, their integrity as well as their intelligence, and their ability to wait and work for what they want as well as their ability to enjoy the good things that have been given to them, you will be in little danger of spoiling them.

Why Parents Spoil

Parents spoil their children by giving too much and by giving in to too many demands. They reinforce the idea that power resides with the child, not the parent. They help a child internalize messages like: "I can have whatever I want. I don't have to listen to anybody or show any respect to others. I can be selfish and everyone is there to serve my needs." Such a child is headed for a stressful life; he or she is also guaranteed to make life miserable for others.

Parents, especially, suffer when their children are spoiled. When the Duke of Windsor (the former king of England who married an American divorcée and stepped down from the throne) visited the United States in the 1940s, he is rumored to have remarked, "The thing that impresses me most about America is the way parents obey their children." This is no idle gibe. Fifty years later, it is still a valid comment.

Parents also lose because spoiled children make home life miserable for those who do the spoiling. No one is happy around such a child. The stress is not confined to the spoiled child; it plagues brothers, sisters, Mom, Dad, and everyone else.

With all this at stake, why do parents persist in spoiling children? Here are some common reasons:

(1) *They want to avoid confrontation.* Many parents give in too easily to their children's demands in order to avoid unpleasant fights. Parents fear their child's anger, or, more importantly, their child's rejection. To many parents, "I hate you" is the most dreaded phrase that can come out of a child's mouth. But such an outburst should be welcomed, not feared; it means you are doing your job. It means you have a spine!

(2) *They want to appease their guilt.* Parents feel guilty about many things—not giving enough time to their kids, not providing the best education, or not living in the best neighborhood. To compensate, they give their children material things. The same guilt makes them permissive and lax in discipline. Sadly, many of these children, in later life, will resent having been "bought off" by gifts or allowed so much freedom.

(3) They want to punish someone else. In our world of broken homes and absent parents, spoiling can also be a way of taking revenge on or proving superiority over someone else.

A divorced father may overindulge his son on a visit over the summer. "You see how good I am, son," he says in effect as he spoils his child. "I'm not the terrible person your mother makes me out to be. Don't forget to rub it in when you get home."

A good father? No way! He is sacrificing his son's welfare to prove his own worth and to punish his ex-wife. When his son returns to his regular home, his values will have been compromised, his discipline undermined, and his expectations raised for all sorts of goodies. His mother will then be seen to be the "bad guy." But at whose expense? Who is the real loser here? The son, of course.

(4) They want to manipulate others. "Selective" spoiling—spoiling one child and not others—can be a form of manipulation or control in a family. A mother may give things to one child, for instance, in order to manipulate another child into complying with her wishes. Or the giving may be an attempt to manipulate the child who is being spoiled. Unfortunately, the result is more often a child who is in control of parents, not the other way around.

"Unspoiling" Your Child

If your self-examination has shown that, for whatever reason, you have been spoiling your child, take heart. Your life does not have to be run by selfish, overindulged, inconsiderate offspring. It is *never* too late to "unspoil" your child.

How? Start by accepting that you cannot change your child overnight. There is no pill to take away a demanding attitude nor any magic formula that will change your child's obnoxious behavior. But you can make changes by persistently implementing healthier parenting practices.

Keep reminding yourself that *you*—not your child—are in control. *You* call the shots. *You* make up the rules. Strengthen your conviction that you, and only you, determine what is to be given, permitted, or tolerated; that's part of your responsibility as a parent. If you play helpless here, you are doomed. If you need assistance in getting over your helplessness, then see a therapist. When you do what is healthy for yourself, you *also* do what is healthy for your child.

Once you have determined to be in charge, then apply the following principles as appropriate to your situation:

(1) Make a list of the things you do that spoil your child. Consult friends, neighbors, relatives, your spouse, and even the other children in the family—and *listen* to what they have to say. Be honest with yourself. Be self-critical. Compile as complete a list as you can.

(2) Make a list of your fears about your child. What do you fear will happen if you do not give in to your child's demands? Do you fear his anger? Are you afraid of her depressed moods? Do you think your child will become a dropout—or stop loving you? Examine and evaluate each of these fears carefully. You will discover that many of them are irrational—and many more have become overblown. So try to become more objective about your fears. Talk them over with a friend, pastor, or therapist. Weigh your realistic fears against the negative effects of spoiling and the long-term benefits of raising an unspoiled child. Then determine to risk letting some of your fears come true in the interest of unspoiling your child. This may mean putting up with some pouting or anger, but in the long run your child will be healthier.

(3) Talk over both your spoiling behavior and your fears with your child, if he or she is old enough. Before you start changing your approach, explain clearly *what* you plan to do and *why* you want to do it. Your child may object, may even kick, scream, pout, and give you a classic temper tantrum (the adolescent equivalent is screaming, or the "silent treatment"), but you should just take the mature approach—ignore your child's misbehavior. Insist that you plan to follow through on "unspoiling."

(4) Now, begin to make your changes. Give fewer "things." Set up clear conditions by which certain privileges can be earned. Never, however, expect your child to earn his or her basic keep or to pay for your love and respect by doing chores. Every child is entitled to life's absolute basics (food, clothing, a place to live, an education, and respect) *without* having to earn it. But vacations, a car, designer clothes, special trips, or even pocket money beyond that needed for basic needs should be considered as privileges, not rights, and should be earned by the child if possible.

(5) Refrain from just giving everything asked for. Weigh every request. Examine its necessity and appropriateness. Ask, "Is this a privilege my child should earn?" Getting too much for too little effort never builds motivation and creativity.

Ask your child, "What do you think would be a fair exchange? What would you be willing to do to earn it?"

"But Mom, you can afford it. Why should I have to earn it?"

"Because you will value it more!"

Sign a contract, if necessary, so that there can be no arguments afterward about what was agreed. Then be absolutely consistent in enforcing the contract.

(6) Hold your child personally accountable for his or her actions. Many "spoiler" parents will make excuses, bargain, and even lie to get their children out of trouble. Unfortunately, these children never develop self-discipline. Instead, they come to believe that they will always be rescued, whatever

trouble they are in. Such children become consistent rule breakers who believe they have the power to "fix" any personal problems through manipulation.

The parent who runs interference for a child tampers with that child's normal development. It is far better for your child to take responsibility and suffer the consequences of his or her behavior, while this behavior is still petty and the consequences minor, than to be rescued from the minor misdemeanor and later "nailed" for some major misbehavior. Consistent discipline—seeing that the child *always* suffers the consequence of his or her misbehaviors—is essential to teaching respect for real-world boundaries and helping the child learn greater self-control.

Children Don't Spoil Themselves

It is not a lifestyle of relative affluence that breeds spoiled children who are selfish, unappreciative, and immature. Spoiling is a question of *how* parents respond to the demands and manipulations of their children and *why* they flood them with more goods and gifts than they can appreciate.

Or, to put it more straightforwardly, spoiled children are not born, but created. Parents spoil children; children don't spoil themselves.

This is an important point to remember, as you examine your parenting style. You are your child's most important teacher. Your children not only learn what you teach them, but what you show them. Your values, your faith, your reactions, your patience, and your coping are models they will one day emulate.

But spoiling a child undermines this learning process. In fact, spoiled children have no incentive for learning anything that builds character. Instead, they come to expect the good things of life to be delivered on a platter. They expect instant success and have no emotional tolls for receiving disappointments and failures constructively.

So, start asking yourself: "Is it better for me *not* to give my kids everything they want? Can I be mature and selective enough to only give my children material things that will foster maturity and accountability?" Your answers, and actions, can make the difference between spoiling and not spoiling your children.

If you continue to overindulge your children, you may discover that in adulthood they still depend on your generosity and are unable to make it in the real world. But if you examine your motives and behavior and set limits on your indulgences, both you and your child can enjoy a more stress-free life.

Summary

Spoiling children means giving them everything they want and therefore making them believe they are entitled to have every whim satisfied. Spoiling is stressful for children because it sets them up for frustration and ill equips them to live in the real world. And spoiling is stressful for parents and other family members because a spoiled child is a selfish, inconsiderate, demanding tyrant.

Spoiling a child is not the same thing as indulging a child. A parent can give freely of both love and possessions without spoiling the child if the parent also sets limits and does not give in to the child's every demand.

Parents spoil children for a number of reasons—to avoid confrontation, appease guilt, punish someone else, or manipulate others. Whatever the reason, spoiling harms both parent and child. But a child can be "unspoiled" if the parent is willing to make changes in his or her parenting style. Unspoiling a child involves learning to be lavish with love and respect but thoughtful and firm in dispensing gifts and privileges. If carried out consistently, the unspoiling process can result in a better life for both children and parents.

Discussion Questions

1. Discuss the differences between "spoiling" a child and "indulging" a child. How can you remind yourself of the differences in the heat of battle?

2. Recall your own childhood. To what extent were you spoiled, and how does this influence how you treat your children?

3. If you find you are guilty of spoiling your child, plan an "unspoiling" strategy. List the changes you can make in how you respond to your child's demands and describe how you will implement these changes.

14

Reassuring
the Worried Child

As I was preparing this chapter we suffered a major earthquake in Los Angeles. The whole city shook and rolled; it was terrifying. And this was the second bad earthquake in just a few years. Everyone is jittery as a result.

This past Sunday afternoon, while my two grandsons were visiting with my wife and me, a major aftershock jolted our area. My young grandsons froze; I could see fear in their eyes. So I responded by turning the whole experience into a game. "Who'll be the first one under the dining room table?" I called out. We all laughed and raced for the questionable safety of the rather shaky table which was to serve as our shelter.

When the shake was over my oldest grandson looked worried. "Will there be another one?" he asked nervously. "No, I think it's all over," I replied, "but if it shakes again I'll race you to the dining table—and I'll beat you this time."

We laughed and the tension subsided. But as I reflected on childhood I realized that today's children face a lot of worry and anxiety. I don't just mean earthquakes or natural disasters, although there is hardly a place on earth where one can live without some natural risk. But even if hurricanes, volcanoes, floods, or earthquakes are not a problem, then gang warfare, crimes against children, war or ecological disaster threaten.

Nowhere is safe, it seems. And since we can now see every threat or disaster anywhere in the world as it happens in vivid color on our televisions, children are being exposed more and more to the frightening reality of life on this planet. At an early age they see natural disasters on the news, terrifying violence in TV movies, gruesome murders on "true detective" shows, and family violence on regular drama series. You don't have to live in Los Angeles to feel afraid of earthquakes; you can experience the fear right there in your living room.

It is not surprising, then, that some children become worrywarts. Sadly, this seems to be happening more and more in our culture. More children seem to be anxious, insecure, and worry-prone than ever before. Instead of becoming desensitized by their repeated exposure to threats, these children seem to be experiencing increased sensitivity. We are finding, for instance, that more children cannot tolerate dark bedrooms; parents must provide nightlights to allay anxiety. And more of them are reporting symptoms of elevated anxiety—headaches, gastric problems (even ulcers at an early age), general fatigue, and unhappiness.

In many ways, today's world is a worrisome place for children. Fortunately, however, there is a lot a parent can do to reduce a child's worry, fear, and anxiety. In this chapter I want to examine the most common types of childhood worry and suggest some practical strategies for helping your child handle his or her worries with a minimum of stress.

Worry Breeds Worry

In this chapter, I use the terms *worry*, *anxiety*, and *fear* more or less interchangeably. But it might be helpful at the outset to distinguish between these three closely related emotions.

Fear is an emotional response to a specific threat—the body's signal to flee the danger. Like anger, it serves an important purpose but can be unhealthy if allowed to continue for too long. *Anxiety* is a more pervasive, less specific response—an unfocused sense of foreboding that can be caused by prolonged stress. Anxiety can serve a constructive purpose—prompting us to take action to relieve the anxiety. But anxiety can also become chronic and crippling. (For a more complete discussion of anxiety, see my book, *Overcoming Anxiety*.[1]) *Worry* is a form of anxiety that involves continuous thinking about a stressful subject; worry involves thought patterns as well as emotions. Because worry builds on itself and distracts us from problem solving, worry is almost never healthy.

Children must be helped, from an early age, to learn to cope effectively with fear, anxiety, and worry. Why is this so important? Primarily because most anxiety problems have their roots in childhood fears. If coping skills are not learned early, they are difficult to acquire later. And if the experience of childhood is intensely fearful or anxious, normal coping skills will not be sufficient to build a healthy, happy, and stress-free adult life.

The damaging effects of intense anxiety in childhood may be so great that the person requires a lot of remedial therapy for much of his or her adult life.

Unchecked worry and anxiety in childhood can be very damaging in a developmental sense. After all, the first requisite of maturity is the ability to see oneself and one's world objectively and to make the best of life's realities. Worry, which is fueled by imagination, tends to distort reality and thus hinders the maturing process. Anxiety also may hinder the development of self-confidence by undermining the child's efforts to feel good about him or herself.

Furthermore, anxiety tends to breed *more* anxiety. Worry is not only self-perpetuating, but self-escalating. And the stress that follows creates *more* anxiety, which in turn causes more stress.

Say, for instance, that nine-year-old Mark grows anxious and fearful after watching a terrifying murder mystery on TV. Then his mother asks him to take the garbage out to the curb. As Mark steps out into the dark alone, he will be more prone to jump at the slightest sound. His imagination will feed on the shadows and dark corners. His ears will be more sensitive to the softest of sounds, and his reflexes will be super-quick. If there is an unexpected movement or sound, his fear may well cause him to panic, crippling his reasoning or other abilities to cope with the unknown threats.

The movie was the initial source of Marc's anxiety, but his fear made his alarm system more alert—and the increased state of arousal caused even more fear. Anxiety, therefore, can be a vicious cycle that is sometimes difficult to break.

Finally, the emotions of anxiety, worry, and fear are closely connected to stress. Worry anxiety can be a major cause of overstress, not only because it creates its own stress problems but because it diminishes a child's capacity to cope with the normal stressors of life. When you spend all your energy fighting imaginary foes, you don't have much left to fight real ones.

As we saw in the above example, worry, like anger, triggers the body's emergency response and the resulting stress symptoms. Remember also that ongoing stress can trigger anxiety by depleting the brain's natural tranquilizers. This in turn leads to more worry, and the cycle continues. And all this is even more reason that parents should be alert to signs of worry and anxiety in their children and do all they can to help the children learn to cope.

Stress Test 9 will give you an idea of whether anxiety is a problem for your child. If this test indicates that he or she is becoming a worrier, don't hesitate to take action. This chapter will suggest some helpful strategies for coping with minor forms of worry, but don't hesitate to seek professional help if worry seems to be an acute or ongoing problem. Your child's growing years are too important to be clouded and distorted by worry and anxiety.

Anxiety and Childhood Development

All children experience some fear, worry, and anxiety as part of learning to relate to the world around them. Like anger, however, anxiety is experienced differently by children at different developmental levels. In the next few pages, I want to look at the major anxiety issues of early childhood, middle childhood, and adolescence and suggest some ways parents can prevent the normal worry and anxiety of growing up from becoming a more serious problem.

One caution before we start. In discussing these various anxiety difficulties, I will use rather extreme examples. This helps bring the major causes and effects into sharper focus. Many children, however, will display much milder—and less crippling—forms of the same problems. These children typically respond quite well to parental intervention.

Separation Anxiety: The Earliest Source of Worry

William, who just turned five, suffers from multiple anxiety-related problems. He has many fears—of strangers, of certain types of animals, and even of some colors. He wakes up at least once a week screaming because of nightmares. When his mother tried to enroll him in kindergarten, he became so upset that the teacher arranged for her to stay in the classroom for the first few days. Two weeks later William had to be withdrawn from kindergarten because his mother could not leave him even for a few minutes. Later, when she tried to enroll him in the first grade, William went through the same trauma. The mother had to teach him at home while she sought assistance from the local community clinic.

William suffers from an acute case of *separation anxiety*, which involves intense fears of being abandoned by parents. Separation anxiety is the first major cause of anxiety in the child. Other worry habits will develop later from this root problem.

In William's case, the problems started when he had to be hospitalized for several weeks as a toddler. The prolonged separation from his parents set him up to respond with acute anxiety to any further separation.

This is not unusual in young children—although William's symptoms are especially severe. Any prolonged separation from parents—especially the mother—before the age of five can have a pronounced impact on children. Typically, they first respond to separation by crying and screaming, then they generally withdraw into despair and detachment. After reuniting with the parents, they often become sensitized to and extremely afraid of further separation.

In extreme cases such as William's, these children may develop a *separation anxiety disorder*. They become preoccupied with morbid fears about

Stress Test 9: Is Your Child Very Anxious?

Child's name _____

This questionnaire is designed to measure your child's general level of anxiety. Score each item according to the following scale:

0 = My child never or rarely experiences this.
1 = My child occasionally experiences this, but never complains that it is a problem.
2 = My child often often experiences this and it bothers him or her a little.
3 = Most of the time my child experiences this.

		Rating
1.	My child has dizzy spells.	_____
2.	My child's stomach feels tied up in knots.	_____
3.	My child feels nauseous.	_____
4.	At times my child cannot breathe normally or must go to the window to get air.	_____
5.	My child is afraid of heights or closed places.	_____
6.	My child cannot stay alone for long.	_____
7.	My child cannot go far away from home.	_____
8.	My child has difficulty going to sleep.	_____
9.	My child wakes up early and cannot go back to sleep.	_____
10.	My child fidgets and is restless a lot of the time.	_____
11.	My child doesn't feel confident and is afraid of the future.	_____
12.	My child is afraid of dying.	_____
13.	My child's thoughts run wild and cannot be controlled.	_____
14.	My child experiences spells of panic or terror.	_____
15.	My child avoids large crowds or public places.	_____
16.	My child seems to be having heart pains at times.	_____
17.	My child's insides feel shaky or nervous.	_____
18.	My child has to use tranquilizers or antidepressants to get through the day.	_____
19.	My child reports strange sensations in the body or skin.	_____
20.	My child has difficulty relaxing or doing nothing.	_____

Total Score _____

Test Interpretation

As you can see, the higher the score, the higher will be your child's experience of anxiety. The highest your child can score is 60, and the lowest is 0. In my opinion, no one should score zero on this test; only the dead are free of all anxiety!

The following ranges of response for the total score can generally be accepted:

   0 – 12   A very low anxiety score
  13 – 20   You child's anxiety score is mildly elevated.
  21 – 30   Your child's anxiety score is moderately elevated.
  Over 30   Your child's anxiety score is severely elevated. You need to seek immediate help for him or her—and the sooner the better. Severe anxiety problems, when left untreated, can impair a child's development and even incapacitate him or her as an adult.

---

accidents or illness befalling their parents, themselves, or others to whom they are attached. They fear getting lost and never being able to return to their home. They react violently to traveling away from home or familiar places and may refuse to sleep over at a friend's house, go on errands, or attend camp. They find it difficult to stay in a room alone, and they often display clinging or "shadowing" behavior.

Physical problems accompanying separation-anxiety disorder include stomachaches, headaches, nausea, vomiting, palpitations, dizziness, and faintness—all symptoms of severe stress. Fears and phobias are also common, including fears of animals, monsters, people, and places. Exaggerated fears of burglars, kidnappers, car accidents, or plane travel and even concerns about dying are quite common.

Does it only take the prolonged separation of months of hospitalization or the trauma of being forcibly separated from a mother due to divorce to create such a disorder? Not necessarily. Whether separation causes major anxiety problems for a child depends on several factors:

(1) *Children differ in their sensitivity to separation.* Some children are quite independent from an early age. They don't notice whether you're there or not. They do their own thing. Minor (and even some major) separations may not please them, but they tolerate them well.

Other children are naturally more sensitive. Even as tiny infants, these children notice everything; their little eyes watch every movement in the room. Let Mother or Father leave the room, and all hell breaks loose. Parents may think these sensitive little souls are asleep with the babysitter, but just start the car and listen to the ruckus! Such a child can become separation-sensitive even when the separation is brief.

(2) Parents differ as well. Even a less-sensitive child may be pushed by a parent to the point of anxiety. An extreme case would be where a parent is an alcoholic. Alcoholics tend to be insensitive to the anxiety they create in children.

Stephanie grew up in a home with an alcoholic father. She was a robust girl who could fend for herself, even from her earliest years. She didn't cry easily or fall apart over petty squabbles.

But, strong as Stephanie was, her father's drinking caused her a lot of separation anxiety. He always drank "with the boys," which means he was gone a lot, and she never knew where he was. Her mother would become quite agitated after about nine in the evening if Stephanie's father hadn't come home. When he was late, he was usually drunk—and that meant a fight. Poor Stephanie would also worry. She also prayed a lot, "Please, God, help Daddy to come home early so he won't get drunk." This only heightened the anxiety and fed her fears.

Stephanie's primary fear was that her mother would leave and abandon her to the father. The idea of being separated from the only stable person in her life was extremely frightening to her. Her other fear was that her father would leave and abandon both her and her mother. Under the burden of these worries, Stephanie developed an acute anxiety problem. Who wouldn't?

(3) Circumstances also differ. While some forms of separation are unavoidable, including prolonged illness or the death of the parents, many forms *can* be avoided if parents are intentional about their lives. Of the ten million children in the United States who lose a parent, for instance, most lose the parent through separation and divorce, not death[2]—and divorce is a major causative force in the development of separation anxiety in young children. Caring parents, even if their marriage is not working out, can usually manage to delay separating until their child is past the critical age for developing a separation anxiety problem. If separation is inevitable, special provision should be made to allay separation anxiety.

A poor parent-child relationship can also be a factor in separation anxiety. If a parent is cold, unresponsive, and distant, or if a baby turns out to be cranky and difficult to manage, a parent may unwittingly withdraw from the child. Cuddling becomes infrequent. For the infant this is no different to being separated physically. Anxiety will almost certainly be a consequence.

Generalized Anxiety: Worry in Older Children

While separation anxiety appears to be the earliest form of childhood anxiety, later childhood (say from four years of age to about nine or ten) is a rich and fertile soil for an anxiety problem called "generalized anxiety disorder." This problem is characterized by a long-standing anxiety, worry, and apprehensiveness which is not attached to any particular threat. The anxiety is pervasive and "free floating"—that is, it can attach itself to almost anything. A child with generalized anxiety is the true "worrywart."

At ten years of age, Denise is quite bright and energetic, but she is handicapped by severe anxiety. Typically, Denise wakes very early. Her mind is racing, worrying about what the day will bring. Is her homework all done? What will happen in class? How will her friends treat her? Will her dress be just right? She hates playing jump rope; will her friends push her to play it again? These questions bug Denise even before she wakes up—or at least she feels that way. They never leave her at peace to get a full night's rest.

Breakfast is a chore for Denise because she usually doesn't feel like eating. If she eats too much, she gets nauseous and sometimes even throws up. If she doesn't eat enough, she gets weak and feels faint later. But who can eat when her stomach is all tied up in knots? And what if the bus is late? What if it doesn't come? What if today is really a holiday and she goes to school and no one is there? (Sometimes, Denise's mother tells her, her worries can be quite ridiculous.)

School itself is not too bad. Denise is good at school and usually gets through her classes quite easily. But recess is usually a pain because she starts worrying again. Will she fall and break an arm if she runs too much? What are her friends thinking? Why is that boy teasing her?

Denise's heart races. She feels a tightness in her chest. And sometimes she is overcome by thoughts of terrible things that might happen. Once, while playing, she was overcome by an intense fear that something had happened to her mother. She could not resist the urge and ran all the way home from school (several miles) to be with her mother. Then she felt so embarrassed she wanted to die.

And so Denise's day progresses. Right through to bedtime, it is filled with sometimes vague, sometimes specific, but always present worry. Obviously, the worry causes her a lot of stress. Headaches are frequent. Her stomach is almost in continuous turmoil. She is sick a lot. Unless she gets help, continuous anxiety is likely to torture her through adolescence and into adulthood.

What causes such pervasive anxiety in a child? There is usually no single cause. Several factors conspire together to create this debilitating disorder with its many variations. These factors in milder forms may account for less pronounced forms of anxiety in older children. They include:

(1) Rejection. Parental rejection can be a prime factor in causing a generalized anxiety problem. Separation from the parent can sometimes be interpreted as rejection, but emotional coldness and indifference are more

Anxiety-Free Separations

Separation anxiety is most intense when a parent is absent for a prolonged period of time. But what about briefer periods of separation such as occurs on a daily basis with children in day care or kindergarten?

These brief separations are not usually a major or long-term problem, provided parents handle them wisely. (Sometimes the anxiety is as much the parents' as the child's.) The age of the child is, of course, a major consideration, as is also the manner in which the separation is effected. The younger a child is, the more careful you have to be about instituting the separation. After age five, every child should be able to tolerate some separation. Remember that after age three, the primary problem is the *anxiety*, not just the physical separation. To minimize the anxiety caused by your absence, here are a few dos and don'ts:

- *Do take things slowly.* Take time to reassure your child before you leave. Explain exactly when you will return. Try to develop a little ritual for separating, like "three kisses and a wave good-bye." Such rituals will help comfort your child and remind him that you do return when you say you will.

- *Do take time to familiarize your child with the person or place where you are leaving him or her.* If possible, spend some time there with your child for a few days ahead of the separation so that the child associates you with the new person or place.

- *Do make your reunion a fun time.* Developing little "hello" rituals—a long hug and a brief talk about the day—gives the child something to look forward to and a comforting sense of routine.

- *Don't just sneak away.* Be sure to say good-bye, even if the child becomes upset. Suddenly realizing you are gone can produce a lot of anxiety in a child.

- *Don't get angry or frustrated because your child clings and protests your departure.* Reassure him or her that you are coming back. Then give your child an extra hug before handing him or her over to the caregiver. (And comfort yourself, as you leave, with the observed fact that your child will probably get over his distress very quickly.)

- *Don't be irregular in fetching your child.* If a child has to wait for you, anxiety rises dramatically.

- *Don't be upset if your child hides from you or gets angry at you because you've been away.* Just accept this behavior as a sign of your child's love for you and allow some time to get reacquainted.

likely causes. An unpleasant emotional climate in early childhood can cause feeding problems, persistent bedwetting, excessive fear, and slow development. Later these problems turn into pervasive anxiety.

Parents who themselves have been the victims of rejection often become rejecting parents. Lack of love, unfortunately, is a "communicable disease." Young parents tend to repeat their own parents' patterns unconsciously, even those that caused them pain.

(2) *Overprotection*. "Smothering" a child doesn't always make him or her feel more secure. Because overprotected children don't learn how to defend themselves, they can become anxious unnecessarily or fear something that is not likely to happen. In particular, they are prone to become worried when parents are not there to continue the protection.

One study of the family background of children suffering from "overanxiety" consistently found an overprotective mother in the background.[3] Other studies corroborate this finding. Of course, cause and effect are not always easy to separate; some mothers could become overprotective *because* their children are overly anxious. The overprotectiveness, however, does not help fix the problem either.

(3) *Unrealistic demands*. Parents who place excessive pressure on their children can generate a lot of anxiety. Expectations should be realistic and matched to the child's age *and* abilities. If nothing a child does is good enough, parents promote feelings of failure and not success. Almost invariably, anxiety increases.

(4) *Modeling*. Again and again, as one reviews the research on anxiety, the role of modeling is highlighted. A tense and anxious parent may impart some of the genes responsible for this tension to his or her child, but the parent also transmits the anxiety *by example*. When you show high anxiety, you teach high anxiety. Your child learns to react to the same fears you do.

I remember this phenomenon well from my own childhood. For some reason I never discerned, my mother was deathly afraid of hearses. I have very early memories of her reacting anxiously whenever a funeral procession drove past our house. The hearse was always a black station-wagon kind of vehicle with fancy trimmings. My mother hated them. And by age six or seven, I hated them also. I would avoid looking at them. When I was older, I even avoided going to funerals, not because I couldn't stand dead bodies, but because I had this inexplicable fear of black station-wagon-type vehicles.

Where did I learn this fear? Obviously, from my mother. What basis did this fear have in reality? None. I had never touched a hearse nor been inside one. And the only way I could be hurt by one was to lie down in front of it. By the time I was twelve, fortunately, I had outgrown this fear. But there are many anxieties we learn from parental modeling that we don't outgrow.

(5) *Prior trauma*. Stressful life events, experienced very early and in excess of what a child can reasonably cope with, can elicit severe tension and set up a generalized anxiety disorder. Being locked in a cupboard, held in a stuck elevator, injured in a car accident, or sexually abused by a parent can be the cause of severe anxiety problems.

No matter what the cause of the anxiety, the consequences are invariably the same: Anxious people develop feelings of inadequacy, oversensitivity, and a low tolerance for stress. Tormented by inner and outer dangers they cope with life apprehensively. Given the bad start most of them have had as children, one must admire the courage and endurance they show in facing up to life as they perceive it.

The Worry of Adolescence

Many children who may have escaped developing the childhood forms of anxiety face yet another period of uncertainty and insecurity when they reach their teenage years. Adolescence, typically, is an unsettled period. Rapid physical growth renders the body awkward. Hormone levels become unbalanced, causing emotional turmoil. Socially, the child is growing up, but he or she still faces restrictions at home and school.

There is no "rite of passage" in our culture that celebrates becoming an adult. Standards of appropriate behavior for the emerging young adult don't exist, or they differ from family to family. Children in our culture never know at what point they can claim the privileges of adulthood—and this uncertainty causes much confusion and conflict.

Psychologically, adolescence is a time for self-discovery. Ideally, the adolescent should move progressively to a greater level of self-acceptance as he or she becomes more self-aware. But our culture defines the standards of acceptability so unrealistically—you must have a perfect body or a beautiful appearance—that practically every adolescent becomes self-rejecting. Very few can honestly say, "I really like myself. I don't want to be anyone else."

Coupled with these developmental issues is the likelihood that the family is not functioning well. The adolescent years often coincide with a critical time for the parents' marriage. If it has survived to this point, it may be conflicted and full of tension. (Some of this tension, of course, is *caused* by the tumult of having an adolescent in the house.) If the parents have divorced and remarried, the teenager is likely to have become a pawn in the ongoing battle between the parents or to be faced with adjusting to a stepfamily. Anxiety, and with it a lower tolerance for stress, mounts rapidly in such circumstances.

For Sylvia, the stress and anxiety in her family just became too much. An attractive girl who looked older than her twelve years, she came to the attention of the juvenile authorities when her parents reported her as a runaway. Three times previously she had also run away, but these occasions had never been reported because, in each case, Sylvia had been found at the home of a friend. This time, however, no one knew where she was. And they didn't find her until a week later, in another city. She had hitchhiked there with an older boy. When she was found, Sylvia showed all the signs of high anxiety and stress: nail biting, minor tics, fidgetiness, and hyper-vigilance (rapid looking about as if some danger were to befall her).

Why did Sylvia run away? She was having difficulty in school but, more importantly, she could not tolerate the bickering, fighting, dissension, and criticism that went on in her home. "I just took off one day," she explained. "Didn't really care where I went or what happened to me. I just can't stand the tension at home. It makes me nervous all the time. I'd rather be on the streets than live at home." Her running away helped her parents to look more honestly at their dysfunctional relationship and they sought out family counseling.

There are several typical reasons why adolescents run away. Many, like Sylvia, are trying to escape a destructive family system. Some leave to escape sexual advances or abuse by someone in the family or stepfamily. Some are trying to avoid facing the consequences of a major problem (such as making someone pregnant) or to find another setting for working out a problem (such as being pregnant). Teenagers from poor families often run away to improve their circumstances. And some teenagers accompany someone else who is running away. Finally, some teenagers who run away are actually "throwaways." There are parents who deliberately make life so miserable that the teenager takes it upon him or herself to find a foster home.

All of these factors are worth noting, because the same factors can cause severe anxiety even for children who don't take the drastic measures of leaving home. Drawing from this list, then, we can isolate some of the primary sources of adolescent anxiety:

- family conflict or tension,
- sexual pressure or confusion,
- pressure to achieve,
- behavioral challenges,
- financial difficulties, and
- peer pressure.

The years of adolescence, therefore, are full of potential for anxiety. Chronic worry can easily become a lifelong pattern that is difficult to break. But healthy coping at this stage can also set a lifelong pattern for handling worry.

Minimizing Childhood Worry

How can a parent help a child overcome worry?

To begin with, it is important to remember that even chronic worriers do have times when they don't worry. There are brief periods when their minds are at rest and nothing is bugging them. These are the times when the worrier needs to prepare his or her mind for the battle ahead. It is in times of calm that one plans strategies and rehearses the behavior or thinking patterns that will overcome the anxiety.

I am assuming, of course, that if the cause of the worry lies in disruptive or damaging family circumstances, these problems will be attended to. No matter what you teach your child, little progress can be made if the home continues to be a threatening place. If you need assistance in dealing with a bad home situation, the best I can do is recommend that you get some professional help. You owe it to your child to provide a safe and secure home environment where normal development can take place.

For now, then, let me focus just on the child and lay out some ways you can help your child be less of a worrier—and, hopefully, less stressed as well.

(1) Deal with every worry circumstance immediately. Whenever a child experiences some anxiety or begins to worry, move in courageously to deal with the worry.

Let's assume, for instance, that your marriage is shaky and that you and your spouse are in counseling. Your child overhears you discussing some issue that came up in marital counseling. You didn't intend your child to overhear the conversation because it makes mention of a possible temporary separation and you know your child will worry about it. Now that he knows, however, it's best to move in and deal with the issue directly.

(2) Be honest. All humans cope better with reality than with imagination. In the situation mentioned above, explain to your child what is going on and why you discussed a possible temporary separation. Don't paint the worst-case scenario, but don't water down the truth, either. Describe what is going to happen and when. If the issue is still up in the air, then say so. And whatever you decide to do, *please* take into consideration the impact it will have on your child.

(3) Don't allow your child to brood. Research has shown that short periods of worrying (say, for less than ten minutes) or very long periods (say, over thirty minutes) tend *not* to induce worry habits as easily as the "in between" periods. It is moderate periods of worry (say, between ten minutes and thirty minutes) that produce deep-seated worry. This effect is called "incubation." When the worrying is maintained for just the right period of time, it tends to "hatch" into full-blown anxiety.

This makes sense, really. If we worried *all* the time, our worry would probably extinguish itself. If we worried for just a few minutes at a time, worry wouldn't get a foothold. But the pattern of worrying for a moderate period of time, then not worrying, then returning to our worries tends to entrench our anxious feelings into a permanent pattern.

It's like painting a barn door. If you just put on one thin coat of paint, the paint will probably dry and wear away quite quickly. If you apply a heavy coat, the paint will peel and drop off before long. The best way to get the paint to stay on for a long time is to apply it in successive layers of just the right thickness, allowing each layer to dry before you put on the next. This way you build up a strong, impermeable, and almost indestructible covering. If you worry the same way, you will also make it a strong, impermeable, and indestructible part of your personality!

How, then, does a child become a worrywart? By worrying for a while, letting the worry "dry out," then applying some more worry. Such a pattern can make a worry habit stick with a child the rest of his or her life.

And how you do prevent a child from becoming a worry-riddled person? You reverse this process. If you find that your child looks bothered by something, encourage him or her to *share it* with you. This helps to *externalize* the worry and also relieves it. Then distract your child. Change the subject. Suggest an exciting activity to get his or her mind off the subject. Try to keep all worry periods short.

Alternatively, you can try to create a continuous worry period. It sounds paradoxical, but it works like this: After your child has shared what he or she is worried about, suggest that you both sit there and worry about it for an extended period of time. "Let's just keep worrying about it. I'll worry and you worry. Together we'll keep it going. Now, tell me once again what it is you are worrying about?"

How long do you think you can keep this game going? Believe me, *not very long*. Worry thrives on *avoidance*. When a child manages to face his or her worries courageously, they lose their power. Try this technique on yourself. It's amazing how your mind gives up the worry and turns to other matters when you stop being afraid of worrying.

(3) *Teach your child to put things in perspective.* Most of the things we worry about *never happen*. Why? Because most worry is based on fantasy, not reality. Even if the things we worry about do happen, the consequences are seldom as bad as we feared.

Reviewing past worries and their outcome with your child can be especially useful in helping him or her develop perspective. This is why a caring parent needs to know what is on the mind of a worry-prone child. When you know that your child was worried about a certain exam, for instance, you can use the results of the exam to show your child that the worry was pointless.

What if he or she failed the exam? Does this prove that the worry was justified? Not at all. The worry itself may have interfered with the child's performance. By reviewing the impact of worry on your child's experience with the exam, you can still help your child see that worry has little value in helping us avoid what we fear.

Street Smart, But Not Stressed Out

We live in a dangerous world, and responsible parenting includes teaching children to be alert for dangerous situations. Children need to know, for instance, that they should never accept a ride from a stranger or pick up a dirty needle. They need to understand that they need not accept unwelcome sexual advances, or play games that involve touching parts of the body, even when initiated by someone they know.

But how do you prepare your child to cope with potential dangers without overstressing him or her? You want to raise a safe, happy child, not a stressed out, mistrustful, and fearful one. Here are some suggestions for preparing your child to live in the real world without putting too much pressure on him or her:

1. Don't make young children responsible for keeping themselves safe. By all means teach your preschoolers some basic rules of self-protection, but avoid making them feel that keeping themselves safe is their responsibility. Instead, emphasize that you are there to protect them.

2. Emphasize how to cope, not what could happen. Instead of dwelling on the possible consequences, tell the child you will help him or her know what to do in an emergency. Use make believe and pretend as a way of practicing emergency responses, and praise your child as he or she learns.

3. Shield your child from too much exposure to worrying circumstances on TV. Little children, especially, just don't need to know the gory details of the mass murder a hundred miles away, even if it is real news and not make-believe.

4. Talk about news stories or TV dramas you feel may worry your child. For instance, if you do see your child's attention riveted on a news account about child abuse, AIDS, or environmental poisoning, bring the subject up. (Your child may worry about it but not know how to talk about it.) Talking about potentially worrying information helps correct misinformation and to place the problem where it belongs. Explain to your child what happened in simple terms. Talk about what is being done to solve the case and protect other people, and reiterate the fact that you will protect the child.

5. Use the "few bad apples" analogy to avoid instilling mistrust. When you caution your child about talking to strangers, accepting candy or rides, and so on, try not to imply that all strangers are automatically bad. You want your child to be careful, not fearful. Teach your child that while *most* people are friendly, there are a few people who might hurt them, and it's not always easy to tell which is which. For that reason, they should be cautious around anyone they don't know.

6. Pay attention to your children's response when you are teaching them about possible dangers. Be alert to signs of anxiety so you can help the child deal with his or her fears.

7. Let your child see you working to make the world safer. Involve yourself in projects designed to stop drunk driving, promote drug awareness, stop hunger, or prevent nuclear holocaust—whatever cause draws your interest and concern. Teach your child that individuals *can* make a difference; we are not just victims of people and forces that might hurt us.

(4) *Teach your child how to use anxiety constructively.* Some *anxiety* is normal, necessary, and even constructive. If I am not anxious about an upcoming examination, I may not study for the exam; it would be disastrous not to have some concern. Worry, however, sabotages this constructive anxiety by diverting the energy that could be applied to solving the problem.

A certain amount of anxiety over what I have to do is quite healthy and necessary. But as with every other useful emotion, this anxiety must be kept within limits. When it is so limited, it moves me to action instead of fueling more worry.

Parents can help a child by pointing out that the anxiety or vague tension he or she is feeling is *a call to action.* "If you study more, you won't have a problem with the exam. Your anxiety is just a friendly reminder that you should be better prepared."

(5) *Teach your child to turn worry into concern.* Worry in and of itself is really a pointless activity. When we worry, we are just spinning our mental wheels. Worry (as opposed to constructive anxiety) does not help in the actual performance of this action.

Once I sit down to study, for instance, worry serves no further purpose except, perhaps, to point me back to the underlying anxiety. The stress it causes might even get in the way and rob me of my ability to study. The fretting and ruminating that goes with worry robs me of energy and leaves me weakened. It also causes a stress reaction throughout the body.

There is a healthier response to threat or challenge than worry; I call it concern. Concern is different from worry in that it takes the underlying anxiety and transforms it into an honest recognition that action is needed. I may continue to feel some internal tension and pressure to maintain the action, but I will not feel the same kind of damaging stress. By learning to express my anxiety in the form of concern rather than anxiety, I can be more creative in resolving that anxiety.

To use the examination illustration again, once your child has knuckled down to some hard study, he or she doesn't need the worry any more. What your child needs is an ongoing concern to keep him or her focused on studying. Your child's *worry*, which is pointless, useless, and stressful, needs to be converted to *concern*, which is constructive and focused on action.

How can you help a child turn worry into concern?

- *Whenever your child is worrying, ask, "What is the real issue? What are you really afraid of?"* Your goal is to clarify the fear. If your child is worried about an exam, the answer may well be, "I'm afraid I will fail the exam." The *concern* here, then, is *failing*. If the answer is, "I'm afraid Daddy will be mad," the concern is a different one—it is fear of a father's temper. Helping your child discover the *real issue* behind the worry helps focus the anxiety and points the way to resolving the issue.

- *Once you know the real issue, help your child plan a course of action.* Set out the options as clearly as you can. "What can you do," you can ask your child, "to avoid failing the exam?" The answer is obvious—study more. What about Father's anger? "You could sit down with Dad and explain to him that you are worrying about the exam because you fear what he will say if you fail. Explain to him that your worrying is getting in the way. More than likely, this will result in a lot of reassurance from Dad."

(6) *Help your child evaluate the outcome of what is feared.* It helps to consider a worst-case scenario. I do this often in therapy with a client. The most common result is a reduction of anxiety.

A teenager, for instance, may come to me with worries about her part-time job. She doesn't think she is doing so well. She fears that her boss is watching her closely and that he is going to fire her. Because she is so worried, her performance deteriorates. And this in turn causes more worry—and more mistakes.

"What is the worst that can happen?" I ask.

"I don't know. I suppose it's that I'll lose my job."

"What then?"

"I won't be able to get another one."

"What then?"

"I won't have enough extra money saved for college."

"What then?" (I tend to be stubborn!)

"I suppose I might have to get a part-time job in college sooner than I'd hoped."

By this point I can begin to see the relief on her face. "That's not a catastrophe," I suggest. "You'll get by. You don't have to work so hard now. You can probably earn more for less time in college than you can now. Besides, your folks will always be there to help in an emergency."

When we honestly follow through on our worries and explore the final consequences, many of them turn out not to be as frightening as we think. Besides, as indicated above, the very process of facing the worries helps alleviate the stress they cause.

Summary

Childhood ought to be a period of relative freedom from worry. A child does not need to experience a lot of anxiety just to learn what the world is like. Unfortunately, it is difficult to keep children from worrying in this dangerous age. But while we cannot protect our children from all anxiety, we can do much to minimize unnecessary fear and debilitating worry. Too much anxiety leads to excessive rumination about unlikely happenings. It feeds unrealistic fears. Worry does not help to mature a child. Rather, it curtails a child's development and prevents the formation of independence and coping skills. Highly stressed adults often point back to childhoods that were overly anxious and fearful. The best way to avoid much adult stress is to learn healthy ways to cope with childhood anxiety and to build a self-image that is sturdy enough to face whatever life has to offer—good or bad.

Discussion Questions

1. What are some of the causes of childhood anxiety, and how can they be prevented from turning a child into a worrywart?

2. Some anxiety is necessary, even healthy for a child. What purpose does healthy anxiety serve in a child's development?

3. Adolescence can be a time for intensified anxiety. What worried you when you were an adolescent? Can you see similarities between your teenage worries and those of today's adolescents? How is the picture different for teenagers today?

Concluding Note
to Parents

I hope this book has been a source of encouragement to you as a parent and that it has shown you ways to raise healthier and less-stressed children. I certainly hope it has not contributed to your stress by making you feel guilty about the parenting mistakes you have made. If it has, resolve not to let your guilt get the best of you. What matters is that you recognize what needs to be changed and then summon the courage to go ahead and make the change.

Attitude is all-important in parenting. If you are painridden, confused, and overwhelmed by parenting responsibilities, chances are you have the wrong attitude. You need to correct your mind-set or posture toward parenting and toward your child.

So how should you think about yourself as a parent, about your child, and about the environment you create for your child in your home? In these concluding remarks allow me to make some suggestions that can help orient your attitude to what you seek to do as a parent.

Concerning your attitude toward *yourself* as a parent, I would repeat what I have said many times in this book: Give yourself permission to be imperfect and make mistakes. If you try too hard to get everything right, you are bound to make even more mistakes. If you think other parents are doing a better job with their kids, you are probably mistaken. Be liberal with self-forgiveness, and don't waste your energy on pointless self-incrimination. Do the best you can—and leave it there.

Concerning *your child*, remember that he or she is a gift from God, "on loan" to you for a brief period of your life. Remember, also that each child is a unique individual and should be permitted to become who he or she really is. Your responsibility is not to turn your children into something of your own design, but to help them become themselves. More stress is caused by trying to crush a child's spirit or to force him or her into a mold that doesn't fit than by almost anything else parents can do.

Concerning *the home environment*, try to think of it as a laboratory instead of a factory. There is no production schedule, no predetermined product, no schedule for completion. Instead, the home is a place for experimenting, for discovering the possibilities of your "product" and for trying out techniques and methods for improving it. Factories can tolerate no mistakes and are overly concerned about quality control and schedules. As a result, they are places of high stress. Factorylike homes produce the same stress. But laboratories thrive on mistakes. More is discovered through error than by deliberate design. Children thrive best in such an atmosphere.

If you have only one parenting goal, make that goal to be a person of *integrity*. If you make a promise, keep it. If you give your word, honor it. If your child asks for an honest opinion, don't withhold it. Parents with integrity are parents who command trust and respect. And the children of such parents are bound to walk in their parents' stress-free footsteps.

Notes

Introduction

    1. Proverbs 22:6.

Chapter 1

    1. Statistics released by Children's Defense Fund, Washington, D.C., on 8 January 1990.

    2. Ron Harris, "Youth Isn't Kid Stuff These Days," *Los Angeles Times,* 12 May 1991, A1.

    3. Harris, "Youth Isn't Kid Stuff," A1. Sources cited are the Center for Demography and Ecology, University of Wisconsin, Madison; the Child Welfare League; and the United States Department of Labor Statistics.

    4. Harris, "Youth Isn't Kid Stuff," A21.

Chapter 2

    1. Meyer Friedman and Ray Rosenman, *Type-A Behavior and Your Heart* (New York: Knopf, 1974), 178.

    2. John R. Aiello, Gregory Nicosia, and Donna E. Thompson, "Psychological, Social and Behavioral Consequences of Crowding on Children and Adolescents," *Social-Development* 50 (March 1979): 195–202.

    3. Ephesians 5:26 LB.

4. See Archibald D. Hart, *Healing Life's Hidden Addictions* (Ann Arbor, Mich.: Servant, 1990), esp. pp. 1–21.

5. John Leo, "Looking for a Life of Thrills," *Time*, 15 April 1990, 92.

6. Mark 6:31.

Chapter 3

1. Archibald D. Hart, *Overcoming Anxiety* (Dallas: Word, 1989), 14–16.

2. Hart, *Overcoming Anxiety*, 14–16.

3. For a more detailed discussion of anxiety, see chapter 14, "The Worried Child"; see also Hart, *Overcoming Anxiety* (cited above).

4. T. H. Holmes and R. H. Rahe, "The Social Readjustment Rating Scale," *Journal of Psychosomatic Research* 11 (1967): 213–18.

Chapter 4

1. Harold D. Fishbein, "The Identified Patient and Stage of Family Development," *Journal of Marital and Family Therapy* 8 (January 1982): 57–61.

2. Mark A. Stewart, Ann Goth, and Elizabeth Hierowski, "Differences Between Girls and Boys Admitted to a Child Psychiatry Ward," *Journal of Clinical Psychiatry* 42, no. 10 (October 1981): 386–88.

Chapter 5

1. Stanley Turecki, *The Difficult Child* (New York: Bantam Books, 1985).

2. Bernard Ohanian and Greta Vollmer, "Born to Be," *Parenting*, November 1990, 92.

3. Archibald D. Hart, *The Hidden Link Between Adrenaline and Stress* (Waco, Tex.: Word, 1986), 41–54.

Chapter 6

1. Thomas J. Moore, "The Cholesterol Myth," *Atlantic Monthly*, September 1989, 39.

2. "Lowering Blood Cholesterol to Prevent Heart Disease," *Journal of the American Medical Association* 253, no. 14: 2080.

3. R. L. Holman, "Atherosclerosis: A Pediatric Nutrition Problem?" *American Journal of Clinical Nutrition* 9 (1961): 565–69.

4. Paul Y. Qaqundah, preface to Robert E. Kowalski, *Cholesterol and Children* (Sydney, Australia: Bantam, 1988), xvi.

5. Anastasia Toufexis, "Watch What You Eat, Kid," *Time*, 22 April 1991, 76.

6. Anastasia Toufexis, "Watch What You Eat," 76.

7. Quoted in *Science Digest*, April 1985, 35.

8. V. Van Doorner and K. Orlebeke, *Journal of Human Stress* 12 (December 1981): 25–26.

9. Toufexis, "Watch What You Eat," 76.

10. W. Gifford-Jones, "Too Much TV Leads to Bad Health," *Pasadena Star News*, 27 May 1991, B1.

Chapter 7

1. Karen Croke, "Don't Wake Him, a Nap May Be Just What He Needs" *Pasadena* [California] *Star-News*, 19 February 1990, C1.

2. Hart, Archibald D., *The Hidden Link Between Adrenaline and Stress* (Waco, Tex.: Word, 1986), 122–26.

3. Richard Bedner, Gawain M. Wells, and Scott R. Peterson, *Self-Esteem, Paradoxes and Innovations in Clinical Theory and Practice* (Washington, D.C.: American Psychological Association, 1989), 4.

4. Bedner, Wells, and Peterson, *Self-Esteem*, 8.

5. Bedner, Wells, and Peterson, *Self-Esteem*, 10.

6. Bedner, Wells, and Peterson, *Self-Esteem*, 13.

Chapter 8

1. Ann Landers, *The Ann Landers Encyclopedia* (New York: Ballantine, 1978), 831.

2. Nick Jordon, "Minding Your Health," *Psychology Today*, June 1989, 16.

3. George Wood and Bernard Schwartz, "I Mean Now," *Psychology Today*, July 1977, 113–16.

4. John Rosemond, "The Answer Is 'Because I Say So,'" *Pasadena* [California] *Star-News*, 29 January, 1991, B1.

Chapter 9

1. Joseph Adler, "A Lesson Plan for Kid Stress," *Los Angeles Times Magazine*, 7 October 1990, pt. 2, 22.

2. Emmy E. Werner, "Stress and Protective Factors in Children's Lives," in *Longitudinal Studies in Child Psychology and Psychiatry* (New York: Wiley, 1982), 195.

3. Adler, "A Lesson Plan," 22.

4. Archibald D. Hart, *Fifteen Principles for Achieving Happiness* (Dallas: Word, 1988), 6.

5. Charles Sheldon, *In His Steps* (Westwood, N.J.: Barbour and Co., 1977).

6. Ephesians 1:7.

7. Bertrand Russell, *Conquest of Happiness* (New York: Liveright, 1930), 17.

8. Harold Kushner, *Who Needs God* (New York: Simon & Schuster, 1989), 26.

9. John 14:27.

10. See Matthew 18:21–35.

Chapter 10

1. Josef Rogner and Heinz W. Kronhe, "Relationships Between Parental Child-Rearing Style Types and Stress Coping Modes of the Child," reported in *Journal of Divorce* 12, nos. 2/3 (1988/89): 139.

2. 1 Corinthians 13:4–5 NIV.

3. Archibald D. Hart, *Children and Divorce* (Dallas: Word, 1982, rev. 1989).

Chapter 11

1. Bettijane Levine, "The Family and Relationships," *Los Angeles Times*, 2 September 1990, E11.

2. Levine, "Family and Relationships," E11.

3. Levine, "Family and Relationships," E11.

Chapter 12

1. Carol Tavris, *Anger, the Misunderstood Emotion* (New York: Simon and Schuster/Touchstone, 1982), 83.

2. Tavris, *Anger*, 83.

3. Tavris, *Anger*, cited above.

4. Carol Tavris, "Anger Defused," *Psychology Today*, November 1982, 25.

5. Tavris, "Anger Defused," 33.

6. Tavris, "Anger Defused," 33.

7. Ephesians 4:31–32 REB.

Chapter 13

1. Kathy Henderson, "Indulged? Or Just Plain Spoiled?" *Psychology Today*, June 1989, 28.

Chapter 14

    1. Archibald D. Hart, *Overcoming Anxiety* (Dallas: Word, 1989).

    2. James Coleman, James Butcher, and Robert Carson, *Abnormal Psychology and Modern Life* (Glenview, Ill.: Scott, Foresman, 1980), 144.

    3. Coleman, Butcher, and Carson, *Abnormal Psychology*, 146.